PETER LOVERING

CHELSEA

PLAYER BY PLAYER

GUINNESS PUBLISHING

ACKNOWLEDGEMENTS

The author would like to thank the following for their encouragement and assistance:
Frank Blunstone, Barry Bridges, Joe Fascione, Ron Harris, Colin Lee, John Mortimore,
Ken Shellito, Peter Sillett, David Webb, Ray Wilkins, Steve Small, Ivan Ponting,
Deirdre Fenney, Andy Cowie and all at Colorsport, Charles Richards and Simon Duncan.

The author is also grateful for permission to reproduce photographs. The vast majority are
from Colorsport, with additional contributions from Allsport and Ron Hockings.

Efforts have been made to trace copyright holders of all photographs used in this book.
We apologise for any omissions, which are unintentional, and would be pleased to include
an appropriate acknowledgement in any subsequent edition.

Pictured on the front cover are: Jimmy Greaves *(top left)*; Peter Osgood *(centre left)*;
Peter Bonetti *(centre right)*; Bobby Tambling *(centre)*; Ron Harris *(top right)*;
Ray Wilkins *(lower left)*; Frank Blunstone *(bottom left)*; Charlie Cooke *(bottom centre)*
and Andy Townsend *(bottom right)*.

On the back are: Paul Elliott *(top left)*; Alan Hudson *(top centre)*;
David Speedie *(top right)*; Pat Nevin *(centre left)*; John Hollins *(centre)*;
Kerry Dixon *(centre right)*; Micky Droy *(bottom left)* and David Webb *(bottom)*.

First published in 1993 by
GUINNESS PUBLISHING
33 London Road, Enfield
Middlesex, EN2 6DJ

Designed and typeset by Steve Small

Text copyright © 1993 by Peter Lovering

Illustrations copyright © 1993 as credited

A catalogue record for this book is available
from the British Library

Printed and bound in Great Britain by The Bath Press, Avon

'Guinness' is a registered trademark
of Guinness Publishing Ltd

ISBN: 0-85112-510-7

INTRODUCTION

A fan may become devoted to a particular team for any number of reasons. Some are attracted by a club's colours or its name; others have a weakness for underdogs and feel drawn to those who struggle gallantly with no realistic hope of ever tasting glory; while some shallow, misguided souls simply wish to be associated with success, and attach themselves to the side favoured by fortune at the time their passion for football is first aroused. My case, however, was different. I had no real choice in the matter, as my father had been a fervent Chelsea supporter since the 1920s. I was a dutiful child, and it no more occurred to me to abandon the faith I had been born into than it did to apply for the citizenship of some far-distant country.

I have no complaints about my fate. Chelsea's triumphs have been few and far between but hope has continued to burn in the hearts of the Blues' supporters. At times the flame has blazed brightly, occasionally it has flickered, but it has never been extinguished, and those rare successes have been all the sweeter for the periods of misery that have separated them.

In this book I have taken a detailed look at the men who have played for the Blues since I first became aware that Chelsea were 'my team'. As a starting point I have chosen 1960/61, the season that saw the departure from Stamford Bridge of Jimmy Greaves, the arrival of Tommy Docherty and the start of the club's modern era. My aim has been to capture the essence of each player, but where he has made so few appearances that a considered assessment is not possible I have confined myself to the facts and figures of his career.

A number of excellent statistical works on Chelsea are already available so I have provided only the essential statistical information: games played (with appearances as a substitute shown in brackets), goals scored, other clubs, and so on. The figures quoted for each player's Chelsea career refer to matches played in League football (including the play-off matches in 1987/88), the FA Cup, League Cup, Full Members' Cup and European competitions but not the FA Charity Shield. A full breakdown is given at the back of the book. The records quoted for other clubs refer to League matches only (excluding play-offs). The dates in large type indicate the seasons during which each player appeared in the Blues' first team, not when he joined or left the club. Honours listed are those won as a Chelsea player with the exception of international caps. The years mentioned after the number of caps won indicate the date of the player's first and last international appearances. Statistics are complete to 17 May 1993. Transfer fees quoted are those given in the press at the time.

Although *Chelsea – Player by Player* is devoted to the period since 1960/61, I have prefaced this cavalcade of heroes with a glance at some stalwarts from the 1950s – in particular the redoubtable side that captured the League Championship in 1955. In common with every Chelsea fan, I am hoping that it will not be too long before the Blues manage to emulate their achievement.

Peter Lovering
London
May 1993

CONTENTS

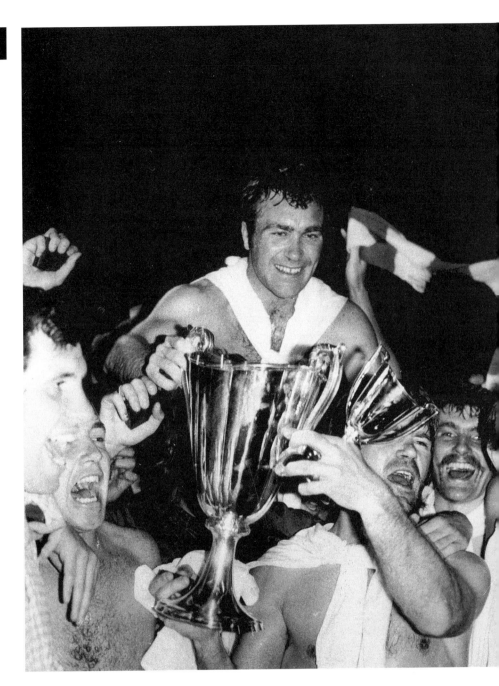

FIFTIES FAITHFULS

The high-water mark of Ted Drake's nine-year reign as Chelsea manager was undoubtedly the League Championship triumph in 1954/55. Combining several dependable stalwarts he had inherited with an array of imaginative signings, Drake had welded together a resolute, purposeful team that managed to carry off the title with an impressive surge in the second half of the season. As that side broke up, seemingly unable to sustain the mighty effort that had brought them glory, he placed his faith in youthful exuberance, and many of Drake's Ducklings are featured in the main part of this book.

However, a number of players who provided sterling service during the second half of the fifties did not survive into the new decade. Some were talented youngsters who failed to command a regular first-team place and soon moved on, others were solid journeymen who lacked the qualities required for a long career at the top; a few of them are featured here, together with the men who brought the Championship to Stamford Bridge, to set the scene for what follows.

Back row *(left to right):*

KEN ARMSTRONG (47/8-56/7, wing-half, 401 games, 30 goals).

RON GREENWOOD (52/3-54/5, centre-half, 66 games, 0 goals).

DEREK SAUNDERS (53/4-58/9, wing-half, 222 games, 9 goals).

BILL ROBERTSON (50/1-59/60, goalkeeper, 214 games, 0 goals).

STAN WILLEMSE (49/50-55/6, full-back, 220 games, 2 goals).

PETER SILLETT (53/4-61/2, full-back, 287 games, 34 goals).

Front row:

ERIC PARSONS (50/1-56/7, winger, 176 games, 42 goals).

JOHN McNICHOL (52/3-57/8, inside-forward, 202 games, 66 goals).

ROY BENTLEY (47/8-56/7, forward, 366 games, 149 goals).

LES STUBBS (52/3-58/9, inside-forward, 122 games, 35 goals).

JIM LEWIS (52/3-57/8, winger, 95 games, 40 goals).

LEAGUE CHAMPIONS 1954/55

STAN WICKS

SEAMUS O'CONNELL

CHICK THOMSON

DICK WHITTAKER

LEN CASEY

IAN MacFARLANE

ALAN DICKS

LES ALLEN

AN WICKS (54/5-56/7, centre-half,
games, 1 goal).

AMUS O'CONNELL (54/5-55/6,
side-forward, 17 games, 12 goals).

HICK THOMSON (52/3-55/6,
alkeeper, 59 games, 0 goals).

OHN HARRIS (45/6-55/6, centre-
lf/full-back, 364 games, 14 goals).

JOHN HARRIS

DICK WHITTAKER (55/6-59/60,
full-back, 51 games, 0 goals).

LEN CASEY (55/6-58/9,
wing-half, 37 games, 0 goals).

IAN MacFARLANE (56/7-57/8,
full-back, 43 games, 0 goals).

ALAN DICKS (52/3-57/8,
centre-half, 38 games, 1 goal).

LES ALLEN (56/7-59/60,
forward, 49 games, 11 goals).

PETER SILLETT

Rather like a Rolls-Royce, there was nothing showy or flamboyant about Peter Sillett but his quality was readily apparent to the discerning observer. Placid and undemonstrative, he remained resolute and imperturbable in the heat of battle, calmly intervening to avert disaster when there was panic and confusion all around, but it could be argued that his sane, civilised attitude to the game prevented the powerfully built full-back from doing complete justice to his exceptional natural talent.

Peter joined Chelsea in May 1953 for £12,000, renewing a family link with Ted Drake, who had played alongside his father at the Dell in the early thirties. In his first season at Stamford Bridge he made only a dozen League appearances but he broke into the team midway through the next campaign and made a significant contribution to the Blues' mould-breaking Championship triumph.

A hard, uncompromising defender who feared no one, Peter was not particularly quick nor was he an exceptional tackler but his complete mastery of the subtle arts of full-back play meant that wily opponents like Stanley Matthews and Tom Finney rarely escaped his shackles. He kicked the ball beautifully, picking out his man with precision, and his ferociously struck free-kicks yielded a number of highly spectacular goals, none better than an astounding effort from 40 yards against Manchester United in September 1959 that flew past the startled goalkeeper into the top left-hand corner of the net. However, he is probably best remembered as a deadly penalty-taker. He took on the potentially embarrassing role after five successive misses by John Harris and Roy Bentley had threatened to undermine the Blues' growing Championship challenge and performed it with characteristic aplomb. Never was his nerve subjected to a more rigorous examination than when he was given the chance to settle an enthralling and potentially decisive encounter with Wolves on Easter Saturday from the spot with 15 minutes remaining, but his trusty right foot did not fail him. The ball rocketed past Bert Williams, the 75,000 crowd erupted and the title was within Chelsea's grasp.

Peter was an automatic choice for the next six seasons, his only significant absence coming at the start of 1956/57 following a knee operation. Although he preferred to play on the right, Chelsea's failure to find a long-term replacement for Stan Willemse meant that he was often obliged to switch to the other flank, where he performed with equal distinction. His versatility ensured that he was a regular member of the party selected for international matches – he travelled to the 1958 World Cup in Sweden, for instance, without getting a game – but the lack of a steady partner at club level may well have hampered his efforts to add to the three full England caps he won on the summer tour in 1955.

The rapid break-up of the Championship-winning team meant that within a few seasons of joining the Blues as a 20-year-old Peter was one of the few seasoned professionals on the Stamford Bridge staff and his encouragement made an invaluable contribution to the development of many of the club's young players, including his eventual successor Ken Shellito. Sillett succeeded Derek Saunders as captain in 1959 but a broken leg sustained in the third game of 1961/62 effectively ended his Chelsea career. He had recovered by the end of the season but there was no place for him under the Docherty regime and he joined Guildford City that summer, a lack of confidence in the leg prompting him to decline offers from a number of League clubs. He was only 29 and it was a decision he subsequently regretted, but it was characteristic of the man that he should have accepted the cards he had been dealt without complaint.

BORN: Southampton, 1.2.33.
GAMES: 287. GOALS: 34.
HONOURS: League Championship 54/5.
3 England caps (55).
OTHER CLUBS: Southampton 51/2-52/3 (59, 4).

1953/54-1961/62

PETER BRABROOK

It is easy to forget that Peter Brabrook was still a month short of his 25th birthday when he left Stamford Bridge in October 1962. He had been unchallenged as the Blues' first-choice right-winger for five seasons and the torrent of goals that, for most of that period, had successfully compensated for the side's defensive shortcomings owed much to the enterprising East Ender's skill and consistency.

Peter was 17 when he was given his first taste of League football, making three appearances at inside-left as the 1954/55 Championship battle neared its climax, and the following season he shared the number eight shirt with Johnny McNichol. However, in November 1956 he was switched to outside-right in place of Eric Parsons and it was soon apparent that he had found his true position. Few of Drake's Ducklings were to make the transition to senior football with such assurance and within two seasons he had become the first product of the Chelsea Juniors to play for England, making his full international debut in the play-off against the Soviet Union in the 1958 World Cup in Sweden.

Pace and good ball control with either foot made Brabrook a formidable opponent. He was a direct, attacking winger who ran at defences and frequently left them trailing bemused in his wake, never more impressively than when he beat three men before pushing the ball past the 'keeper at Upton Park in February 1960. He crossed the ball well, his centres helping Ron Tindall to many of his goals, and if he didn't have Frank Blunstone's tenacity – well, there were very few who did. He was also a reliable goalscorer, regularly meeting crosses from the left with a well-placed header.

However, the departure of Ted Drake and the appointment of Tommy Docherty prompted wholesale changes at Stamford Bridge. When Brabrook was left out of the team at the start of 1962/63 it became clear that his departure would not be long delayed and within weeks he had been transferred to West Ham United for £35,000.

BORN: Greenwich, 8.11.37.
GAMES: 270. GOALS: 57.
HONOURS: 3 England caps (58-60).
OTHER CLUBS: West Ham United 62/3-67/8 (167, 33);
Leyton Orient 68/9-70/1 (72, 6).

1954/55-1961/62

Moving to Stamford Bridge was probably the biggest mistake Reg Matthews ever made.

A magnificent natural goalkeeper with quite astonishing reflexes, he had begun his career with his home-town club, Third Division Coventry City, and performed so impressively that he earned five England caps without the benefit of the publicity surrounding more fashionable teams. When he joined Chelsea in November 1956 he became the most expensive 'keeper in the country, but he was unable to settle in London and continued to live in Coventry. As a result he could not train with his team-mates regularly and, not surprisingly in the circumstances, he produced his best form only intermittently during his time with the Blues, although in mitigation it should be said that the protection he received from his defence was often rudimentary.

Reg was a little round-shouldered with an ambling gait that scarcely betrayed the fact that he was a professional athlete, but once he donned the green jersey he was transformed. Agile and acrobatic, he was at his best on his line but came out for crosses with authority and was utterly fearless when diving at the feet of onrushing forwards. He smoked heavily to calm his jangling nerves and his excitability caused more than a few anxious moments for his defenders, but he generally emerged from the frequent goalmouth mêlées clutching the ball.

Significantly, Reg's best performances for the Blues came on visits to the Midlands, with a superlative display in a rousing 2-1 win against Wolves in January 1959 outstanding, and by the closing weeks of 1959/60 his position as Chelsea's first-choice 'keeper was in doubt. A bruised ankle allowed Peter Bonetti to prove his class and Matthews was able to reclaim the position only briefly before moving on to Derby County in October 1961.

BORN: Coventry, 20.12.33.
GAMES: 148. GOALS: 0.
HONOURS: 5 England caps (56).
OTHER CLUBS: Coventry City 52/3-56/7 (111, 0);
Derby County 61/2-67/8 (225, 0).

1956/57-1960/61

JOHN SILLETT

Few wingers enjoyed playing against John Sillett. He possessed only a fraction of his elder brother Peter's abundant natural talent but made far greater use of the ability he had been granted, his determination and unquenchable aggression ensuring that his technical limitations were rarely exploited.

John started his career with Southampton and joined Chelsea as a 16-year-old when Peter moved to Stamford Bridge from the south coast club. At that stage he was a bustling centre-forward but by the time he made his League debut at Old Trafford on New Year's Day 1957 he had been converted to full-back. A dislocated kneecap that September delayed his progress and he was 22 by the time he was given his first extended run in the side at the beginning of the 1958/59 season. He started on the left with Peter at right-back, but John was happier on the other flank (and less adaptable than his brother) and therefore made the majority of his appearances over the next three years in the number two shirt.

Ferocious in the tackle and utterly fearless, John invariably performed with passion and unwavering commitment, rapidly coming to be recognised as one of football's hard men. He lacked his brother's composure but had the pace to sprint back and close the door when a rash lunge appeared to have left it wide open. He lost his place after a 6-0 defeat at Bolton in March 1959 but fought his way back into the side the following season and for the next 18 months the pairing of Sillett (P) and Sillett (J) was broken only when the junior partner was held to be responsible for some particularly painful thrashing and consigned to the reserves for a few weeks.

John's technique may have been unsophisticated but he was a solid professional who worked hard at his game. However, when Tommy Docherty succeeded Ted Drake he quickly decided that Ken Shellito was the better long-term prospect and in April 1962 Sillett was transferred to Third Division Coventry City.

BORN: Southampton, 20.7.36.
GAMES: 102. GOALS: 1.
OTHER CLUBS: Coventry City 61/2-65/6 (109, 1);
Plymouth Argyle 66/7-67/8 (38, 1).
MANAGER: Hereford United (74-78 and 91-92);
Coventry City (87-90).

1956/57-1961/62

MEL SCOTT

Mel Scott was given his chance to claim a first-team place against Wolves in March 1958 and seized the opportunity so impressively that by the following September he had graduated to the England under-23 side. Quick and agile, the 18-year-old centre-half was remarkably assured and appeared to possess all the qualities required for success. He had a good touch and read the game well, favouring the timely interception rather than the crunching tackle, and if his distribution was only fair no doubt that would improve with experience.

However, there was a fundamental weakness that would prove to be Mel's undoing: he was not quite tall enough to dominate in the air and lacked the physical presence to handle big, aggressive centre-forwards. He was the first-choice number five for most of the following season but the Blues' unswerving commitment to attack meant that the defence was often hopelessly exposed and, with the goals-against tally steadily mounting, his confidence was gradually eroded. For all his undoubted ability, the youngster was making too many mistakes, although his pace often allowed him to retrieve the situation. He gave the impression of being content to rely on the natural gifts he had been granted, rather than working to make the fullest possible use of his talent – or perhaps it was simply that too much had been demanded of him so early in his career. Following the arrival of Sylvan Anderton in March, Ted Drake decided to switch John Mortimore back into the middle and for the next two years Scott was consigned to the reserves.

Mel reclaimed his place towards the end of 1960/61 and played regularly the following season but was unable to recapture the form that had marked his arrival in the First Division. He was once again displaced by Mortimore and it became increasingly apparent that he had no future at Stamford Bridge. In March 1963 he joined Brentford, a move which did little to revive his fading career.

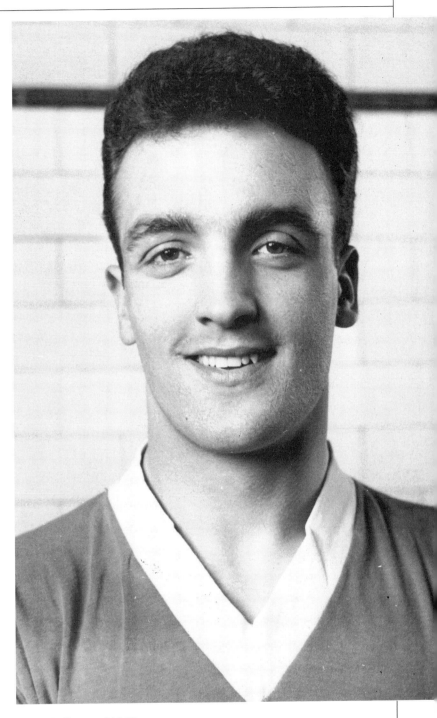

BORN: Claygate, 26.9.39.
GAMES: 104. GOALS: 0.
OTHER CLUBS: Brentford 62/3-66/7 (156, 2);
Chicago Sting; Oakland Clippers.

1957/58-1961/62

RON TINDALL

Chelsea have had many centre-forwards more gifted than Ron Tindall, but none who has tried harder. Popular in the dressing room and utterly selfless on the pitch, he was a true 'team man', who could be relied upon to play his part to the full.

Ron scored on his debut, at home to West Bromwich Albion in November 1955, but even after Roy Bentley's departure to Fulham the following September he had to fight to retain his grip on the number nine shirt, as first Les Allen and then Charlie Livesey attempted to snatch it from him. It was as if Ted Drake felt he ought to be able to find someone more stylish to fill the position, but soon discovered that the replacements, no matter how stylish, were less effective than the original incumbent.

Tindall was the ideal target man, with the strength to hold the ball before bringing team-mates into the game, and harassed colleagues knew that he would be easy to find with a long pass. Brave and athletic, he was majestic in the air and most of his goals were scored with his head, including a hat-trick against Newcastle in November 1960. Less adept when the ball was on the ground, he was not the quickest or most elegant of movers, but formed a formidable attacking partnership with Jimmy Greaves, his flicks presenting Jimmy with many of his openings.

It was entirely characteristic that Ron, a natural all-round sportsman who played cricket for Surrey during the summer, should take on the role of emergency goalkeeper and perform it with distinction, and he gave further evidence of his boundless versatility by moving to left-back for a while in the autumn of 1959 following the arrival of Livesey from Southampton.

Tindall was one of a number of players to leave Stamford Bridge following Drake's replacement by Tommy Docherty, moving to West Ham United in November 1961 in part-exchange for Andy Malcolm.

BORN: Streatham, 23.9.35.
GAMES: 174. GOALS: 70.
OTHER CLUBS: West Ham United 61/2 (13, 3);
Reading 62/3-63/4 (36, 12);
Portsmouth 64/5-69/70 (161, 7).
MANAGER: Portsmouth (70-73).

1955/56-1961/62

JOHN MORTIMORE

John Mortimore's Chelsea career divides neatly into two halves – separated by a frustrating two-year sojourn in the wilderness when he was probably at his peak.

After a distinguished spell as an amateur with Woking, during the course of which he made three League appearances for the Blues, John joined the professional staff at Stamford Bridge in August 1957, although he continued to pursue his career as a teacher for several years. He had been signed as a replacement for Ken Armstrong at right-half, but proved to be most effective when playing in the centre of the defence. Dominant in the air, he was a tight marker with a firm tackle who used the ball constructively but lacked the pace to be a top-class wing-half.

Solid and dependable, Mortimore was a first-team regular for three seasons but then found himself out of favour as first Bobby Evans and then Mel Scott – neither of whom excelled 'upstairs' – occupied the number five shirt. John came close to joining Chester as player-manager but resumed his duties at centre-half in the last three matches of 1961/62 and lent some much-needed experience and composure to Docherty's exuberant young side over the next three seasons. A League Cup winner's medal in 1965 was a richly deserved reward for the tall defender's loyalty, and only an over-zealous referee's whistle prevented him from giving the Blues the lead in that season's FA Cup semi-final against Liverpool.

John had been appointed coach in succession to Dave Sexton earlier that year but was reluctant to accept Docherty's suggestion that he should give up playing to concentrate on his new role, and when he was left out in favour of Marvin Hinton at the start of the following season he decided to move on to Queens Park Rangers, subsequently embarking on a highly successful coaching career, much of which has been spent as assistant manager of Southampton.

BORN: Farnborough, 23.9.34.
GAMES: 279. GOALS: 10.
OTHER CLUBS: Queens Park Rangers 65/6 (10, 0); Sunderland (0, 0).
MANAGER: Ethnikos, Greece (twice); Portsmouth (73-74);
Benfica (twice); Real Betis, Spain; Belenenses, Portugal.

1955/56-1964/65

TONY NICHOLAS

While physical prowess alone can bring considerable success at junior level, something more is needed if a youngster is to make a similar impact in League football and it was the absence of this extra dimension from his game that prevented Tony Nicholas from fulfilling his undoubted potential. A strong, powerfully built inside-forward with two good feet, he had pace and covered a lot of ground in 90 minutes, but his athleticism could not conceal the fact that he was essentially an instinctive player who lacked the speed of thought and tactical awareness needed to trouble First Division defences and he failed to maintain his early progress.

Nicholas was given his senior baptism in August 1956 as Ted Drake set about the wholesale reconstruction of his Championship-winning side, and he had several extended runs in the first team over the next four seasons but never succeeded in making his place secure. His most productive spell was in the autumn of 1957 when he scored six goals in nine appearances including a splendid individual effort in a 6-1 win against Burnley, but the pressing need was for someone to supply the ammunition for Jimmy Greaves. The arrival of Johnny Brooks in December 1959 effectively spelled the end of Tony's chances at Stamford Bridge and the following November he was transferred to Brighton.

BORN: West Ham, 16.4.38.
GAMES: 63. GOALS: 20.
OTHER CLUBS: Brighton and Hove Albion 60/1-61/2 (65, 22);
Leyton Orient 65/6 (9, 2).

1956/57-1960/61

DEREK GIBBS

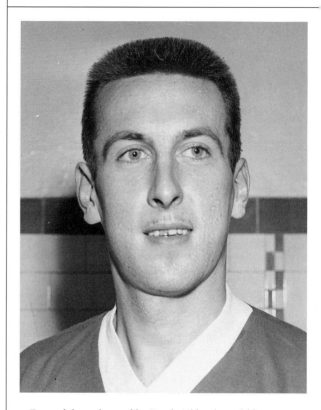

Every club needs men like Derek Gibbs, dependable reserves who will give everything they have on the rare occasions they are called up to fill a gap in the first team. A hard-working, dogged inside-forward, he was a big, strong player who could run all day, shuttling up and down the pitch, but possessed only a fraction of the talent of contemporaries such as Jimmy Greaves and David Cliss. Although he occasionally looked clumsy, he passed the ball neatly enough but his yeoman qualities were never sufficient to win him a recognised place in the side and he was restricted to a total of 25 senior appearances spread over five seasons, scoring six times.

Derek's best season was probably 1958/59, with the high spot being a third round FA Cup tie against Newcastle at St James's Park when the Blues defied a passionate Geordie crowd to record a famous 4-1 win, Gibbs scoring the third goal when he ran onto a pass from Stan Crowther and beat the advancing 'keeper, not long after he had hit the bar with a venomous drive. Defeat at the hands of Aston Villa in the next round ended dreams of Wembley for another year and shortly afterwards Gibbs returned to the reserves.

The arrival of Johnny Brooks only added to the competition for inside-forward places and in November 1960 Derek moved to Leyton Orient, but he failed to make the impression in the lower divisions that one might have anticipated.

BORN: Fulham, 22.12.34. GAMES: 25. GOALS: 6.
OTHER CLUBS: Leyton Orient 60/1-62/3 (33, 4);
Queens Park Rangers 63/4-64/5 (27, 0).

1956/57-1960/61

SYLVAN ANDERTON

Sylvan Anderton was one of football's drudges, an honest toiler who went about his work with the unobtrusive efficiency of a diligent clerk perched high upon a stool in some sepulchral Victorian office, his quill moving ceaselessly across the pages of a weighty ledger.

Signed by Ted Drake from the club he had managed before taking over at Stamford Bridge, Reading, shortly before the transfer deadline in March 1959 to reinforce a team that had lost its way after a bright and breezy start to the season, Sylvan proved to be a sound, dependable right-half who used the ball well and covered conscientiously. Although he was a little short of drive and aggression, he contributed to a worthwhile upturn in the Blues' fortunes in the closing weeks of 1958/59 and missed only two League games the following season, forming a solid if somewhat pedestrian half-back partnership with Stan Crowther.

Powerless to resist the challenge of 17-year-old Terry Venables, a player of infinitely greater gifts, Anderton began the next campaign in the reserves but fought back with characteristic tenacity to claim a place at left-half after Christmas. Tommy Docherty's elevation to the position of chief coach presented a chance to reassert his claims but the arrival of Andy Malcolm dashed Sylvan's hopes and in January 1962 he joined Queens Park Rangers.

BORN: Reading, 23.11.34.
GAMES: 82. GOALS: 2.
OTHER CLUBS: Reading 52/3-58/9 (155, 18);
Queens Park Rangers 61/2 (4, 0).

1958/59-1961/62

STAN CROWTHER

A powerful, aggressive wing-half with a reputation as a hard man, Stan Crowther was signed from Manchester United shortly before Christmas 1958 in an effort to reinforce a defence that had been conceding too many soft goals, particularly away from home. Although he was only 23, he had already had an eventful career: having helped Aston Villa win the FA Cup in 1957, he had moved to Old Trafford in the aftermath of the Munich disaster and reached Wembley once again, becoming the first man to play in the competition for two different clubs in the same season.

Apart from a spell at the beginning of 1959/60 when he was sidelined by injury, Stan was the Blues' regular left-half for the next 18 months but he lacked the natural ability of the man he had replaced, Derek Saunders, and could not summon the self-discipline to make the fullest use of the talent he possessed. For all the Midlander's fierce tackling and unwavering commitment, the torrent of goals conceded continued unabated and at the start of 1960/61 Ted Drake looked to Terry Bradbury.

Crowther made only one more first-team appearance for Chelsea, in a League Cup tie against Workington that October, and in March 1961 he was transferred to Second Division Brighton, subsequently dropping out of League football.

BORN: Bilston, 3.9.35.
GAMES: 58. GOALS: 0.
OTHER CLUBS: Aston Villa 56/7-57/8 (50, 4);
Manchester United 57/8-58/9 (13, 0);
Brighton and Hove Albion 60/1 (4, 0).

1958/59-1960/61

JIMMY GREAVES

Jimmy Greaves is widely acknowledged as the greatest goalscorer that English football has ever produced but, in the eyes of the Stamford Bridge faithful at least, he never quite recaptured the precocious brilliance he showed during his four seasons in the Chelsea first team prior to his departure for Italy in the summer of 1961. He was rarely to be seen dropping back to help his defenders and could scarcely be described as a model professional off the field, but none of that mattered; he was a match-winner whose pace and deft control made him almost impossible to contain.

Jimmy made his League debut at White Hart Lane in the first game of 1957/58, having scored more than a century of goals as a junior the previous season, and crowned a sparkling performance by tucking home the equaliser with the precision that was to become so familiar with five minutes remaining. However, the Greaves legend really began to take shape when he returned to the side on Christmas morning after a brief spell on the sidelines, the audacious 17-year-old scoring four times in a festive romp against Portsmouth.

Greaves scored 132 goals in 169 games for Chelsea, an astonishing rate of return that kept the Blues afloat despite the manifest inadequacies of their defence. He hit five in a match on three occasions, including a remarkable 5-4 win at Deepdale in December 1959 when he appeared to score at will every time Preston drew level. A hat-trick against Manchester City in November 1960 made him the first man to score a hundred League goals before the age of 21 and it seems highly unlikely that his club record of 41 League goals in 1960/61 will ever be beaten.

The statistics of Jimmy's career are enough to reduce every striker currently plying his trade in the Premier League to abject despair, but figures alone cannot do justice to the imperious style in which his goals were taken. Not for him the ego-boosting blast into the roof of the net; he had the confidence to select his spot and roll the ball home, often having wrong-footed the hapless 'keeper. Blessed with remarkable anticipation, he was a clinical, razor-sharp finisher who pounced eagerly on the half-chance at close quarters, ruthlessly punishing the slightest lapse. He relished every opportunity to run at defences, heading for goal with characteristic singleness of purpose, and had the skill to go past his man, as he demonstrated against Birmingham in September 1959 when he picked the ball up in his own half and weaved his way past five defenders before leaving the 'keeper helpless with a stinging shot. But, above all, he made it look absurdly, joyously easy . . .

Greaves won his first full international cap against Peru in May 1959 and was a regular member of Walter Winterbottom's side thereafter, but Chelsea's failure to build a winning team around their extraordinary young marksman made it inevitable that they would lose him. In Italian football he could command vastly more than the modest sum the Blues were permitted to offer him and it was eventually agreed that he would join AC Milan for £80,000 at the end of the 1960/61 season. His last game for the club was against Nottingham Forest at Stamford Bridge and he marked the occasion in characteristically dramatic fashion by scoring all four goals in a 4-3 win. It was an emotional occasion, for the little genius had been enormously popular with fans and team-mates alike and the future looked bleak without him. However, while the Stamford Bridge crowd mourned the loss of their saviour, few could pretend that in his place their decision would have been any different.

Like many football expatriates since, Jimmy did not enjoy his stay in Italy but by the following December the maximum wage had been lifted and he was back in London – but with Tottenham, not Chelsea.

BORN: East Ham, 20.2.40.
GAMES: 169. GOALS: 132.
HONOURS: 57 England caps (59-67).
OTHER CLUBS: AC Milan;
Tottenham Hotspur 61/2-69/70 (321, 220);
West Ham United 69/70-70/71 (38, 13).

1957/58-1960/61

CHARLIE LIVESEY

The two seasons Charlie Livesey spent at Stamford Bridge represented a wasted opportunity for a player of considerable natural ability. A speedy, powerfully built centre-forward, he had failed to make the grade with the Blues as a schoolboy but was signed from Southampton in May 1959 in a part-exchange deal involving Cliff Huxford after an impressive first season in League football which had also attracted the interest of Arsenal and Birmingham City.

Charlie began his Chelsea career with something of a flourish, contributing to a bright start to the new campaign with eight goals in his first 14 appearances, including a coolly taken individual effort against West Bromwich Albion in October, but his stay with the club was to be blighted by inconsistency. All too often a good performance would be followed by a match in which he remained largely anonymous, as if he felt he had nothing left to prove, and it seemed that only when he was dropped was he prepared to assert himself.

Although he was not the most ruthless of goalscorers, Livesey possessed a cultured left foot and, like any worthwhile number nine of the period, posed a threat when the ball was in the air, but these qualities were not enough to guarantee his place and after a lively start to the following season he was once again omitted in favour of Ron Tindall, eventually joining Gillingham in August 1961.

BORN: West Ham, 6.2.38. GAMES: 42. GOALS: 18.
OTHER CLUBS: Southampton 58/9 (25, 14);
Gillingham 61/2-62/3 (47, 17); Watford 62/3-63/4 (64, 26);
Northampton Town 64/5-65/6 (28, 4);
Brighton and Hove Albion 65/6-68/9 (125, 30).

1959/60-1960/61

JOHNNY BROOKS

One of a number of players brought to Stamford Bridge by Ted Drake who had started their careers under his tutelage during his five-year spell in charge at Reading, Johnny Brooks was a stylish inside-forward whose delicate ball skills and imperious distribution had earned him three England caps at the high point of a largely successful stay with Tottenham. However, by the time he joined Chelsea in December 1959 in an exchange deal which took Les Allen to White Hart Lane – where he would earn a place in the history books as a member of Spurs' double-winning team – his career was in what would prove to be an irreversible decline.

There was no doubt of Johnny's talent. His ability to prise open even the stubbornest defence with a majestic swerve or to switch the point of attack with a crisply struck 40-yard pass should have ensured that Jimmy Greaves was kept supplied with a steady stream of goalscoring opportunities, but in a struggling team the newcomer's fragile confidence crumbled away, prompting his detractors to mutter about a lack of heart and courage.

Drake kept faith with Brooks for a year or so but his belief that he could help the 28-year-old rediscover his lost form proved unfounded. In the spring of 1961 Johnny was ousted from the first team by young Bobby Tambling and shortly after the start of the following season he moved on to Brentford.

BORN: Reading, 23.12.31.
GAMES: 52. GOALS: 7.
HONOURS: 3 England caps (56).
OTHER CLUBS: Reading 49/50-52/3 (46, 5);
Tottenham Hotspur 52/3-59/60 (166, 46);
Brentford 61/2-63/4 (83, 36); Crystal Palace 63/4 (7, 0).

1959/60-1960/61

MIKE HARRISON

Mike Harrison was a strong, athletic left-winger whose pace and powerful running troubled all but the most accomplished defenders, but he lacked the delicate skills and indomitable spirit of Frank Blunstone and was never able to establish himself as Chelsea's first-choice number 11. He made his debut at Blackpool in April 1957 when he was still five days short of his 17th birthday but had to wait until the closing weeks of the 1958/59 season before he was given an extended run in the side. He did well enough to prompt Ted Drake to accommodate Blunstone at inside-left, but the following season Harrison made only five appearances and thereafter he was firmly cast in the role of understudy.

His direct style created a steady stream of goalscoring opportunities for his team-mates but Mike is best remembered for his ability to test goalkeepers from prodigious distances with his mighty left foot, a remarkable swerving effort against Arsenal in March 1962, for example, leaving the unfortunate Jack Kelsey utterly bewildered.

Blunstone's frequent absences allowed Harrison a fairly regular taste of League football, but the arrival of Tommy Knox in the summer of 1962 marked the end of his hopes at Stamford Bridge and he soon moved on to Blackburn, giving the Lancashire club excellent service over the next five years.

BORN: Ilford, 18.4.40.
GAMES: 64. GOALS: 9.
OTHER CLUBS: Blackburn Rovers 62/3-67/8 (160, 40);
Plymouth Argyle 67/8 (15, 3);
Luton Town 68/9-69/70 (32, 6).

1956/57-1962/63

MICKY BLOCK

It seems cruel that the door to the Chelsea first team should have been opened to Micky Block so early in his career, only to be slammed in his face before he had reached his 19th birthday. His tantalising taste of First Division football was an indirect result of the injury which was to sideline Frank Blunstone for the best part of two years, the powerfully built youngster making his debut on the left wing in September 1957 and going on to record a total of 20 League appearances that season. Direct and persistent, Block possessed few of Frank's intricate skills, his preferred strategy being to run at his full-back, then knock the ball past him and use his pace to get clear, but he had a left foot of great power and precision and was not afraid to try his luck from distance.

Micky continued his public apprenticeship the following autumn, although he now faced competition for the number 11 shirt from Mike Harrison, a player of similar style who was three months younger. However, it was the return of Blunstone to fitness at the end of November that really marked the turning-point in Block's fortunes, the likeable teenager quickly finding himself relegated to the position of third choice. He remained at Stamford Bridge for another three years, making just five more League appearances, but the appointment of Tommy Docherty prompted widespread changes to the Blues' playing staff and in January 1962 he was transferred to Brentford.

BORN: Ipswich, 28.1.40.
GAMES: 40. GOALS: 6.
OTHER CLUBS: Brentford 61/2-65/6 (146, 30);
Watford 66/7 (13, 2).

1957/58-1961/62

DAVID CLISS

There have been any number of Chelsea players who have failed to do justice to their talent down the years, but rarely has the gulf between potential and achievement been wider than in the case of David Cliss. A diminutive inside-forward with the sort of audacious, delicate skills the Stamford Bridge crowd have always relished, he made his first-team debut against Preston in February 1958 and his stylish display in a 3-1 win at Villa Park two weeks later suggested that a star was in the making.

However, despite the 18-year-old's plentiful exuberance, Ted Drake appeared to feel that his lack of weight and power was an insuperable handicap and Cliss soon gave way to more robust performers. He made only seven appearances during the next two seasons and a broken leg in the first reserve match of 1960/61 dashed hopes that the experience he had gained playing in America during the summer would enable him finally to make the breakthrough.

Fully recovered, David started the following campaign in the side but the departure of Drake ended his chances of establishing himself, and in the summer he slipped into non-League football. With more application, and better luck, it could have been different . . .

BORN: Enfield, 15.11.39.
GAMES: 24. GOALS: 1.

1957/58-1961/62

TERRY BRADBURY

Brimming with youthful enthusiasm, Terry Bradbury was a tall, aggressive wing-half who was destined to discover that an abundance of effort alone could not compensate for the absence from his game of the kind of refinement generally considered essential to a First Division career.

Having waited rather longer than many of his contemporaries for his chance in the first team, he started the 1960/61 season in a completely remodelled half-back line that was completed by the Scottish veteran Bobby Evans and, on the right, 17-year-old Terry Venables. An eager, determined ball-winner who was blessed with considerable self-confidence, Bradbury tackled with great spirit and had the maturity to play within his limitations, sensibly opting for the simple pass to a colleague rather than attempting – in vain – something more ambitious, but after nine games which saw 24 goals conceded, he gave way to Sylvan Anderton. Six further appearances followed later in the campaign but consistency remained elusive.

Terry was given another run in the side during the Blues' dismal relegation battle the following winter but when he failed to win a place in Tommy Docherty's revamped team at the beginning of 1962/63 it became apparent that it was time to move on and in September he joined Southend United.

BORN: Paddington, 15.11.39. GAMES: 29. GOALS: 1.
OTHER CLUBS: Southend United 62/3-65/6 (161, 19);
Leyton Orient 66/7 (27, 0); Wrexham 67/8-68/9 (78, 4);
Chester 69/70-70/1 (90, 2).

1960/61-1961/62

ANDY MALCOLM

When Tommy Docherty succeeded Ted Drake in September 1961 it was already apparent that the team would have to be strengthened if the Blues were to avoid relegation. That verdict can only have been reinforced by a sequence of four defeats and a draw in his first five matches in charge, and in an effort to halt the slide he signed Andy Malcolm from West Ham in a deal which took Ron Tindall to Upton Park in part-exchange.

A strong, aggressive right-half with a reputation as a tight marker, Malcolm was a seasoned campaigner and there seemed to be every hope that the experience and resolve he brought to a tactically naive team might make a decisive difference when his debut at Highbury yielded a 3-0 win, Chelsea's first away victory of the season. Comfortable in possession and always wanting the ball, Malcolm soon made the number four shirt his own, assuming the captaincy in the absence of Peter Sillett, but the revival could not be sustained and relegation soon became virtually inevitable.

A fine solo goal in a 4-3 win at Fulham was probably the best moment of Andy's short stay at Stamford Bridge, but there was no place for him in the remodelled team unveiled by Docherty at the start of the following season and that October he moved on to Queens Park Rangers.

BORN: West Ham, 4.5.33.
GAMES: 28. GOALS: 1.
OTHER CLUBS: West Ham United 53/4-61/2 (283, 4);
Queens Park Rangers 62/3-64/5 (84, 4);
Port Elizabeth, South Africa.

1961/62

BOBBY EVANS

When Chelsea signed Bobby Evans in May 1960 they were buying a player of proven class. A Scottish international for more than a decade, he had served Glasgow Celtic with distinction for 16 seasons, helping the Parkhead club to a league and cup double in 1954 with a series of imposing displays at right-half before switching successfully to the number five shirt, but the Stamford Bridge crowd were to see little of the doughty tackling and measured passing that had won him such respect north of the border.

Bobby was already past his 33rd birthday when he trotted out for the first game of the new season and it soon became apparent that he was a spent force, the veteran finding it impossible to adapt to the greater pace of English football at this stage in his career. No doubt Ted Drake had hoped that his enormous experience would advance the football education of the youngsters in the team but, with Evans struggling to keep his head above water as a flood of goals were conceded, he was able to offer little assistance to others.

Bobby retained his place at centre-half until March but he was painfully aware that he had not lived up to his reputation, and in the closing weeks of the season he made way for Mel Scott before joining Newport County as player-manager in the summer.

BORN: Glasgow, 16.7.27. GAMES: 37. GOALS: 1.
HONOURS: 48 Scotland caps (48-60).
OTHER CLUBS: Glasgow Celtic;
Newport County 61/2 (31, 0);
Morton; Third Lanark; Raith Rovers.
MANAGER: Newport County (61-62); Third Lanark.

1960/61

TOMMY DOCHERTY

GORDON BOLLAND

DENNIS SORRELL

TOMMY DOCHERTY 1961/62

Wing-half. BORN: Glasgow, 24.8.28.
GAMES: 4. GOALS: 0.
HONOURS: 25 Scotland caps (51-59).
OTHER CLUBS: Glasgow Celtic; Preston North End 49/50-57/8 (324, 5);
Arsenal 58/9-60/1 (83, 1).
MANAGER: Chelsea (62-67); Rotherham United (67-68);
Queens Park Rangers (68 and 79-80); Aston Villa (68-70);
Oporto, Portugal; Scotland (71-72); Manchester United (72-77);
Derby County (77-79); Sydney Olympic, Australia;
Preston North End (81); Wolverhampton Wanderers (84-85).

DENNIS BUTLER 1961/62-1962/63

Full-back. BORN: Fulham, 7.3.43.
GAMES: 18. GOALS: 0.
OTHER CLUBS: Hull City 63/4-69/70 (217, 0);
Reading 69/70-73/4 (170, 0).

GORDON BOLLAND 1961/62

Inside-forward. BORN: Boston, 12.8.43.
GAMES: 2. GOALS: 0.
OTHER CLUBS: Leyton Orient 61/2-63/4 (63, 19);
Norwich City 63/4-67/8 (105, 29);
Charlton Athletic 67/8-68/9 (11, 2);
Millwall 68/9-74/5 (244, 62).

COLIN SHAW 1961/62

Centre-forward. BORN: St Albans, 19.6.43.
GAMES: 1. GOALS: 0.
OTHER CLUBS: Norwich City 63/4-64/5 (3, 0);
Leyton Orient 65/6 (7, 0); Natal, South Africa.

DENNIS SORRELL 1961/62-1963/64

Wing-half. BORN: Lambeth, 7.10.40.
GAMES: 4. GOALS: 1.
OTHER CLUBS: Leyton Orient 58/9-60/1 (37, 1) and
64/5-66/7 (74, 3).

ERROL McNALLY 1961/62-1963/64

Goalkeeper. BORN: Lurgan, 27.8.43.
GAMES: 9. GOALS: 0.
OTHER CLUBS: Portadown; Glenavon.

DENNIS BUTLER

COLIN SHAW

ERROL McNALLY

MICHAEL PINNER

JOHN DUNN

DENNIS BROWN

JIM MULHOLLAND

JOHN O'ROURKE

IAN WATSON

MICHAEL PINNER 1961/62

Goalkeeper. BORN: Boston, 16.2.34.
GAMES: 1. GOALS: 0.
OTHER CLUBS: Aston Villa 54/5-56/7 (4, 0);
Sheffield Wednesday 57/8-58/9 (7, 0);
Queens Park Rangers 59/60 (19, 0);
Manchester United 60/1 (4, 0); Swansea City 61/2 (1, 0);
Leyton Orient 62/3-64/5 (77, 0).

JOHN DUNN 1962/63-1965/66

Goalkeeper. BORN: Barking, 21.6.44.
GAMES: 16. GOALS: 0.
OTHER CLUBS: Torquay United 66/7-67/8 (44, 0);
Aston Villa 67/8-70/1 (101, 0); Charlton Athletic 71/2-74/5 (104, 0).

JIM MULHOLLAND 1962/63-1963/64

Forward. BORN: Knightswood, 10.4.38.
GAMES: 12. GOALS: 3.
OTHER CLUBS: East Stirling; Morton;
Barrow 65/6-68/9 (134, 47); Stockport County 68/9-69/70 (33, 5);
Crewe Alexandra 70/1 (10, 0).

DENNIS BROWN 1963/64-1964/65

Inside-forward. BORN: Reading, 8.2.44.
GAMES: 13. GOALS: 2.
OTHER CLUBS: Swindon Town 64/5-66/7 (92, 38);
Northampton Town 66/7-68/9 (46, 10);
Aldershot 69/70-74/5 (245, 56).

IAN WATSON 1962/63-1964/65

Full-back. BORN: Hammersmith, 7.1.44.
GAMES: 9. GOALS: 1.
OTHER CLUBS: Queens Park Rangers 65/6-73/4 (203, 1).

JOHN O'ROURKE 1963/64

Centre-forward. BORN: Northampton, 11.2.45.
GAMES: 1. GOALS: 0.
OTHER CLUBS: Luton Town 63/4-65/6 (84, 64);
Middlesbrough 66/7-67/8 (64, 38);
Ipswich Town 67/8-69/70 (69, 30);
Coventry City 69/70-71/2 (54, 17);
Queens Park Rangers 71/2-72/3 (34, 12);
AFC Bournemouth 73/4-74/5 (22, 4).

FRANK UPTON

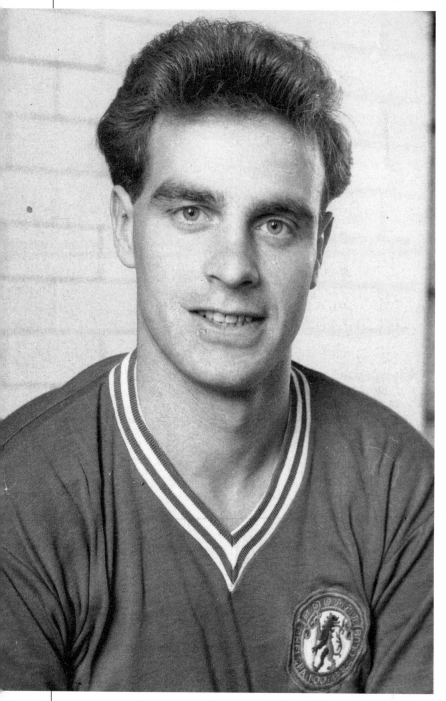

A burly, tough left-half who delighted in his reputation as a hard man, Frank Upton was possibly the least gifted member of the Chelsea team that gained promotion from the Second Division in 1962/63 but his contribution was vital. Signed from Derby County shortly before the start of the previous season, he had been dropped after just three matches and remained out of favour until the following March, when he was recalled at centre-forward in a desperate bid to drag the Blues away from the foot of the table. The move was not a success, but when Tommy Docherty paired Frank with John Mortimore at the centre of the defence in the closing fixtures he had at last discovered a foundation on which he could build a winning team.

There were no frills to Upton's game, but he was a fearsome competitor who could be depended upon to give everything he had. Good in the air and a doughty tackler, he played to his strengths, winning the ball and giving it to a colleague better equipped to do something constructive with it. His influence on his young team-mates was invaluable, and anyone he suspected of not matching his own total commitment could expect to have it drawn to his attention in no uncertain terms.

Frank scored three goals that season from carefully planned free-kick moves, but his most celebrated contribution came in the epic battle at Roker Park in May which opened the door to the First Division. Handed the number nine shirt and instructed to unsettle Charlie Hurley, the creative Sunderland centre-half, he carried out his task with undisguised relish, characteristically shaking off a knee injury to finish the game on one leg.

Having lost his place in defence to Ron Harris, Frank returned to the side the following November after a tactical reshuffle and helped the Blues establish themselves as a force to be reckoned with, but with Docherty trying to build a team that would challenge for honours, there was no long-term future for him at the Bridge and he rejoined Derby in September 1965. He later had a spell on the Chelsea coaching staff and was caretaker manager – for a day – after the departure of Ken Shellito.

BORN: Nuneaton, 18.10.34.
GAMES: 86. GOALS: 3.
OTHER CLUBS: Northampton Town 52/3-53/4 (17, 1);
Derby County 54/5-60/1 (224, 12) and 65/6-66/7 (35, 5);
Notts County 66/7 (34, 3); Workington 67/8 (7, 0).
MANAGER: Workington (68).

1961/62-1964/65

ALLAN HARRIS

During his two spells at Stamford Bridge Allan Harris was a valued member of the first-team squad but never quite succeeded in making his place in the side secure. A cool, thoughtful full-back, he was loyal and uncomplaining and could be depended upon to give his all whenever he was called upon, but perhaps lacked the aggression needed to succeed at the highest level.

A member of the Chelsea side that won the FA Youth Cup in 1960 and 1961, Allan made his senior debut as a 17-year-old in a League Cup tie against Workington in October 1960 and went on to make a total of 21 appearances that season, all of them on the left – his preferred position, even though he was naturally right-footed. When Peter Sillett broke his leg the following August the youngster was presented with an opportunity to make the position his own and impressed many observers with his composure and maturity. Although he was occasionally betrayed by over-confidence when in possession, his reading of the game, sound positional play and measured passing suggested a bright future, but the arrival of Eddie McCreadie from East Stirling that April effectively blocked his progress.

Harris found himself in the thankless role of understudy over the next two seasons and eventually moved to Second Division Coventry City in November 1964 in search of first-team football. Eighteen months later he was back at the Bridge, deputising for McCreadie in the second leg of the Fairs Cup semi-final against Barcelona and the subsequent play-off in Spain, but for much of the following season he was on the sidelines once more. He returned to the first team at right-back in time to help the Blues to the FA Cup Final, but the frustrating 2-1 defeat at the hands of Tottenham was to be his last game for the club as he was transferred to Queens Park Rangers that summer.

BORN: Northampton, 28.12.42.
GAMES: 98 (4). GOALS: 1.
OTHER CLUBS: Coventry City 64/5-65/6 (60, 0);
Queens Park Rangers 67/8-70/1 (93, 0);
Plymouth Argyle 70/1-72/3 (64, 0);
Cambridge United 73/4 (6, 0).
MANAGER: Español, Spain.

1960/61-1964/65 & 1965/66-1966/67

DEREK KEVAN

When it became apparent that the sparkling form that had taken Chelsea six points clear of their nearest rivals at the top of the Second Division table at Christmas had disappeared during the Big Freeze that brought English football to a virtual standstill in the first two months of 1963, Tommy Docherty's characteristically bold response was to pay West Bromwich Albion £45,000 for the services of Derek Kevan, their powerfully built centre-forward. The 28-year-old England international had a highly impressive scoring record but he was none too mobile and thus had great difficulty in adapting to his new team's close-passing style, which depended on seemingly non-stop running. For all his physical strength and ability to win the ball in the air, Derek was largely dependent on others to create chances for him and in a side that had lost its confidence and rhythm the service he received was predictably scanty.

Kevan experienced similar difficulty in accustoming himself to the strict discipline and demanding training Docherty had introduced to Stamford Bridge, and his Chelsea career was to be brief and unrewarding. The single goal he scored for the club could scarcely have been more important, his header after 90 seconds paving the way for the 7-0 win over Portsmouth that clinched the Blues' return to the First Division, but on the eve of the following season he was transferred to Manchester City.

BORN: Ripon, 6.3.35. GAMES: 7. GOALS: 1.
HONOURS: 14 England caps (57-61).
OTHER CLUBS: Bradford Park Avenue 52/3 (15, 8);
West Bromwich Albion 55/6-62/3 (262, 157);
Manchester City 63/4-64/5 (67, 48); Crystal Palace 65/6 (21, 5);
Peterborough United 65/6-66/7 (17, 2); Luton Town 66/7 (11, 4);
Stockport County 66/7-67/8 (40, 10).

1962/63

TOMMY HARMER

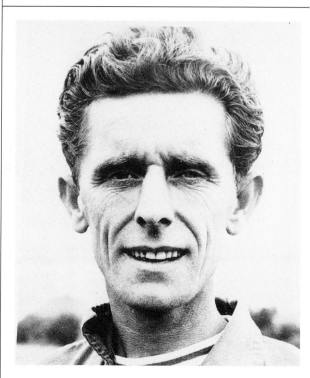

An old-fashioned ball playing inside-forward who had graced White Hart Lane in the late fifties with his close control and superb passing, Tommy Harmer was 34 when he joined Chelsea from Watford in September 1962, expecting to play in the reserves and further the education of the Stamford Bridge youngsters. Slight and frail-looking, with a deeply lined face that suggested profound knowledge acquired over many years, 'Tiny Tom' seemed ideally cast as a dressing-room sage but in the event he made five League appearances that season and finished on the winning side every time.

Although he needed a cigarette before a game to calm his jangling nerves, Tommy was a steadying influence out on the pitch, slowing things down if the pace became too frantic. He was no athlete, but his ability to hold the ball despite the earnest attentions of opponents seemingly twice his size and find a colleague with a telling pass proved invaluable as the tension mounted, especially in the epic struggle at Roker Park, where his goal – deflected into the net from a Tambling corner – earned the Blues the victory they needed to keep their promotion hopes alive.

'Charmer' Harmer played three times in the First Division the following season, having a hand in both goals in a 2-1 win at Tottenham, and remained on the Chelsea coaching staff until 1967.

BORN: Hackney, 2.2.28.
GAMES: 9. GOALS: 1.
OTHER CLUBS: Tottenham Hotspur 51/2-59/60 (205, 47);
Watford 60/1-61/2 (63, 6).

1962/63-1963/64

KEN SHELLITO

The injury which wrecked Ken Shellito's career robbed Chelsea of a richly talented right-back and left a gap in Tommy Docherty's emerging team which was never adequately filled. Having been introduced to first-team football in April 1959, Ken spent most of the next two seasons in the reserves, honing his technique, but when the chance he had been waiting for finally arrived in the wake of Ted Drake's departure he was ready to make the most of it, the 21-year-old securing his place with a series of polished displays.

However, it was during the Blues' whirlwind tour of the Second Division that Shellito's reputation began to blossom, his partnership with Eddie McCreadie quickly becoming one of the most respected in the country. An accomplished defender, he was not outstandingly quick but his positional play and reading of the game reflected a solid grounding in the traditional full-back skills and he relished a struggle for supremacy with a tricky winger. In a team committed to playing constructive football with a measured build-up from the back, his role in launching attacks was crucial, and he rarely wasted possession, picking out his man with a precise pass. Encouraged by Docherty and his coach, Dave Sexton, to support the attack at every opportunity, Ken helped pioneer the overlap, surging down the right flank, linking with his forwards and delivering a telling centre.

Shellito won what promised to be the first of many England caps on the 1963 summer tour and took over the Chelsea captaincy early the following season, but then in October he damaged his left knee against Sheffield Wednesday. He underwent four cartilage operations in the next three years as he battled with extraordinary courage and tenacity to save his career, but the knee was never right and the home leg of the Fairs Cup tie against Wiener of Austria in December 1965 proved to be his last competitive first-team match for the Blues. Finally forced to abandon his dogged fight for fitness in January 1969, he joined the Stamford Bridge coaching staff, succeeding his old full-back partner as manager in 1977.

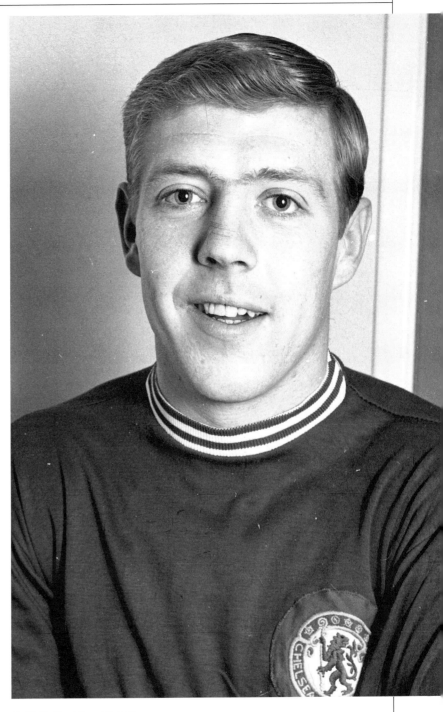

BORN: East Ham, 18.4.40.
GAMES: 123. GOALS: 2.
HONOURS: 1 England cap (63).
MANAGER: Chelsea (77-78);
Cambridge United (85).

1958/59-1965/66

FRANK BLUNSTONE

Few ball-playing wingers have possessed the indomitable courage of Frank Blunstone. Faced by fearsome full-backs who had no hesitation in carrying out their blood-curdling threats when words alone proved insufficient to intimidate their tormentors, he remained defiant, revelling in the challenge and quite prepared to hand out as many knocks as he took. The frequent injuries that were an inevitable consequence of this aggressive approach he generally shook off without recourse to so much as the trainer's magic sponge, never mind the two weeks' rest that many of his peers might have considered unavoidable, and when a broken leg put him out of the game for nearly two years he fought his way back to fitness with characteristic grit to play the most effective football of his career.

Frank arrived at Stamford Bridge as an 18-year-old in February 1953, having learned his trade in the Third Division North with his home-town club, Crewe Alexandra, and quickly became an automatic choice at outside-left, helped on his way by a goal on his senior debut for the Blues against Tottenham. His return to the side after a lengthy injury lay-off in November was an important factor in the surge that brought the League Championship to SW6 in 1954/55, and his sparkling form that season earned him international honours against Wales, Scotland, France and Portugal. However, he played in around a hundred games in not much more than six months, many of them for the Army during the course of his National Service, and that was probably an underlying cause of the fracture to his left leg sustained in a fourth round FA Cup tie at White Hart Lane in January 1957. Back in action in a pre-season friendly against Ajax the following August, Frank suffered a recurrence of the injury and this time he was ruled out for more than a year, making his comeback at Everton in November 1958.

It says much for his character that he soon recaptured his best form, ensuring a steady supply of chances that helped Jimmy Greaves make his name and Chelsea stay in the First Division despite the shortcomings of their defence. A bubbly, lively character, full of energy and life, Frank was a direct, attacking winger, famed for a head-down dribbling style that prompted some wits to suggest that he would have ended up out in the Fulham Road if he hadn't counted the white lines as he went. Despite this, he was a good crosser of the ball and had the confidence to keep running at a defence even when things weren't going his way.

Once the baby of the side, Frank was one of the old heads of the team which won promotion in 1962/63, and he confirmed his supreme professionalism by adapting to the new tactics introduced by Tommy Docherty and Dave Sexton which called for him to drop back into midfield and make runs to create space for Eddie McCreadie's overlaps. It was a role that involved a lot of work and little glory but Frank's ability to change the character of a match with a single coruscating flash of skill remained invaluable. His two superb individual goals in a vital 3-1 win against Derby in March were typical, but possibly the best game of his long and distinguished career was the third round FA Cup tie against Spurs at White Hart Lane the following season when his perfect centre gave Bert Murray a magnificent equaliser.

Cruelly, injury was to strike Frank down once again, just as he was poised to share in the Blues' exciting pursuit of honours, a ruptured Achilles tendon suffered during a tour of the Caribbean in the summer of 1964 ending his career when he still had a huge amount to offer. After his retirement he helped with the coaching of Chelsea's young players, subsequently managing Brentford and working with Tommy Docherty at Manchester United and Derby, but he prudently declined the offer of the manager's chair at Stamford Bridge in the wake of Dave Sexton's departure.

BORN: Crewe, 17.10.34.
GAMES: 346. GOALS: 53.
HONOURS: League Championship 54/5.
5 England caps (54-56).
OTHER CLUBS: Crewe Alexandra 51/2-52/3 (48, 12).
MANAGER: Brentford (69-73).

1952/53 - 1963/64

BERT MURRAY

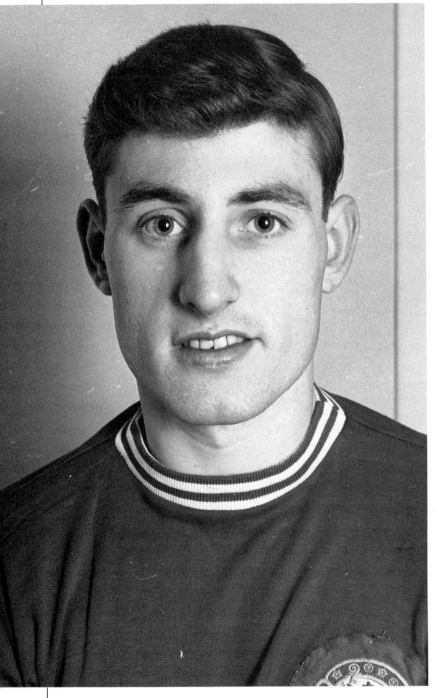

The Stamford Bridge crowd never really warmed to Bert Murray, failing to appreciate the contribution made by his unstinting efforts on the right flank to the overall effectiveness of a side justly admired for its team-work. He was regarded as an orthodox winger when he made his League debut in October 1961 but it was his ability to adapt to the more demanding role envisaged by Tommy Docherty and Dave Sexton the following season that enabled him to establish himself in the team at the expense of Peter Brabrook.

Shuttling up and down the pitch, Bert formed a formidable partnership with Ken Shellito, making runs to create space for the full-back when he broke forward, and tackling back when possession was lost. Quick and direct, with two good feet, he provided a steady service to his forwards, playing the ball in early with no unnecessary frills, and scored more than his fair share of goals, many with his head, including the equaliser in a hard-fought third round FA Cup tie at White Hart Lane in January 1964 and the winner in the replay.

When Tommy Docherty adopted a 4-3-3 formation in the wake of the injury which ended Frank Blunstone's career, 'Ruby' was called upon to show his versatility once more and abandon the flanks for a new role in midfield, to the bewilderment of some of the club's less knowledgeable followers who, seemingly oblivious to the tactical revolution that had swept English football in recent years, demanded to know why their number seven was 'never on his bloody wing'. Bert was a regular member of the side which pursued a magnificent treble that season, contributing 17 goals in 40 League appearances, a total many a striker would envy, but his involvement in the celebrated Blackpool Incident inevitably soured relations with his uncompromising manager. The emergence of Peter Osgood in 1965/66 ultimately cost Bert his place and at the end of the season, with the side that had brought the Blues so close to success breaking up as the simmering Stamford Bridge saucepan boiled over, he followed Barry Bridges to Second Division Birmingham City.

BORN: Hoxton, 22.9.42.
GAMES: 179 (4). GOALS: 44.
HONOURS: League Cup 64/5.
OTHER CLUBS: Birmingham City 66/7-70/1 (132, 22);
Brighton and Hove Albion 70/1-73/4 (102, 25);
Peterborough United 73/4-75/6 (123, 10).

1961/62-1965/66

GRAHAM MOORE

Graham Moore arrived at Stamford Bridge with a big reputation to live up to, and it would be fair to say he didn't quite manage it. He did a respectable job during his two-year stay in London, but possessed the natural talent to have achieved rather more.

A powerfully built Welsh international forward, Graham was signed from Cardiff City in December 1961 for £35,000, a club record fee at the time. The 20-year-old went straight into the first team at centre-forward and two thunderously struck goals in his third game, a 5-2 defeat at White Hart Lane, suggested that he would make a valuable contribution to the grim fight against relegation which faced the Blues in the second half of the season. However, he failed to add to them and the lack of a goalscoring touch was to prove one of his greatest weaknesses.

'Archie' had exceptional skill for a player of his size and was highly effective as a target man, receiving the ball with his back to goal, shielding it and laying it off to colleagues with aplomb. A little ponderous, he didn't have too much pace and struggled the following season as Tommy Docherty and Dave Sexton pioneered their new style of football based on constant movement. Nevertheless he played in all but six League matches, usually in the number ten shirt, and formed an effective partnership with Barry Bridges and Bobby Tambling.

Always popular in the dressing room, Graham retained his place as the Blues attempted to establish themselves in the First Division the following autumn but still the goals wouldn't come and when Docherty made a tactical switch, restoring Frank Upton to the team at the expense of a forward, he was the one to go, despite scoring twice in what was to be his last match for Chelsea, a 3-2 home defeat at the hands of Birmingham in November. Shortly afterwards he was on his way to Manchester United, where further disappointment awaited him.

BORN: Hengoed, 7.3.41. GAMES: 72. GOALS: 14.
HONOURS: 21 Wales caps (59-70).
OTHER CLUBS: Cardiff City 58/9-61/2 (85, 23);
Manchester United 63/4 (18, 4);
Northampton Town 65/6-66/7 (53, 10);
Charlton Athletic 67/8-70/1 (110, 8);
Doncaster Rovers 71/2-73/4 (69, 3).

1961/62-1963/64

BARRY BRIDGES

A potent cocktail of electrifying pace and the predatory instincts of a natural goalscorer made Barry Bridges a key member of the Chelsea team for much of the turbulent Docherty era. He was by no means a complete striker – a tendency to spurn simple chances in favour of those that looked impossible comes to mind – but he certainly made the fullest possible use of the gifts he possessed, his determination and sheer effort compensating for any deficiencies in his technique.

Although Barry made his senior debut when he was 17, scoring in a 3-2 win against West Ham in February 1959, more than two years would pass before he was given a real chance to prove himself during the Blues' miserable slide towards relegation in 1961/62. His tally of 19 goals in 32 League appearances represented an impressive achievement in a poor side, but he was unable to maintain that striking rate in the Second Division and was dropped for the decisive matches against Sunderland and Portsmouth in May to accommodate Frank Upton. When Jimmy Mulholland was preferred at the start of the following season, Bridges understandably concluded that there was no future for him at Stamford Bridge but he quickly regained his place and resumed his prolific partnership with Bobby Tambling.

Many of Barry's goals were scored at close range, his speed and outstanding awareness enabling him to pounce on a ball played into the goalmouth before anyone else had moved, as he demonstrated with the Blues' fourth goal in the FA Cup quarter-final against Peterborough in March 1965. However, he was probably at his most dangerous when running onto a through-pass down the middle and thrived on the superb service supplied by Terry Venables, although he was sometimes guilty of over-eagerness, mistiming his move and being caught offside as a result.

Barry's consistency won him full international honours against Scotland, Hungary and Yugoslavia in 1964/65 but at the end of that season he was one of eight players sent home from Blackpool after they had broken a curfew imposed by Tommy Docherty and his relations with the autocratic Scotsman were never the same again. The following October he was recalled to the England team to face Austria but three days later he was dropped from the Chelsea starting line-up against Leicester to make room for Peter Osgood, who was promised a run of a dozen games in the side. Bridges, upset that his World Cup chances were being jeopardised, asked for a transfer but, following a petition by fans outraged at the thought that their hero might be allowed to leave the club, it was decided that he should stay and he switched to a wandering role at the expense of Bert Murray, enjoying considerable success.

Two goals, the second a swerving right-foot drive, in the fifth round of the FA Cup against Shrewsbury confirmed Barry's continuing usefulness, but he was left out once more after the semi-final defeat at the hands of Sheffield Wednesday and when he was sent home from the airport prior to the first leg of the Fairs Cup tie with Barcelona there was little doubt that he would soon be moving on. Somewhat surprisingly, he went to Second Division Birmingham City and, although he had the satisfaction of playing on the winning side when Chelsea visited St Andrews in the sixth round of the FA Cup in 1968, he never really recaptured the form he had shown during his years at Stamford Bridge.

BORN: Horsford, 29.4.41.
GAMES: 203 (2). GOALS: 93.
HONOURS: League Cup 64/5.
4 England caps (65).
OTHER CLUBS: Birmingham City 66/7-68/9 (83, 37);
Queens Park Rangers 68/9-70/1 (72, 32);
Millwall 70/1-71/2 (77, 27);
Brighton and Hove Albion 72/3-73/4 (66, 14);
Highlands Park, South Africa.

1958/59-1965/66

EDDIE McCREADIE

Tommy Docherty was in the habit of describing Eddie McCreadie as the best left-back in Europe and, while that may be regarded as an example of the Doc's fondness for hyperbole, there is no doubt that the £6,000 fee he paid East Stirling for the 22-year-old Scot's services in April 1962 was one of the more successful bits of transfer business he did during his years at Stamford Bridge.

A rugged defender whose trademark was a ferocious sliding tackle, Eddie was not the most astute reader of the game in the early stages of his career but he made the transition from part-time football in Scotland to the heat of the Second Division promotion battle with characteristic assurance, immediately striking up a formidable partnership with Ken Shellito. He was inclined to be impetuous, diving in when he would have done better to have held off and settled for containing his winger, and this weakness was to prove his undoing when Stoke visited Stamford Bridge at the end of the season for a match that was crucial to the Blues' fading hopes. Stanley Matthews, by then a veteran of 48, teased and taunted Eddie like a wily bullfighter, the supremacy he gained helping the leaders to a vital 1-0 win. However, McCreadie was blessed with tremendous pace and his exceptional powers of recovery generally allowed him to repair the damage done by his impulsiveness.

Although he possessed a good left foot, Eddie's distribution was indifferent, but he took delight in every opportunity to get forward, surging down the flank with great panache. Unfortunately, he tended to lose composure when he got into the last third of the field, sometimes opting for a wildly optimistic shot from 40 yards when the situation called for a measured pass to a better-placed team-mate, but in the first leg of the League Cup final against Leicester in 1965 all his dreams of glory were realised when, playing at centre-forward in the absence of Barry Bridges, he scored the winning goal after an epic solo run that carried him the length of the pitch.

Eddie was an emotional man with a fiery temper and he was inevitably involved in regular clashes with Tommy Docherty, another Scot with a combustible temperament. His role in the ill-starred Blackpool Affair in April 1965 did nothing to improve matters and during the next year McCreadie fired off no fewer than five transfer requests, but they were all turned down and eventually an uneasy peace was restored.

Good-humoured and popular with the Stamford Bridge crowd, Eddie won his first international cap against England two weeks before the dramatic events at Blackpool and regularly represented his country for the next four years, while his flair, aggression and dauntless spirit were central to the Blues' challenge for honours during the mid-sixties. However, the later stages of McCreadie's career were to be plagued by a cruel series of injuries. He was able to play in the 1970 FA Cup final only after he had courageously decided to postpone abdominal surgery and he missed much of the following season as a result of a persistent ankle problem, but his contribution behind the scenes was invaluable and in March 1972 he was appointed club captain in succession to Ron Harris. He was able to lead the side out onto the field for much of the next campaign but his playing days were nearing their end, and his appointment as reserve team coach in the summer of 1974 marked the start of a new challenge which would see this passionate, highly intelligent man assume the arduous task of keeping the Blues in the First Division before the season was out.

BORN: Glasgow, 15.4.40.
GAMES: 405 (5). GOALS: 5.
HONOURS: FA Cup 69/70; League Cup 64/5.
23 Scotland caps (65-69).
OTHER CLUBS: East Stirling.
MANAGER: Chelsea (75-77); Memphis Rogues.

1962/63-1973/74

JOHN BOYLE

Although his unspectacular contribution went largely unnoticed by the press and the majority of the Stamford Bridge crowd, John Boyle was a key member of Tommy Docherty's squad in the mid-sixties. Tigerish tackling and unrelenting effort were the solid foundations upon which his game was built, but he possessed more ability than he was generally given credit for and his versatility ensured that he was rarely out of the team.

John arrived in senior football in style, scoring the winning goal in the first leg of the League Cup semi-final against Aston Villa in January 1965 from 25 yards, and quickly established himself as Ron Harris's deputy in the middle of the defence. With Harris spending much of the following campaign at full-back, the Scottish teenager had every opportunity to impress and his sterling performance against AC Milan at Stamford Bridge provided ample evidence of his rapid progress. However, John was most effective when employed as a ball-winner in midfield and that was where he made most of his appearances over the next three seasons, his non-stop running and neat distribution helping the Blues to the FA Cup final in 1967. Head injuries sustained in a road accident the following March interrupted his progress when he appeared to have wrested the number four shirt from John Hollins and, with Dave Sexton introducing a slightly more adventurous, cavalier style, his place came under increasing pressure.

A cartilage operation in the summer of 1969 seemed to rob Boyle's career of much of its momentum and, after a year in the shadows, he came close to joining Sheffield Wednesday in August 1970. He was recalled to the first team at right-back a couple of months later in place of the injured Paddy Mulligan and acquitted himself with distinction despite his lack of pace, but his adaptability continued to hamper his efforts to win a secure place in the starting line-up and he gradually slipped out of contention. In 1972/73 he made only a handful of appearances and, following a spell on loan at Brighton, he was transferred to Orient for a nominal fee in December 1973.

BORN: Motherwell, 25.12.46.
GAMES: 253 (13). GOALS: 12.
HONOURS: European Cup-Winners' Cup 70/1;
League Cup 64/5.
OTHER CLUBS: Brighton and Hove Albion *on loan* 73/4 (10, 0);
Leyton Orient 73/4-74/5 (18, 0); Tampa Bay Rowdies.

1964/65-1973/74

GEORGE GRAHAM

The casting of Tommy Docherty, the martinet of Stamford Bridge, in the role of the fairy godmother may appear unpromising, but there is nevertheless something in the dramatic elevation of George Graham, from the drudgery of Aston Villa reserves to a key role in a side chasing an unprecedented treble, that prompts thoughts of Cinderella. Signed for a modest £5,000 in June 1964, the 19-year-old striker made a promising start to his Chelsea career, scoring on his debut, and became established in the first team when his demanding manager decided that neither of the replacements available was going to be able to fill the boots of the injured Frank Blunstone on the left wing and switched to a 4-3-3 formation to accommodate the young Scotsman.

Poised and stylish, George always seemed to have time to spare, his air of aristocratic languor earning him the richly evocative sobriquet 'Stroller'. Although he was no great runner and lacked pace, he proved to be a prolific marksman, finding the net 17 times in 30 League appearances in 1964/65, but just as important was his role as a provider. Blessed with immaculate ball control, he was a highly effective target man and acted as the pivot of the Blues' well-balanced attack, supplying the ammunition for Barry Bridges and Bobby Tambling, whose speed was the ideal complement to Graham's guile.

The strongly built youngster was majestic in the air, his unstoppable header in the first leg of the Fairs Cup tie against AC Milan in the San Siro stadium in February 1966 – and an equally spectacular effort in the second match a week later – demonstrating the value of perfect timing. His total of 23 goals in all competitions that season was not bettered, but the team that had brought the Blues within touching distance of glory was breaking up amid mounting dressing-room disharmony. Graham's transfer request was initially refused but, with the new campaign six weeks old, he was allowed to join Arsenal, Tommy Baldwin moving to Stamford Bridge in part-exchange.

BORN: Bargeddie, 30.11.44. GAMES: 102. GOALS: 46.
HONOURS: League Cup 64/5.
12 Scotland caps (71-73).
OTHER CLUBS: Aston Villa 62/3-63/4 (8, 2); Arsenal 66/7-72/3 (227, 59);
Manchester United 72/3-74/5 (43, 2); Portsmouth 74/5-76/7 (61, 5);
Crystal Palace 76/7-77/8 (44, 2).
MANAGER: Millwall (82-86); Arsenal (86-).

1964/65-1966/67

ALAN YOUNG

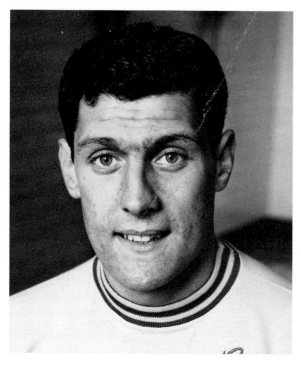

During his seven years with Chelsea Alan Young made just 26 first-team appearances but that bare statement conceals a fair amount of drama as well as much invaluable work assisting the development of the club's young players in the reserves. A strapping, six-foot centre-half who was effective in the air but rather less assured when the ball was on the floor, he was brought to Stamford Bridge as a 20-year-old by his former Arsenal team-mate Tommy Docherty shortly after the abrasive Scot had replaced Ted Drake, but failed to win a place in a struggling side and soon slipped into obscurity.

A brief taste of the limelight came when Alan was recalled for the first leg of the League Cup final against Leicester three years later but he was injured after 13 minutes and had little reason to remember the Blues' courageous win with pleasure. The departure of Frank Upton and John Mortimore early the following season opened the door for him, however, and he enjoyed a run of nine League games in the autumn and also played in the Fairs Cup ties against Roma and Wiener, later emerging with credit from the 2-0 defeat at the hands of Barcelona in the first leg of the semi-final. During Chelsea's run to the FA Cup final in 1966/67 Young played – and scored – in a fourth round replay against Brighton but that was to be his last senior appearance, and after another two years of loyal and dependable service behind the scenes he moved on to Torquay United in search of new challenges.

BORN: Hornsey, 20.1.41.
GAMES: 26. GOALS: 1.
OTHER CLUBS: Arsenal 60/1 (4, 0);
Torquay United 68/9-71/2 (59, 1).

1961/62-1966/67

TOMMY KNOX

Tommy Knox had to wait two seasons for a real chance to prove himself in the Blues' first team, and when the opportunity he had waited for for so long finally arrived he was found wanting. A traditional left-winger with good close control, he had followed his former East Stirling club-mate Eddie McCreadie to Stamford Bridge in the summer of 1962 and made six Second Division appearances the following season without suggesting that he would earn a regular place in the side. Tommy was called upon only once in 1963/64 and it seemed that his Chelsea career would bring nothing but frustration, but the injury to Frank Blunstone during the summer tour of the Caribbean meant that the Scotsman started the new campaign in the number 11 shirt with every prospect of an extended run in the side.

When Tommy was able to jink his way past his full-back he could be a considerable asset, as he demonstrated when making a goal for George Graham in a 3-2 win at Hillsborough, but if that ploy failed he had little else to offer. Had he been able to reproduce the form he showed in training things might have turned out differently, but his overall contribution was disappointing and when Tommy Docherty changed his tactics to accommodate three strikers there was no longer a place for an orthodox winger in the side. The following February Knox moved to Newcastle United to seek greater success in the lower divisions.

BORN: Glasgow, 5.9.39. GAMES: 21. GOALS: 0.
OTHER CLUBS: East Stirling;
Newcastle United 64/5-66/7 (25, 1);
Mansfield Town 66/7-67/8 (34, 5);
Northampton Town 67/8-68/9 (29, 0).

1962/63-1964/65

JIM McCALLIOG

Jim McCalliog was a potentially outstanding player who might well have enjoyed great success at Stamford Bridge had he been prepared to wait a little longer for the regular first-team place he felt he deserved. A midfielder of style and authority, he became Terry Venables's acknowledged understudy in 1964/65, making his League debut against Birmingham City in November and scoring twice in a 6-1 win. Having played regularly in the early rounds of the League Cup, the young Scot did not figure in the two-legged final against Leicester City, but his ability to spot an opening and exploit it with a measured pass pointed to a bright future.

McCalliog was given the attacking role usually filled by George Graham on the opening day of the following season but it was apparent that he was most effective when employed as a midfield general, dictating the shape of the game with his cool and assured distribution. However, there seemed little prospect of a vacancy arising in that department, and the 19-year-old's mounting frustration prompted him to fire off a volley of transfer requests. Tommy Docherty was reluctant to lose a player of such ability and there was much dark muttering about the teenager having been 'tapped', but in October 1965 Jim moved to Sheffield Wednesday in a £37,500 deal and proved a point by scoring the Owls' second goal when they beat Chelsea in the FA Cup semi-final at Villa Park in April.

BORN: Glasgow, 23.9.46. GAMES: 12. GOALS: 3.
HONOURS: 5 Scotland caps (67-71).
OTHER CLUBS: Sheffield Wednesday 65/6-68/9 (150, 19);
Wolverhampton Wanderers 69/70-73/4 (163, 34);
Manchester United 73/4-74/5 (31, 7); Southampton 74/5-76/7
(72, 8); Chicago Sting; Lincoln City 78/9 (9, 0).
MANAGER: Halifax Town (90-91).

1964/65-1965/66

JOE FASCIONE

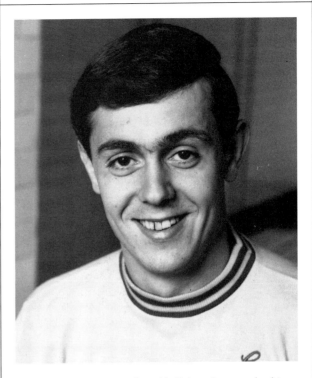

Joe Fascione can count himself a little unfortunate that his years at Stamford Bridge did not bring him greater reward. A small, skilful winger who could play on either flank, he was signed from Scottish club Kirkintilloch Rob Roy as a 17-year-old and, like his fellow countryman Jim McCalliog, had his first taste of top-flight football in the early rounds of the League Cup in 1964/65. His League baptism at Highbury the following September could scarcely have been more encouraging, the energetic youngster scoring the Blues' second goal with a glancing header from Bert Murray's corner, then helping create the third for Barry Bridges. A series of impressive displays followed, but Joe's enterprising forays down the flanks and tireless covering in midfield were not enough to secure his place in the reshuffle that followed the advent of Peter Osgood. Understandably miffed, he retired to the shadows.

Fascione was given a second chance when Dave Sexton succeeded Tommy Docherty almost two years later, but he was unable to reproduce the sure touch in front of goal that had served him so well in the reserves and after a run of six games he was displaced once again, Sexton bringing Alan Birchenall down from Sheffield United in an effort to boost the team's firepower. That was effectively the end of the road for the talented Scot and in the summer of 1969 he decided to try his luck with Durban City in South Africa.

BORN: Coatbridge, 5.2.45.
GAMES: 27 (7). GOALS: 1.
OTHER CLUBS: Durban City.

1964/65-1968/69

JOHN HOLLINS

The phrase 'model professional' is used somewhat glibly, but there is no doubt that in the case of John Hollins it is fully justified. His boundless energy and unfailing enthusiasm made him a cornerstone of the Chelsea midfield for eleven seasons, but his most remarkable achievement is to have accomplished so much in a fiercely competitive environment yet remained universally liked and respected.

Strangely enough, the three senior appearances he made as a 17-year-old in 1963/64 all ended in defeat, but he was handed the number four shirt at the start of the following season and quickly became a key component in Tommy Docherty's high-revving machine. In the early stages of his career John played his football at such a frantic pace that mistakes were inevitable, but his fizzing vitality more than compensated for his tactical naivety and over the years he would develop a more considered, focused style. His dynamic displays earned him a place in the England side that faced Spain at Wembley in May 1967, four days after he had played there for the Blues in the FA Cup final, but that was to be his only appearance in a full international – to the bewilderment of his legions of admirers at Stamford Bridge.

John had a spell at right-back in 1967/68 and found himself there again the following season when he was unable to reclaim his usual place from Peter Osgood after he had been sidelined by injury for a month, but it was not a role he enjoyed. He appeared to have lost much of his old zest but bounced back to produce the best football of his career, showing a new maturity and consistency, and was voted the fans' Player of the Year for two seasons in succession. In five seasons 'Holly' missed only four matches – the result of an ankle ligament injury in April 1971. Typically, he fought hard to get fit to take his place against Real Madrid in Athens and it was cruel that a recurrence prevented him from playing in the replay.

Sharp and alert, John was quick to pounce on any stray passes but his own distribution was not always as accurate as it might have been, largely because of over-eagerness. However, he was constantly involved, covering defenders when they went forward, tackling relentlessly in the middle of the field and making surging runs that helped create space for the forwards, and his selfless efforts were of immeasurable value to the side. He also scored many memorable goals for the Blues, none better than a spectacular solo effort against Arsenal in August 1970 that was a reward for remarkable persistence, and possessed a stunning shot, his venomously struck penalties helping him to a total of 18 goals in all competitions in 1971/72.

John's cheerful personality had always had a beneficial effect on morale in the dressing room and he was handed the captaincy at the start of 1974/75, having led the side during Eddie McCreadie's frequent absences, but his long love-affair with the Blues was destined to end unhappily. With the team struggling, his form suffered and he was rested for a spell to help him get over a niggling knee problem. The final blow came when McCreadie, the newly appointed manager, left him out for the three matches at the end of the season that would determine whether the club stayed in the First Division and that summer he followed Dave Sexton to Queens Park Rangers.

After distinguished service at Loftus Road and then at Highbury, Hollins returned to Stamford Bridge as player-coach in the summer of 1983 and, playing at right-back, was enormously influential in welding together the side which won the Second Division Championship. After Christmas he gave way to Colin Lee to concentrate on a coaching career which seemed certain to prove no less successful.

BORN: Guildford, 16.7.46.
GAMES: 591. GOALS: 64.
HONOURS: FA Cup 69/70; League Cup 64/5;
Second Division Championship 83/4.
1 England cap (67).
OTHER CLUBS: Queens Park Rangers 75/6-78/9 (151, 5);
Arsenal 79/80-82/3 (127, 9).
MANAGER: Chelsea (85-88).

1963/64-1974/75 & 1983/84

TERRY VENABLES

It is customary to describe outstanding midfield players as 'influential' but the word is more than merely a conventional acknowledgement of exceptional ability when applied to Terry Venables. During four breathlessly exciting seasons which saw Chelsea throw off their old inertia and emerge, newly minted, as serious contenders for football's glittering prizes, he exercised a dominion at Stamford Bridge that helped forge a vibrant new identity for the club and presented a challenge to the authority of Tommy Docherty that the strong-willed Scotsman ultimately found intolerable.

When the Blues were playing well, Venables was the hub around which their football revolved. He craved constant involvement, dropping deep to collect the ball from his defenders, and his ability to pierce a defence with a superbly weighted pass ensured that Barry Bridges and Bobby Tambling received a steady flow of openings. A keen student of the game, Terry took a lively interest in the tactical innovations introduced by Tommy Docherty and Dave Sexton and delighted in helping to devise free-kick routines of the kind that gave him two of his three goals in the first leg of a bad-tempered Fairs Cup tie against Roma in September 1965. The skill with which he marshalled his depleted forces that night, after Eddie McCreadie had been sent off with less than thirty minutes played, provided a perfect example of the tactical awareness that made him such an effective midfield general, but there were occasions when it seemed that the Blues had become over-reliant upon their master-strategist. When he had a poor game, as he did against Liverpool in the FA Cup semi-final the previous season, Chelsea appeared to be lost, the well-oiled machine rendered impotent by the malfunctioning of the single component that brought all the rest to life.

Venables first appeared regularly in senior football as a brilliantly precocious 17-year-old in 1960/61, his assured displays at right-half belying his inexperience, but when Tommy Docherty succeeded Ted Drake he plausibly judged that the immediate crisis called for maturity and resilience rather than the rich potential of golden youth and he lost no time in acquiring the services of Andy Malcolm from West Ham. Relegation confirmed the folly of such caution and the following season the right-flank triangle of Venables, Shellito and Murray performed with exemplary consistency as the Blues surged back into the First Division. However, it was when he was handed the number ten shirt at the expense of Graham Moore in November 1963 that Terry really began to dictate the shape of the game, his commanding displays in the middle of the pitch earning him England caps against Belgium and Holland a year later.

A born leader, Venables had become a dominant figure in the dressing room and he took over as captain when Ken Shellito was sidelined by injury, but his outstanding football brain, sharp wit and forceful personality meant that conflict with Docherty was virtually inevitable. In the wake of the semi-final defeat at the hands of Liverpool in 1964/65 he was dropped for a game that was crucial to Chelsea's hopes of winning the Championship and his involvement in the notorious Blackpool Incident shortly afterwards added to the mounting tension. With his form suffering, Terry was stripped of the captaincy in the new year and shortly before the third game against AC Milan two months later it was announced that he had been put up for sale.

Although it was subsequently decided that there would be no departures while the Blues were still pursuing honours, there seemed little hope that Terry's differences with Docherty could be resolved and before the season was over he had been transferred to Tottenham for a fee of £80,000.

BORN: Bethnal Green, 6.1.43.
GAMES: 237. GOALS: 31.
HONOURS: League Cup 64/5.
2 England caps (64).
OTHER CLUBS: Tottenham Hotspur 65/6-68/9 (115, 5);
Queens Park Rangers 69/70-74/5 (179, 19); Crystal Palace 74/5 (14, 0).
MANAGER: Crystal Palace (76-80); Queens Park Rangers (80-84); Barcelona;
Tottenham Hotspur (87-91).

1959/60-1965/66

PETER BONETTI

A vital save can determine the outcome of a game just as decisively as the highly publicised efforts of the men commanding massive transfer fees at the other end of the pitch, and there is no doubt that in Peter Bonetti Chelsea were blessed with a real match-winner. In a first-team career that spanned 20 seasons and comprised more than 700 appearances, his professionalism and dependability provided the unshakeable foundations of a succession of famous triumphs and helped to avert at least as many humiliating disasters.

Peter was first thrust into the limelight as an 18-year-old against Manchester City in April 1960 when both Reg Matthews and his deputy Bill Robertson were injured, and performed with such verve and assurance that he quickly made the position his own. Playing behind a notoriously leaky defence, he lost no time in establishing a reputation as one of the best shot-stoppers in English football, although it is true that in the early stages of his career the astonishing agility that had earned him the nickname 'Catty' was sometimes required to compensate for positioning that betrayed his inexperience.

Peter's strength of character was never seen more clearly than during the Blues' exhilarating promotion campaign in 1962/63 when he shrugged off a couple of costly mistakes that had prompted Tommy Docherty to leave him out of the side and produced a performance in the decisive match at Roker Park in May that was nothing less than heroic, a flying leap in injury time to deny Sunderland winger George Mulhall crowning an outstanding second-half display that had seen him resist relentless pressure seemingly single-handed. The gale howling down the pitch that day exposed the weakness of his kicking, but his ability to catch the ball and hurl it out to his full-backs with pinpoint accuracy in a single flowing movement was the springboard of many attacks down the years.

Over the next three seasons, Bonetti played a key role in Chelsea's quest for honours, but amid the turmoil that engulfed Stamford Bridge in the wake of the semi-final defeat at the hands of Sheffield Wednesday in 1966 he was one of many players to seek a transfer, and when Alex Stepney was signed from Millwall it seemed certain that he would be allowed to leave. However, Peter began the following campaign in the scintillating form that had earned him the first of his seven full England caps during the summer and it was Stepney who moved on, having made just one first-team appearance.

Slim and lithe, Peter was almost boyish in appearance and there was something uncanny about the way he would repeatedly emerge with the ball clutched securely to his chest after a high centre had been swung into the Blues' penalty area, his immaculate timing and adhesive handling frustrating burly forwards who seemed certain to overwhelm him with their height and aggression. His spectacular performance in the FA Cup final in 1970 was instrumental in earning the Blues a replay and his extraordinary courage was no less crucial to the emotional triumph at Old Trafford 18 days later, Peter making a number of vital saves despite a first-half injury which impaired his mobility.

As a result of his unfailing daring, Bonetti picked up more than his fair share of injuries over the years and, with signs of fallibility beginning to appear, he came under increasing pressure from John Phillips in the early seventies. When it was announced in March 1975 that he was to be awarded a free transfer at the end of the season it appeared that his long association with the club was at an end, but after a summer in American football Peter returned to Stamford Bridge, initially on a monthly contract, and his brilliant goalkeeping helped Eddie McCreadie's young team gain promotion in 1976/77. He continued to battle for a first-team place over the next two seasons before moving to the Isle of Mull in 1979, combining life as a guest-house proprietor with appearances for Dundee United. He has since acted as a goalkeeping coach to a number of clubs, including Chelsea, and is currently involved with the England set-up.

BORN: Putney, 27.9.41.
GAMES: 728. GOALS: 0.
HONOURS: European Cup-Winners' Cup 70/1; FA Cup 69/70; League Cup 64/5.
7 England caps (66-70).
OTHER CLUBS: St Louis Stars; Dundee United.

1959/60-1978/79

TONY HATELEY

In his proper element, Tony Hateley was highly effective, if not exactly decorative. When the ball was flighted to the far post he was magnificent, all menace and power, but his lack of mobility and failure to master even the basics of ball control meant that on the floor he posed as much threat as a shark in a desert. It will be apparent, therefore, that he was a strange choice to replace Peter Osgood when the sublimely gifted youngster broke his leg in October 1966, but of course Tommy Docherty was nothing if not unpredictable.

Signed from Aston Villa for £100,000, the highest fee the club had ever paid, Tony never looked likely to prosper at Stamford Bridge, for the Blues' recent success had been based upon fluid passing movements and the speedy interchange of forwards, a style totally alien to the ungainly six-footer. He scored twice against Fulham three days after his arrival, his second goal the product of a soaring leap and a header of brutal force, but much of the time he was a spectator as his colleagues weaved their familiar patterns. Docherty encouraged his team to exploit the newcomer's strengths, sometimes to the exclusion of any other strategy, but this reaped only limited rewards as Hateley rarely received the sort of inviting crosses he needed if he was to thrive. Too often the ball was knocked forward from deep positions, denying him the opportunity to build up momentum and handing the initiative to the defence.

Tony made a valuable contribution to Chelsea's progress to the FA Cup final that season, his superb header from Bobby Tambling's centre in the fifth round against Sheffield United demonstrating how dangerous he could be, and his goal against Leeds in the semi-final – despatched past Sprake with an imperious thrust of the forehead – earned him an enduring place in the hearts of the faithful. However, nine goals in 33 appearances was not an encouraging return and at the end of the season, with Osgood approaching fitness, he was transferred to Liverpool, where he enjoyed scarcely more success.

BORN: Derby, 13.6.41.
GAMES: 32 (1). GOALS: 9.
OTHER CLUBS: Notts County 58/9-62/3 (131, 77) and 70/1-71/2 (57, 32);
Aston Villa 63/4-66/7 (127, 68); Liverpool 67/8-68/9 (42, 17);
Coventry City 68/9 (17, 4); Birmingham City 69/70-70/1 (28, 6);
Oldham Athletic 73/4 (5, 1).

1966/67

JOE KIRKUP

Signed from West Ham United in March 1966 to reinforce a squad depleted by a recurrence of Ken Shellito's knee trouble, Joe Kirkup was a polished, cultured right-back who epitomised the artistic approach to the game for which the Upton Park side were once renowned. A member of the Hammers team which had lifted the European Cup-Winners' Cup the previous spring, he settled into the Chelsea defence with a characteristic absence of fuss, making an assured debut in front of a 60,000 crowd against Manchester United, and played in all the Blues' remaining fixtures that season.

Joe was at his most impressive when he was coming forward, using the ball well and linking effectively with the attack, as when he fired home from ten yards against Blackburn after a sweeping move involving Ron Harris and Bert Murray. He sometimes appeared a little vulnerable in defence, his lack of aggression presenting a distinct contrast with the style of his full-back partner Eddie McCreadie, but he was nevertheless unfortunate to lose his place to Jim Thomson the following November. He remained out of favour for nearly a year, returning to the team on a regular basis only when Dave Sexton replaced Tommy Docherty, but the reprieve was to be short-lived and in February 1968 he was transferred to Southampton in part-exchange for David Webb, subsequently enjoying considerable success at the Dell.

BORN: Hexham, 17.12.39.
GAMES: 62 (7). GOALS: 2.
OTHER CLUBS: West Ham United 58/9-65/6 (165, 6);
Southampton 67/8-73/4 (169, 3).

1965/66-1967/68

JIM THOMSON

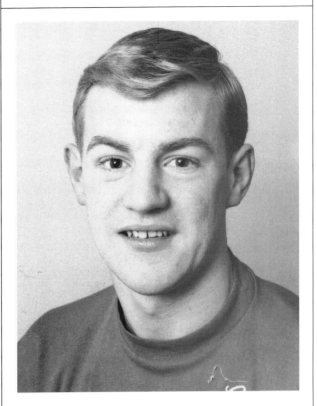

One of the many young Scots brought to Stamford Bridge by Tommy Docherty, Jim Thomson was perhaps the victim of his own versatility, for in the course of the 40 first-team games he started for the Blues he wore seven different shirts without ever looking likely to establish a lasting grip on any of them. A solid defender with few pretensions to creativity, his best position was probably in the middle of the back four, but the majority of his senior appearances during his time at Stamford Bridge were at right-back, while on occasion he was pressed into service in midfield, where he inevitably looked ill at ease.

After a couple of outings towards the end of 1965/66, Jim's real break came early the following season when John Hollins was dropped after asking for a transfer, Docherty insisting that when the rebel was recalled it would not be at the expense of the new boy, as if to stress that loyalty would be rewarded. Thomson played fairly regularly thereafter, his enthusiasm and unflagging effort going some way to compensate for a lack of finesse, and he was unfortunate to miss out on the Blues' appearance at Wembley in May, but he remained prone to silly mistakes. After Dave Sexton took over as manager in October 1967 Thomson's opportunities became rarer and the following September he was transferred to Burnley, where he performed valiantly for more than a decade.

BORN: Glasgow, 1.10.46.
GAMES: 40 (7). GOALS: 1.
OTHER CLUBS: Burnley 68/9-80/1 (297, 3).

1965/66-1967/68

BOBBY TAMBLING

When Jimmy Greaves packed his bags and headed for Italy in 1961 he left a gap in the Chelsea forward line that no mere mortal could reasonably be expected to fill, and it is a measure of Bobby Tambling's remarkable goalscoring prowess that within a year the Stamford Bridge crowd had ceased to mourn the loss of their old favourite and were instead hailing the emergence of a new hero. He may have been blessed with only a fraction of his illustrious predecessor's magical gifts, but Bobby's courage, spirit and cool finishing were essential ingredients in the most successful decade in the Blues' history and his total of 202 goals remains a club record.

Tambling had his first taste of senior football as a 17-year-old against West Ham in February 1959 and, like his fellow debutant Barry Bridges, scored in a 3-2 win, but it was in 1960/61 that he began to appear regularly in the first team, initially on the left wing (he remained a good crosser of the ball throughout his career) then at inside-forward. Greaves's defection that summer thrust Bobby into the limelight but he coped magnificently with the burden placed on his young shoulders, emerging from the Blues' grim battle against relegation as top scorer with 20 goals in 34 appearances, and the following season he became, at 21, the youngest player to have captained a promotion-winning side, having been appointed to succeed Peter Sillett. Needless to say, he led from the front, scoring 35 League goals, 25 of them in the 22 matches he played before the Big Freeze interrupted the team's rhythm, and his sparkling form earned him full England honours against Wales and France.

A modest, popular man, Bobby did not really enjoy the pressures of captaincy and was happy to accept Tommy Docherty's suggestion that he should pass the job on to Ken Shellito when he found goals hard to come by in the opening weeks of 1963/64. Dry spells of this kind tended to worry him, but they were to be rare occurrences over the next six seasons. Like Greaves, Tambling had days when he could do no wrong and the goals kept flying in. He scored four in a match on four occasions, most dramatically in the final game of 1962/63 when victory against Portsmouth was essential to clinch promotion, and against Aston Villa in 1966 he plundered five goals – all straightforward chances, perhaps, but all of them ruthlessly taken.

Tambling had a splendid left foot and some of his goals were highly spectacular, like the stunning free-kick he swerved round the defensive wall against Sheffield Wednesday in the fifth round of the FA Cup in 1968, but more typical was the winner against Leeds in the fourth round two years before, knocked in from close range with the minimum of fuss after George Graham had struck a post. He could usually be relied upon to hit the target when presented with an opening, and was quite prepared to accept a knock for the satisfaction of seeing the ball nestling in the back of the net, but he was at his most effective when employed as a front-runner on the left of the attack, using his pace to get clear of the defenders as he pursued a through-ball from George Graham or Terry Venables.

As his career progressed, Bobby did not enjoy the best of luck with injuries, a hamstring strain affecting him in 1965/66, abdominal problems requiring surgery on two occasions two seasons later, and a cartilage operation costing him his first-team place in August 1969. By the time he had recovered, Ian Hutchinson and Peter Osgood had formed their formidable partnership, and Bobby, having lost a little pace perhaps, was unable to force his way back in. He went to Crystal Palace on a month's loan, and then, having decided to remain in football despite his involvement with the Jehovah's Witnesses movement, made a permanent switch to Selhurst Park in June 1970.

BORN: Storrington, 18.9.41.
GAMES: 366 (4). GOALS: 202.
HONOURS: League Cup 64/5.
3 England caps (62-66).
OTHER CLUBS: Crystal Palace 69/70-73/4 (68, 12);
Cork Celtic; Waterford; Shamrock Rovers.
MANAGER: Cork Celtic.

1958/59-1969/70

52

JIM SMART 1964/65

Forward. BORN: Dundee, 9.1.47.
GAMES: 1. GOALS: 0.
OTHER CLUBS: Morton; Highlands Park, South Africa.

BILLY SINCLAIR 1964/65

Midfielder. BORN: Glasgow, 21.3.47.
GAMES: 1. GOALS: 0.
OTHER CLUBS: Morton; Glentoran.

TOMMY ROBSON 1965/66

Winger. BORN: Gateshead, 31.7.44.
GAMES: 6 (1). GOALS: 0.
OTHER CLUBS: Northampton Town 61/2-65/6 (74, 20);
Newcastle United 66/7-68/9 (48, 11);
Peterborough United 68/9-80/1 (482, 113).

JIM BARRON 1965/66

Goalkeeper. BORN: Tantobie, 19.10.43.
GAMES: 1. GOALS: 0.
OTHER CLUBS: Wolverhampton Wanderers 63/4-64/5 (8, 0);
Oxford United 65/6-69/70 (152, 0);
Nottingham Forest 70/1-73/4 (155, 0);
Swindon Town 74/5-76/7 (79, 0);
Peterborough United 77/8-80/1 (21, 0).

BARRY LLOYD 1966/67-1968/69

Midfielder. BORN: Hillingdon, 19.2.49.
GAMES: 8 (2). GOALS: 0.
OTHER CLUBS: Fulham 68/9-75/6 (257, 29);
Hereford United 76/7 (14, 0); Brentford 77/8 (31, 4).
MANAGER: Brighton and Hove Albion (87-).

CHICO HAMILTON 1966/67

Midfielder. BORN: Streatham, 31.10.50.
GAMES: 3 (2). GOALS: 2.
OTHER CLUBS: Southend United 68/9 (37, 11);
Aston Villa 69/70-75/6 (208, 40);
Sheffield United 76/7-77/8 (60, 13); Minnesota Kicks;
San José Earthquakes.

GEORGE LUKE 1966/67

Wing-half. BORN: Hetton-le-Hole, 9.11.48.
GAMES: 1. GOALS: 0.
OTHER CLUBS: Newcastle United (0, 0);
Durban City.

JIM SMART

TOMMY ROBSON

BARRY LLOYD

BILLY SINCLAIR

JIM BARRON

CHICO HAMILTON

GEORGE LUKE

ALEX STEPNEY

ROGER WOSAHLO

GEOFF BUTLER

PAUL McMILLAN

ALEX STEPNEY 1966/67

Goalkeeper. BORN: Mitcham, 18.9.42.
GAMES: 1. GOALS: 0. HONOURS: 1 England cap (68).
OTHER CLUBS: Millwall 63/4-65/6 (137, 0);
Manchester United 66/7-77/8 (433, 2); Dallas Tornadoes.

KINGSLEY WHIFFEN 1966/67

Goalkeeper. BORN: Welshpool, 3.12.50.
GAMES: 1. GOALS: 0.
OTHER CLUBS: Plymouth Argyle (0, 0).

ROGER WOSAHLO 1966/67

Winger. BORN: Cambridge, 11.9.47.
GAMES: 0 (1). GOALS: 0.
OTHER CLUBS: Ipswich Town 67/8 (1, 0) and 69/70 (1, 0);
Peterborough United 68/9 (15, 1).

COLIN WALDRON 1967/68

Centre-half. BORN: Bristol, 22.6.48.
GAMES: 10. GOALS: 0.
OTHER CLUBS: Bury 66/7 (20, 1); Burnley 67/8-75/6 (308, 16);
Manchester United 76/7 (3, 0); Sunderland 76/7-77/8 (20, 1);
Tulsa Roughnecks; Atlanta Chiefs (twice); Rochdale 79/80 (19, 1);
Philadelphia Furies.

GEOFF BUTLER 1967/68

Full-back. BORN: Middlesbrough, 29.9.46.
GAMES: 8 (1). GOALS: 0.
OTHER CLUBS: Middlesbrough 65/6-67/8 (55, 1);
Sunderland 67/8-68/9 (3, 0); Norwich City 68/9-75/6 (153, 1);
Baltimore Rockets; AFC Bournemouth 75/6-80/1 (119, 1);
Peterborough United 81/2 (39, 0).

STEWART HOUSTON 1967/68-1970/71

Defender. BORN: Dunoon, 20.8.49.
GAMES: 10 (4). GOALS: 0.
HONOURS: 1 Scotland cap (75).
OTHER CLUBS: Brentford 71/2-73/4 (77, 9);
Manchester United 73/4-79/80 (205, 13);
Sheffield United 80/1-82/3 (94, 1);
Colchester United 83/4-85/6 (107, 5).

PAUL McMILLAN 1967/68

Centre-half. BORN: Lennoxtown, 13.7.50.
GAMES: 1. GOALS: 0.
OTHER CLUBS: Clydebank.

KINGSLEY WHIFFEN

COLIN WALDRON

STEWART HOUSTON

ALAN BIRCHENALL

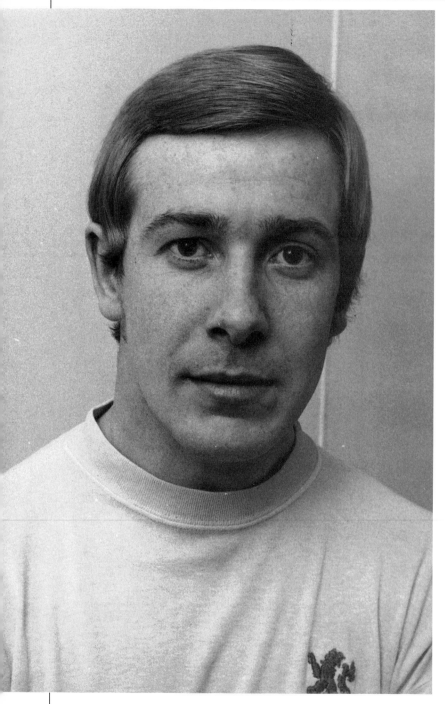

Alan Birchenall felt that he was playing the best football of his career in the autumn of 1969. He had scored with a well-struck shot in the third round of the League Cup against Leeds at Elland Road and followed that up by clinching the Blues' victory in the replay with a thumping left-foot volley. In between, the big striker had come up with two goals in a 3-0 home win against Arsenal, the first being a powerful header at the far post that had Stamford Bridge roaring its approval. All seemed to be well with the powerfully built 24-year-old's world.

Then, cruelly, it all went wrong. 'Birch' hurt his knee against WBA at the Bridge in October and was out of action for three months. While he was sidelined, Ian Hutchinson and Peter Osgood struck up their spectacular double act, but when they had to miss the home game against Newcastle in February, Alan was recalled and hoped to make enough of an impression to reclaim his place.

Instead, having looked sharp, he was carried from the field after 51 minutes with a badly gashed knee following a clash with goalkeeper Iam McFaul. The blond Midlander recovered in time to play twice more before the end of the season, but the arrival of Keith Weller confirmed that he had no future with Chelsea and in June 1970 he was transferred to Crystal Palace.

A stylist who delighted in receiving the ball with his back to goal and spreading it wide with his cultured left foot, Birchenall had been Dave Sexton's first signing for the Blues when he moved from Sheffield United in a £100,000 deal in November 1967, but his instinctive tendency to drop back into midfield meant that he was not the ideal partner for Osgood, who in this respect was a similar player. Alan's effectiveness in the air and persistent running made him popular with the fans despite his indifferent goalscoring record, and it is unfortunate that his progress should have been interrupted at a crucial stage of his career.

BORN: East Ham, 22.8.45.
GAMES: 95 (1). GOALS: 28.
OTHER CLUBS: Sheffield United 64/5-67/8 (107, 31);
Crystal Palace 70/1-71/2 (41, 11); Leicester City 71/2-76/7 (163, 12);
Notts County 75/6 *on loan* (5, 0); San José Earthquakes; Notts County 77/8 (28, 0);
Memphis Rogues; Blackburn Rovers 78/9 (18, 0); Luton Town 78/9-79/80 (10, 0);
Hereford United 79/80 (11, 0).

1967/68-1969/70

JOHN DEMPSEY

During his three and a half seasons as Chelsea's regular centre-half John Dempsey played in three major cup finals, but he was somewhat overshadowed by his more flamboyant team-mates and never received the credit he deserved for his part in the club's success. A £70,000 signing from Fulham in January 1969, the Irish international was a dependable defender who felt no embarrassment about putting the ball into touch whenever danger threatened and favoured an uncomplicated approach to the job in hand which led one journalist to describe his resolute display in the 1970 FA Cup final at Wembley as 'splendidly functional'.

Quick on the turn and able to hold his own with most forwards over short distances, John was a good close marker, with a firm tackle and plenty of strength. He was not particularly dominant in the air but when David Webb switched from full-back to join him in the middle of the back four the pair presented a formidable barrier, as well as posing a considerable threat at the other end of the field.

John is probably best remembered for the superb volley which gave the Blues the lead in the 1971 European Cup-Winners' Cup final replay in Athens, a goal which must have come as something of a relief to the undemonstrative Londoner since it was his unlucky slip deep into stoppage time at end of the first game which had allowed Zoco to equalise for Real Madrid. However, in August 1972 he suffered the first of the catalogue of serious injuries which were to blight the remainder of his career. He made just 31 first-team appearances in three seasons but appeared to have re-established himself in 1975/76, forming a solid partnership with Micky Droy as Chelsea regrouped in the Second Division. Sadly, a twisted knee cost Dempsey his place and he was unable to force his way back into the side, although he remained at Stamford Bridge for another two years, eventually taking the well-trodden path to America in March 1978.

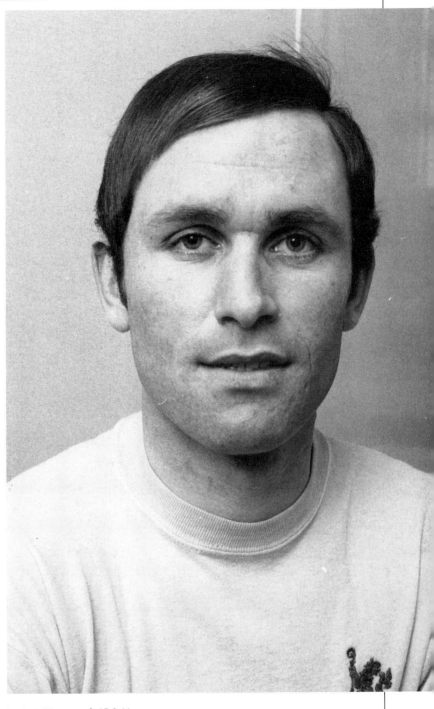

BORN: Hampstead, 15.3.46.
GAMES: 200 (7). GOALS: 7.
HONOURS: European Cup-Winners' Cup 70/1; FA Cup 69/70.
19 Ireland caps.
OTHER CLUBS: Fulham 64/5-68/9 (149, 4);
Philadelphia Furies.

1968/69-1975/76

DAVID WEBB

There was little polish or refinement about David Webb's game, but few players have been more popular with the Stamford Bridge crowd. A rugged defender with the wit, resilience and appetite for life for which East Enders are famed, he had the gift of communicating his warm, roguish personality to the fans, who shared in all his triumphs and disasters. But despite his air of jaunty defiance, Dave was a solid, dependable professional whose infectious enthusiasm made him a cornerstone of Dave Sexton's exciting team.

A hefty six-footer with rough-hewn features that helped earn him the highly apt nickname 'Desperate Dan', Webb was signed from Southampton in February 1968 in a deal which took Joe Kirkup to the Dell in part-exchange. He had played at right-back for the south coast club but Sexton, who had been his manager at Leyton Orient for a few months in 1965, initially employed him at centre-half, which had become something of a problem position. Dave distinguished himself with a swashbuckling hat-trick at Ipswich on Boxing Day, but when John Dempsey arrived shortly afterwards he was handed the number two shirt that had been vacated by Kirkup.

Webb continued to perform with characteristic gusto but he lacked the pace and agility to make a complete success of the role and his limitations were brutally exposed in the 1970 FA Cup final at Wembley when Leeds United's wily left-winger, Eddie Gray, teased and tormented him with a display of traditional wizardry. Dave bore his ordeal with the courage Chelsea fans had come to expect, making a crucial clearance in extra time, and in the replay at Old Trafford he had his revenge. While Ron Harris switched to full-back and subdued Gray in his own inimitable fashion, Webb moved into the middle alongside Dempsey to shackle Clarke, crowning an authoritative performance with the winning goal, bundled in at the far post from Ian Hutchinson's long throw.

Webb was reluctant to return to his old position and after a lame performance there against Everton in the Charity Shield – attributed by some experienced observers to the lush beard he had acquired during the summer – he was dropped, but he soon established himself as Dempsey's regular partner in the centre of the defence and it became clear that he had found his best position. A doughty competitor with unquenchable spirit, he was strong in the air and tackled like an earth-mover, and outstanding displays in both matches against Real Madrid in Athens provided ample confirmation of his growing stature.

Dave continued to score a healthy ration of goals and even made occasional appearances as an emergency striker – to considerable effect – but his willingness to do whatever was asked of him in the Chelsea cause was never seen more clearly than when he played in goal against Ipswich on Boxing Day 1971, taking over the green jersey in the absence of all three senior 'keepers and – needless to say – emerging with a clean sheet. He performed heroics of a rather more familiar kind against Spurs in the League Cup semi-final at White Hart Lane a few days later but in 1972/73 he suffered a brief loss of form and, having regained his place, missed the closing weeks of the campaign through injury.

The following season was not a happy one for the Blues and in the wake of the disharmony that led to Alan Hudson and Peter Osgood leaving Stamford Bridge, Webb became unsettled. He felt that the atmosphere at the club had turned sour, and that summer he was transferred to Queens Park Rangers for £100,000. His departure was a further indication that a golden age was drawing to a close, but he would return to Chelsea nearly twenty years later in the hope of launching another . . .

BORN: Stratford, 9.4.46.
GAMES: 298. GOALS: 33.
HONOURS: European Cup-Winners' Cup 70/1; FA Cup 69/70.
OTHER CLUBS: Leyton Orient 64/5-65/6 (62, 3);
Southampton 65/6-67/8 (75, 2); Queens Park Rangers 74/5-77/8 (116, 7);
Leicester City 77/8-78/9 (33, 0); Derby County 78/9-79/80 (26, 1);
AFC Bournemouth 80/1-82/3 (11, 0); Torquay United 84/5 (2, 1).
MANAGER: AFC Bournemouth (80-82); Torquay United (84-85);
Southend United (86-87 and 88-92); Chelsea (93).

1967/68-1973/74

PETER OSGOOD

The efforts of the terrace choristers are rarely notable for their insight, but the song that hailed Peter Osgood as the King of Stamford Bridge succeeded in capturing the essence of the man. Regal in his bearing, imperious in his manner, he scored unforgettable goals with a swagger that bordered on arrogance, took his revenge with the cruelty of Genghis Khan when his displeasure had been aroused and had a taste for the good things in life that befitted an emperor.

It took Ossie a little time to secure the loyalty of his subjects. He scored twice on his senior debut in a League Cup tie against Workington in December 1964 but had to wait until the following September for another chance to impress, Tommy Docherty promising him a run of a dozen games in the first team. Since this was at the expense of Barry Bridges, the current England centre-forward, the reaction from the terraces was initially hostile but it soon became clear that the 18-year-old was something very special indeed.

A willowy 6ft 3in, Peter had the ability to slice his way through defences with a deceptive swerve, as he demonstrated at Turf Moor the following January when, running from his own half, he beat four Burnley defenders before rounding the keeper and stroking the ball home. He was good in the air and possessed magical ball control, but most remarkable was his gift for spotting openings apparent to no one else.

Osgood's world came crashing down when he broke his right leg in a clash with Blackpool's Emlyn Hughes in October 1966. He missed the rest of the season and during his absence he put on two stone in weight that he never managed to lose, with the result that he was no longer able to run with the ball as he once had. It took him a long time to regain his confidence and it was only after a spell in midfield in 1968/69 that the golden touch began to return. He was most effective when he dropped back a little to collect the ball and he enjoyed the most productive period of his career when he was joined in attack by Ian Hutchinson in November 1969. Ossie scored in every round of the FA Cup that season, plundering a hat-trick at QPR, and crowned it all with a superb diving header in the replay against Leeds at Old Trafford that left David Harvey bewildered.

Osgood travelled to Mexico for the World Cup that summer but he was never the type of player to find favour with Sir Alf Ramsey. Responding to the challenge of a vital match played in front of a big crowd in characteristic style, he returned from a savage eight-week suspension to score twice in the second leg of the Cup-Winners' Cup quarter-final against Bruges the following season and found the net in both matches against Real Madrid in Athens to help another trophy on its way to Stamford Bridge.

However, Peter's relationship with Dave Sexton was never easy and at the start of the next campaign he was transfer-listed for 'lack of effort'. Things were smoothed over on that occasion but the manager finally lost patience with his star player's inconsistency and dropped him, together with three others, for a game at Sheffield United on New Year's Day 1974. Following a training-ground flare-up Ossie was put on the transfer list and, after a long-drawn-out saga which saw his team-mates attempt to engineer a reconciliation, Sexton walk out in a huff and Osgood ask for his cards, he was eventually sold to Southampton for £275,000.

In December 1978 Peter returned to Stamford Bridge but he was unable to recapture the old magic and after ten rather sad months he retired from a game that had been immensely richer for his virtuosity, style and sense of drama.

BORN: Windsor, 20.2.47.
GAMES: 375 (4). GOALS: 150.
HONOURS: European Cup-Winners' Cup 70/1; FA Cup 69/70.
4 England caps (70-73).
OTHER CLUBS: Southampton 73/4-77/8 (126, 28);
Norwich City *on loan* 76/7 (3, 0); Philadelphia Furies.

1964/65-1973/74 & 1978/79-1979/80

KEITH WELLER

When Dave Sexton added Millwall's Keith Weller to his Cup-winning squad in a £100,000 deal in May 1970, he explained that he intended to employ his latest signing as a goalscoring right-winger, a declaration which occasioned some surprise since the chirpy Cockney had made a name for himself at the Den as an enterprising midfield player. However, having been a victim of the star system at White Hart Lane, Weller was desperate to prove himself in the First Division and approached the challenge presented by an unfamiliar role in a positive frame of mind.

At first things went splendidly. He scored twice from Peter Osgood knock-downs to rescue a point at Upton Park in only his third game, and his pace, control and directness made him a consistent threat to opposing defences. His determination won him the respect of his new colleagues and by Christmas the stocky Londoner's decisive finishing had brought him 12 goals, including a spectacular volley at home to Newcastle.

However, in the second half of the season Weller's form wilted. The service he received became fitful, partly as a result of the injuries to key players which continued to disrupt the side, and the goals dried up. Although he emerged as the leading scorer in a team which won the European Cup-Winners' Cup and finished sixth in the League, his confidence had suffered and he was no longer an automatic selection. When discussing his new recruit, Sexton had stressed his versatility, yet he was never given a chance to show what he could do at the heart of the side, which was a pity.

Illness and injury restricted Keith to only two matches in the opening weeks of the following campaign, and when Steve Kember and Chris Garland were signed it became clear that he no longer figured in the manager's plans. Sixteen months after his arrival at Stamford Bridge, he was transferred to Leicester City, where he gave sterling service for eight seasons and became an England player – in midfield.

BORN: Islington, 11.6.46.
GAMES: 48 (5). GOALS: 15.
HONOURS: European Cup-Winners' Cup 70/1.
4 England caps (74).
OTHER CLUBS: Tottenham Hotspur 64/5-66/7 (21, 1); Millwall 67/8-69/70 (121, 40);
Leicester City 71/2-78/9 (262, 37); New England Tea Men; Fort Lauderdale Strikers.

1970/71-1971/72

MARVIN HINTON

As a sweeper, covering behind a well-organised defence, Marvin Hinton had few peers, as he demonstrated when he was used in that role by Tommy Docherty in a number of Fairs Cup ties in 1965/66. Sadly, he was rarely given the chance to exploit his ability in the position in which he excelled.

Marvin had started his career with Charlton Athletic as a centre-half but made most of his appearances during his first two seasons at Stamford Bridge following his £30,000 transfer in August 1963 at right-back, deputising for the injured Ken Shellito. He was then switched to the centre of the back four in place of John Mortimore but was never a truly dominating defender and lacked the height to be commanding in the air.

Although Hinton was short of pace, he possessed an outstanding football brain and read the game so well that he was rarely embarrassed. Steady and totally unflappable, he looked good in possession and used the ball intelligently, and his immaculate displays that season – with an assured, polished performance in the first game against AC Milan in the San Siro stadium outstanding – earned him a place in the squad of 40 players named for the 1966 World Cup.

However, after the arrival of David Webb in February 1968 Marvin was rarely sure of a place in the first team and the following season he started only six League games. A more assertive man would probably have moved to another club in search of the recognition his talent deserved, but 'Lou' was content to remain at the Bridge in the role of understudy and his continuing value to Chelsea was underlined when he came on as a substitute for the last five minutes of extra time in the FA Cup final replay at Old Trafford in 1970 to calm rapidly fraying nerves, both on the pitch and on the terraces.

Hinton made his final senior appearance for the Blues in the last game of 1974/75. He finally left Stamford Bridge twelve months later, aged 36, but continued to play in non-League football for many years.

BORN: Norwood, 2.2.40.
GAMES: 327 (16). GOALS: 4.
HONOURS: FA Cup 69/70; League Cup 64/5.
OTHER CLUBS: Charlton Athletic 57/8-63/4 (131, 2).

1963/64-1974/75

CHARLIE COOKE

If professional football were simply a matter of gifted artists entertaining the paying public with their delightful skills, Charlie Cooke would be revered as one of the finest players ever to have laced on a pair of boots. Instead, results take precedence over every other consideration, and for much of his Stamford Bridge career the mercurial Scotsman was regarded with suspicion by managers frustrated that his exceptional talent was largely ornamental.

A superb dribbler with a gloriously deceptive body swerve, Charlie was signed from Dundee in April 1966 for a club record fee as a direct replacement for Terry Venables, but found it impossible to adapt to the team's established style, which depended on the ball being played early to speedy front-runners. All too often he would weave his way down cul-de-sacs when a simple pass would have opened up a clear path to goal, and when it became apparent that Tony Hateley was helpless without a steady supply of high crosses Charlie was moved to the wing to provide it. A typical wriggle and a pinpoint centre created the winning goal in the FA Cup semi-final against Leeds, but Cooke never produced his best form on the flanks, tending to drift out of matches if he was not at the heart of the action.

Charlie's ball-juggling skills inevitably made him a darling of the Stamford Bridge crowd and he was voted the Blues' Player of the Year the following season, but Dave Sexton was less convinced, feeling that for all his delightful artistry the maestro made insufficient practical contribution to the team. Charlie seemed to accept that he would need to harness his individualism to the collective effort, for in 1969/70 he emerged as a more rounded, complete performer, but he was still at his most effective on those rare occasions when he was given a chance to bring his skills to bear in the middle of the pitch, most memorably in the FA Cup final replay at Old Trafford when he mastered Billy Bremner and created Peter Osgood's equaliser with an exquisite chip.

Always a player to produce his best on the big occasion, Charlie was again outstanding in the matches against Real Madrid in Athens, but he was unable to summon the consistency required to earn a regular place in the Blues' midfield and in September 1972 he followed Paddy Mulligan to Crystal Palace. A deeply intelligent, thoughtful man who was often tortured by self-doubt, Cooke was to have a miserable time at Selhurst Park, but after 15 months he was recalled to the Bridge to provide some much-needed sparkle in the wake of Alan Hudson's departure. The fee of £17,000 was around a fifth of what Chelsea had received and it was soon clear that Sexton had secured a bargain. Charlie had taken a long, hard look at himself and was clearly determined to make the most of his gifts in the years left to him. By the start of the following season he was fitter than he had ever been and his inspired displays on the wing provided a rare glimmer of hope during the Blues' wretched drift towards relegation.

Having rediscovered his old passion for the game, Cooke suffered a series of unfortunate injuries over the next couple of years but he returned to the side during the closing weeks of the tense promotion campaign in 1977 and, at 34, helped steady the nerves of Eddie McCreadie's young team, holding the ball and spraying it around with much of the old assurance. The veteran was destined to enjoy one more day of glory, a delightful 35-minute cameo in the third round of the Cup against Liverpool in January 1978 paving the way for a famous victory, before making a permanent switch to the United States that summer.

BORN: St Monance, Fife, 14.10.42.
GAMES: 360 (13). GOALS: 30.
HONOURS: European Cup-Winners' Cup 70/1; FA Cup 69/70.
16 Scotland caps (65-75).
OTHER CLUBS: Aberdeen; Dundee;
Crystal Palace 72/3-73/4 (44, 0);
Los Angeles Aztecs; Memphis Rogues; California Surf.

1965/66-1972/73 & 1973/74-1977/78

TOMMY BALDWIN

When Tommy Baldwin arrived at Stamford Bridge in September 1966 as part of the deal that took George Graham to Highbury, he had started fewer than 20 League games and was regarded as no more than a makeweight, but his form over the next three seasons left no doubt that once again Tommy Docherty had recognised gold where others had seen only base metal. However, the busy striker failed to maintain his early impetus and was to be no more than a squad player – albeit an important one – for the remainder of his long career with the Blues.

Baldwin scored on his Chelsea debut at Manchester City the day after making the move across London and would prove to be a dependable marksman, his last-minute winner against Sheffield Wednesday in the sixth round of the Cup that season confirming the value of his sharpness at short range. More important, however, was the huge amount of work he got through in 90 minutes, his good close control and determination enabling him to hold the ball under pressure and create openings for others.

The turning-point in Tommy's career came when he was sidelined for four months after damaging his knee against Ipswich on Boxing Day 1968. In his absence Ian Hutchinson emerged as a formidable rival and thereafter 'Sponge' could never be sure of a place in the first team. He was undeniably unlucky with illness and injuries but his inconsistency did nothing to help his chances. When he was recalled to the side he usually performed with much of his old zest at first, but then he seemed to lose interest and, not surprisingly, he was the one to be left out again when things went wrong.

Although he played in all the Blues' cup finals in the early seventies, Baldwin understandably grew increasingly dissatisfied with his role as a reserve and when he was made available in November 1972 it seemed that his departure was unlikely to be long delayed. In the event a series of proposed deals fell through and, after an abortive spell on loan at Manchester United, he was given a free transfer in September 1975.

BORN: Gateshead, 10.6.45.
GAMES: 228 (11). GOALS: 92.
HONOURS: European Cup-Winners' Cup 70/1; FA Cup 69/70.
OTHER CLUBS: Arsenal 64/5-66/7 (17, 7);
Millwall *on loan* 74/5 (6, 1);
Manchester United *on loan* 74/5 (2, 0);
Brentford 77/8 (4, 1).

1966/67-1974/75

STEVE KEMBER

The Crystal Palace fans took Steve Kember to their hearts for his tigerish aggression and when Dave Sexton broke the Chelsea transfer record in September 1971 to take him to Stamford Bridge, the Londoner admitted he was sorry to be leaving the club he had supported from the age of five. Although he was a first-team regular throughout his four seasons with the Blues, the midfielder never looked entirely comfortable in his new surroundings and rarely produced his best form.

At Selhurst Park Steve had been a major influence on a struggling side, and he seemed to be somewhat intimidated by some of the big names and extrovert personalities with whom he now shared a dressing room. It was unfortunate that an appearance for Palace in the early stages of the League Cup prevented him from taking part in Chelsea's run to the final during his first season with the club and no doubt that added to his sense of isolation.

He was marginalised in a rather more literal sense by Sexton, who asked him to play wide on the right rather than in his preferred position at the heart of the action. There was much learned talk about the value of Kember's stamina on the flanks, but he was unable to make much impression and soon became a frustrated and bewildered figure.

Once Sexton had departed, Steve was given his chance to demonstrate his worth in the thick of the midfield battle. His confidence quickly returned and his spirited displays were an inspiration as commitment replaced panache as the Chelsea rallying cry, but it was too late for the sorrowful slide towards relegation to be reversed. Kember's personal renaissance was short-lived, and when the season had reached its melancholy conclusion he was grateful to be given the opportunity to continue his career in the First Division with Leicester City.

BORN: Croydon, 8.12.48.
GAMES: 144 (6). GOALS: 15.
OTHER CLUBS: Crystal Palace 65/6-71/2 (218, 35) and 78/9-79/80 (42, 1);
Leicester City 75/6-78/9 (117, 6);
Vancouver Whitecaps.
MANAGER: Crystal Palace (81-82).

1971/72-1974/75

ALAN HUDSON

The ascent of Alan Hudson from the obscurity of the Football Combination to the
fringe of the England World Cup squad could scarcely have been more spectacular.
Having made his first-team debut in February 1969, the richly talented midfielder seized
the opportunity presented by a wave of injuries that afflicted Stamford Bridge at the start
of the following season to establish himself as an influential member of what was rapidly
developing into a thrilling Chelsea side. No less an authority than Sir Alf Ramsey, not a
man renowned for his oratorical excesses, declared that there was 'no end to what this
boy can achieve', and a quite breathtaking individual goal against Sheffield Wednesday in
March reinforced the gifted 18-year-old's blossoming reputation. Alan was among
the 40 players short-listed for service in Mexico and it seemed that the Blues had
unearthed a player of genuine world class.

With his long hair flapping and his socks around his ankles, Hudson covered a huge
amount of ground during the course of a match, helping out in defence one moment
then surging up the field to create an opening at the other end the next. He read the
game with an astuteness that belied his inexperience, and his willingness to take
responsibility, running at defences before splitting them wide open with an inch-perfect
through-ball, was remarkable in one so young. It is rare indeed for athleticism and artistry
to be combined in such rich measure; it really did seem as though Alan had it all . . .

However, the teenager's apparently irresistible rise was brought to an abrupt halt by a
nasty ankle injury picked up at the Hawthorns on Easter Monday and, despite a
courageous fight, he missed both the epic confrontation with Leeds at Wembley and, to
his intense disappointment, the Old Trafford rematch. Like many young footballers of
exceptional ability since, Hudson, who had been brought up close to London's
fashionable King's Road, just a few minutes' walk from the Blues' ground, did not find it
easy to come to terms with the adulation suddenly thrust upon him, and the rest of his
Chelsea career was to be marred by an exasperating inconsistency. In the end that
golden promise remained largely unfulfilled.

A stress fracture of the shin hampered Alan's recovery from this setback and the form that
had won him such acclaim was rarely seen the following season, but by the second half of
1971/72 he was generally considered to be back at his best. His appetite restored, his passing
more perceptive than ever, Hudson was quite outstanding against Liverpool in March,
dominating the game in majestic style, but that summer he suffered a severe blow when he
was banned from international football for two years after declining to join an under-23 tour.

Alan's fortunes dipped once again the following winter and, frustrated at being asked to
play out of position on the right flank, he demanded a transfer, marking the start of a
battle of wills with Dave Sexton that could have only one outcome. The FA ban was
lifted in July 1973 and, for a few weeks in the autumn, he looked sharp and eager, his
desire rekindled. Chelsea suddenly recaptured much of their old swagger, but the revival
was to be short-lived and Hudson was dropped, together with three others, for the game
at Sheffield United on New Year's Day. He asked for a move once again and within a
fortnight he had been transferred to Stoke City for £240,000, his sparkling performances
for the Potteries club earning him two England caps.

Alan returned to Stamford Bridge in the summer of 1983, but illness and injury sadly
denied him the chance to show whether he could reproduce the magic that had
enthralled the fans a decade earlier.

BORN: Chelsea, 21.6.51.
GAMES: 187 (1). GOALS: 14.
HONOURS: European Cup-Winners' Cup 70/1.
2 England caps (75).
OTHER CLUBS: Stoke City 73/4-76/7 (105, 9) and 83/4-85/6 (39, 0);
Arsenal 76/7-77/8 (36, 0); Hercules, Spain; Seattle Sounders.

1968/69-1973/74

IAN HUTCHINSON

Any centre-half who had spent ninety minutes marking Ian Hutchinson knew he had earned his money. Brave and aggressive, the big striker allowed defenders no respite, constantly harrying them and challenging for every ball played in his direction with a ferocity that made onlookers wince. Accepting injuries as the price that had to be paid if he was to do his job, he rarely emerged from a game unscathed and his uncompromising style made it almost inevitable that his career would be cut short, but during his one full season in the Chelsea first team 'Hutch' produced a series of stirring performances that will not be easily forgotten by those who witnessed them.

Ian gained his football education in a tough school, playing as a part-timer in non-League football with Burton Albion and Cambridge United before moving to Stamford Bridge in a £5,000 deal in July 1968. He was given an extended run in the side in the closing weeks of the following season and made a dramatic impact, scoring six times in 11 appearances and impressing with his strength and enthusiasm, but the real turning-point came when he was paired with Peter Osgood against Sheffield Wednesday at Hillsborough on a cold, wet Saturday in November 1969. It was immediately apparent that their partnership had enormous potential, the lion-hearted 21-year-old drawing the enemy's fire while his stealthy partner crept in unobserved, and the Blues won 3-1, Ian rounding off a splendid display with two well-taken goals.

A superb header of the ball, the powerfully built youngster may have looked a little ungainly on the floor but his control was getting better all the time, as he demonstrated in the FA Cup semi-final against Watford four months later, turning past a bewildered defender before thumping home the Blues' fourth goal and setting up the fifth for Peter Houseman with a delicate lay-off. Then at Wembley he conjured up a last-ditch equaliser with a brave diving header, and his immensely promising season was crowned in the replay at Old Trafford when one of the prodigious long throws which had become his trademark was bundled in at the far post by David Webb for the winner.

Hutchinson looked set to maintain his progress the following winter but in December he received the first of the heartbreaking catalogue of injuries that were to wreck his career. Ironically, in view of the punishment he received every week, it was self-inflicted, a clash with a Nottingham Forest defender who had left him minus a tooth resulting in a broken bone in his arm. Two months later the combative striker damaged his right knee against Southampton and he would not return to first-team action for nearly two years, having broken his leg in a reserve game and subsequently suffered a repeat of the fracture.

Two goals on his comeback against Norwich in December 1972 were quickly forgotten when more trouble with his knee forced Ian back into hospital and he managed only a handful of appearances in 1973/74, but the following season he was able to play more regularly and showed signs of recapturing the drive and commitment that had made him so formidable. Utterly determined to overcome every setback, 'Hutch' seemed to have re-established himself in the side in the autumn of 1975 but his right knee was still causing him a lot of pain and the following February came the final announcement that the joint could take no more abuse.

His long fight for fitness had been characteristically dogged and unflinching, but Eddie McCreadie spoke for many of the fans who had followed Ian's injury-blighted career with boundless admiration when he said that it was a relief that the popular Midlander's ordeal was at an end.

BORN: Derby, 4.8.48.
GAMES: 136 (7). GOALS: 57.
HONOURS: FA Cup 69/70.

1968/69-1975/76

CHRIS GARLAND

Prior to the first leg of the 1971/72 League Cup semi-final against Tottenham at Stamford Bridge on 22 December, Chris Garland had started only four first-team games since his £100,000 transfer from Bristol City at the beginning of September and had yet to score. He had been signed to add depth to the squad, and would probably not have played if Steve Kember had been available, but he seized his chance splendidly by heading home at the near post from Peter Houseman's right-wing corner as Chelsea triumphed 3-2, and finally won over the fans with an unstoppable 20-yard drive at White Hart Lane two weeks later which helped clinch the Blues' place at Wembley.

In the final against Stoke the enthusiastic striker produced another energetic, determined performance and it took a heroic save from Gordon Banks in the closing minutes to deny him a deserved equaliser. However, those three matches were very much the highlights of the athletic blond forward's four-year stay at Stamford Bridge, during which he was rarely certain of a first-team place.

He started the following season with a flurry of goals but then picked up a persistent groin injury which hampered him for the next two years, preventing him from training for much of the time. Chris found it frustrating that Dave Sexton generally asked him to play wide on the left or the right to capitalise on his powerful running, since he felt that his most effective position was in the middle alongside a dominant centre-forward, but in truth he probably did not have the sharpness to be a regular marksman at the top level.

Something of an open-hearted country boy, Garland never really adapted to the cynicism of life in the metropolis and, with Chelsea doomed to relegation, was relieved to be given a chance to revive his career in the provinces by Leicester manager Jimmy Bloomfield in March 1975, subsequently returning to his native Bristol.

BORN: Bristol, 24.4.49.
GAMES: 111 (3). GOALS: 31.
OTHER CLUBS: Bristol City 66/7-71/2 (143, 31) and 76/7-82/3 (64, 11);
Leicester City 74/5-76/7 (55, 15).

1971/72-1974/75

PETER HOUSEMAN

It was Peter Houseman's misfortune to be victimised by a section of the Stamford Bridge crowd who were seemingly alienated by his meticulous, diffident manner – and, more to the point, didn't know a footballer when they saw one – but that should not be allowed to overshadow the outstanding service this talented player gave the Blues in a first-team career that spanned more than a decade.

Peter was still three days short of his 18th birthday when he made his senior debut against Sheffield United in December 1963, but he proved to be something of a late developer and five years would pass before Dave Sexton gave him a permanent place in the side. A cultured performer with a fine left foot, 'Nobby' blossomed as his confidence grew and he didn't miss a match in 1969/70, starting the season in midfield then settling down on the left wing when Alan Hudson broke into the team.

Houseman was a diligent worker who dropped back conscientiously to cover his full-back and his ability to hold the ball was much appreciated by hard-pressed colleagues. When he was in the mood to make the most of his skill he could be a match-winner and he crossed the ball beautifully, although he was sometimes guilty of over-elaboration. He is best remembered for his performances in the FA Cup that year, with a magisterial display on a heavy pitch in the semi-final at White Hart Lane the highlight.

Peter was a fixture in the side for the next two seasons, but as Chelsea started to struggle his own star began to wane and his first-team place came under mounting pressure. Sexton switched him to left-back at the start of 1974/75 but he lacked the aggression for the role and, with a wind of change sweeping through Stamford Bridge, he was transferred to Oxford at the end of the season.

All football's triumphs and disasters were shown for what they are, however, when this quiet, unassuming man was killed together with his wife Sally in a tragic road accident two years later.

BORN: Battersea, 24.12.45.
GAMES: 324 (18). GOALS: 39.
HONOURS: European Cup-Winners' Cup 70/1;
FA Cup 69/70.
OTHER CLUBS: Oxford United 75/6-76/7 (65, 2).

1963/64-1974/75

Judgements of Ron Harris during his playing days tended to reflect the loyalties of the person handing down the verdict. To supporters of other teams he was 'Chopper' Harris, the ruthless destroyer who would use any means, within the laws of the game or otherwise, to subdue his opponent; to the Stamford Bridge crowd he was an indomitable lionheart and probably the best tackler in English football. However, all could agree that he was a consummate professional, seemingly fashioned from toughened steel, who never flinched from a challenge and routinely played when carrying injuries that would have confined lesser men to the comfort of their armchair.

Ron had already made five League appearances for the Blues when he captained the England Youth team that won the Little World Cup at Wembley in April 1963. Tommy Docherty, impressed by the 18-year-old's fierce will to win, decided that he was the man to add resolve to Chelsea's faltering promotion challenge and recalled him to the first team against Preston four days later. He stayed there for 17 years, carrying out his allotted task with uncompromising thoroughness and invariably giving his managers – all seven of them – everything he had to offer.

Ron was at his best playing alongside the centre-half, close-marking the opposition's most dangerous forward. Men like Geoff Hurst and George Best rarely prospered with Harris sticking to them closer than their shadows, and his mastery of Jimmy Greaves was such that the little genius scored just once in more than twenty matches against the Blues and was even heard to ask why Tottenham bothered to pick him against Chelsea. It is true that Ron occasionally did things that made his team-mates cringe and was not above examining the bravery of the players he faced, some of whom were quite content to let him pass his afternoon largely undisturbed. However, he relished the opportunity to test his mettle against an opponent with an equally fearsome reputation, and one bone-splintering challenge for a 50-50 ball with Liverpool's Tommy Smith is not likely to be forgotten by those who witnessed it.

Adaptable and uncomplaining, Ron was regularly switched to full-back to plug gaps caused by injuries or loss of form, but his lack of pace was occasionally exposed in that role and there is no doubt that his willingness to play out of position for the good of the team did little to advance his own career. He replaced Terry Venables as captain in January 1966 and led the Blues to four major cup finals, inspiring his troops by his peerless example rather than the melodramatic fist-waving employed by more flamboyant characters. The much trumpeted 'clean-up' of the early seventies was widely supposed to have blunted Chopper's edge and he was briefly dropped after the crushing disappointment of defeat in the fifth round of the FA Cup and the League Cup final on successive Saturdays in the spring of 1972, the captaincy passing to Eddie McCreadie. However, Ron remained a model of solid pragmatism, content to win the ball with quiet efficiency and play a simple pass to a more gifted colleague.

Harris was named as substitute on no fewer than 30 occasions by McCreadie in 1976/77 but did his usual dependable job when he stood in for David Hay in the tense closing stages of the promotion battle. Three years later he was handed the number 11 shirt by Geoff Hurst and asked to play as a midfield destroyer. At 35, he proved so effective that one wondered what he might have achieved if he had been used in that role a decade earlier, but his relations with his former adversary were not entirely comfortable and at the end of the season he joined Brentford as a player-coach, having made 794 appearances for the Blues, establishing a record that is very unlikely ever to be broken.

BORN: Hackney, 13.11.44.
GAMES: 783 (11). GOALS: 14.
HONOURS: European Cup-Winners' Cup 70/1; FA Cup 69/70; League Cup 64/5.
OTHER CLUBS: Brentford 80/1-83/4 (61, 0).
MANAGER: Aldershot (84-85).

1961/62-1979/80

PETER FEELY

TOMMY ORD

LEE FROST

PETER FEELY 1970/71-1972/73

Forward. BORN: Camden, 3.1.50.
GAMES: 4 (1). GOALS: 2.
OTHER CLUBS: AFC Bournemouth 72/3-73/4 (9, 2);
Fulham (0, 0); Gillingham 74/5-75/6 (41, 22);
Sheffield Wednesday 75/6-76/7 (19, 2);
Stockport County *on loan* 76/7 (2, 0).

TONY POTRAC 1971/72

Forward. BORN: Victoria, 21.1.53.
GAMES: 1. GOALS: 0.
OTHER CLUBS: Durban City.

MIKE BROLLY 1972/73-1973/74

Winger. BORN: Galston, 6.10.54.
GAMES: 8 (1). GOALS: 1.
OTHER CLUBS: Bristol City 74/5-75/6 (30, 2);
Grimsby Town 76/7-81/2 (254, 27);
Derby County 82/3 (42, 4);
Scunthorpe United 83/4-85/6 (95, 15).

TOMMY ORD 1972/73

Forward. BORN: Woolwich, 15.10.52.
GAMES: 3. GOALS: 1.
OTHER CLUBS: Bristol City *on loan* (0, 0);
Montreal Olympic; Rochester Lancers;
New York Cosmos;
Vancouver Whitecaps; Seattle Sounders;
Tulsa Roughnecks;
Atlanta Chiefs.

LEE FROST 1977/78-1979/80

Winger. BORN: Woking, 4.12.57.
GAMES: 12 (3). GOALS: 5.
OTHER CLUBS: Brentford *on loan* 78/9 (6, 0);
Brentford 80/1 (15, 3).

BOB ILES 1978/79-1982/83

Goalkeeper. BORN: Leicester, 2.9.55.
GAMES: 14. GOALS: 0.
OTHER CLUBS: AFC Bournemouth (0, 0).

TONY POTRAC

MIKE BROLLY

BOB ILES

JOHN SITTON

JIM DOCHERTY

JIMMY CLARE

MARK FALCO

JOHN SITTON 1978/79-1979/80

Central defender. BORN: Hackney, 21.10.59.
GAMES: 12 (2). GOALS: 0.
OTHER CLUBS: Millwall 79/80-80/1 (45, 1);
Gillingham 81/2-84/5 (107, 5);
Leyton Orient 85/6-90/1 (170, 7).

GARY JOHNSON 1978/79-1980/81

Forward. BORN: Peckham, 14.9.59.
GAMES: 18 (4). GOALS: 9.
OTHER CLUBS: Crystal Palace *on loan* (0, 0);
Brentford 80/1-82/3 (60, 13); PG Rangers, South Africa;
Aldershot 85/6-87/8 (75, 20).

JIM DOCHERTY 1978/79

Forward. BORN: Broxburn, 8.11.56.
GAMES: 2 (1). GOALS: 0.
OTHER CLUBS: East Stirling; Dundee United.

TIM ELMES 1980/81

Midfielder. BORN: Thornton Heath, 28.9.62.
GAMES: 2 (2). GOALS: 0.
OTHER CLUBS: Leyton Orient (0, 0).

JIMMY CLARE 1980/81

Midfielder. BORN: Islington, 6.11.59.
GAMES: 0 (1). GOALS: 0.
OTHER CLUBS: Charlton Athletic (0, 0).

MARK FALCO 1982/83

Forward. BORN: Hackney, 22.10.60.
GAMES: 3 (*on loan* from Tottenham Hotspur). GOALS: 0.
OTHER CLUBS: Tottenham Hotspur 78/9-86/7 (174, 68);
Watford 86/7 (33, 14); Glasgow Rangers;
Queens Park Rangers 87/8-90/1 (87, 27);
Millwall 91/2 (21, 4).

PAUL WILLIAMS 1982/83

Central defender. BORN: Lambeth, 16.11.62.
GAMES: 1. GOALS: 0.

GARY JOHNSON

TIM ELMES

PAUL WILLIAMS

PADDY MULLIGAN

Before joining Chelsea from Shamrock Rovers in a £17,500 deal in October 1969, Paddy Mulligan had combined football with a job as an office furniture salesman and it took him some time to adapt to the level of fitness expected at Stamford Bridge. The enthusiastic Irishman made only a handful of appearances during his first season but, in the wake of Eddie McCreadie's long-term injury problems, he appeared to have established a regular place in the Blues' first team at right-back the following autumn, his whole-hearted style and adventurous overlapping down the wing making him popular with the fans. He had generally played in the centre of the defence for the Republic of Ireland, but a fine match-winning goal in the home game against Arsenal when he ran onto Peter Osgood's pass, beat McNab and sent a well-struck right-foot shot past Bob Wilson demonstrated his considerable attacking ability.

A torn hamstring sustained in the second leg of the Cup-Winners' Cup tie against CSKA Sofia put him out for two months and on his return he was unable to regain the position, but the following season he started 36 games – all but two of them at right-back – and seemed to be developing into a fine player, adding poise to his natural energy and determination. The injury which kept him off the field for the second half of the League Cup final that year undoubtedly contributed to Chelsea's defeat, yet at the start of the next campaign the amiable Dubliner was in the reserves, and when the chance of a regular first-team place at Crystal Palace was offered to him, he was happy to accept.

While Paddy may not have been the most naturally gifted defender in the Football League, his attitude helped compensate for any shortcomings and his performances at Selhurst Park and, subsequently, West Bromwich Albion confirmed that he had been right to try to prove himself on this side of the Irish Sea.

BORN: Dublin, 17.3.45.
GAMES: 73 (5). GOALS: 2.
HONOURS: 51 Ireland caps.
OTHER CLUBS: Shamrock Rovers (twice); Boston Beacons;
Crystal Palace 72/3-74/5 (57, 2);
West Bromwich Albion 75/6-77/8 (109, 1).

1969/70-1972/73

TOMMY HUGHES

When Chelsea lost 5-2 at home to Leeds United in January 1970, ending all thoughts of a challenge for the Championship, Tommy Hughes was savaged by the Sunday newspapers. The Scottish under-23 international had taken the place of Peter Bonetti, who had flu, and his uncertainty was said to have been responsible for the defeat. However, the young 'keeper, playing only his sixth first-team match, had been the victim of his own courage and sense of duty, as he was also unwell and should really have been tucked up in bed with a hot-water bottle rather than facing Don Revie's men at the height of their powers. He later acknowledged that it had been a mistake to play but, however unfair it might have been, the 'accident prone' label had been firmly attached, and his reputation took a further battering when his fourth game of the season ended in another five-goal drubbing, at the hands of the Champions, Everton.

Dave Sexton still had faith in his ability, but a broken leg sustained when jumping for a high ball in a pre-season friendly against Breda at the end of July effectively ended Tommy's chances of proving his worth at Stamford Bridge. However, the big Scot subsequently established himself at Hereford, where he played for nine seasons before becoming manager.

BORN: Dalmuir, 11.7.47.
GAMES: 11. GOALS: 0.
OTHER CLUBS: Clydebank; Aston Villa 71/2 (16, 0); Brighton and Hove Albion *on loan* 72/3 (3, 0); Hereford United 73/4-81/2 (240, 0).
MANAGER: Hereford United (82-83).

1966/67-1969/70

DEREK SMETHURST

As he collected the medal he had earned when he came on as a substitute in the European Cup-Winners' Cup final replay in Athens in May 1971, Derek Smethurst must have felt that he could look forward to a bright future with the Blues. The 23-year-old South African striker had played in both legs of the semi-final against Manchester City, scoring the only goal of the game at Stamford Bridge when he slid the ball neatly past Joe Corrigan from a pass by stand-in centre-forward David Webb, and had also appeared in the last five League games of the season, collecting two more goals. The new campaign would surely bring many more opportunities to prove his worth . . .

Derek had made his first-team debut at Burnley the previous September, having been signed from Durban City in December 1968, and appeared to have established himself as a valued member of Dave Sexton's squad, signing a professional contract when he had fulfilled a two-year residential requirement. Tall and stylish, he was a little short of pace and lacked the drive and aggression so highly prized in English football, but he certainly had ability and appeared to be a bright prospect.

It was therefore something of a surprise when, having played in the first two games of the new season in place of Keith Weller, Smethurst was transferred to Millwall for £35,000 in September, remaining at the Den for four years before trying his luck in America.

BORN: Durban, South Africa, 24.10.47.
GAMES: 18 (1). GOALS: 5.
HONOURS: European Cup-Winners' Cup 70/71.
OTHER CLUBS: Durban City; Millwall 71/2-74/5 (71, 9); Tampa Bay Rowdies; San Diego Sockers; Seattle Sounders.

1970/71-1971/72

MICKY DROY

Micky Droy's Chelsea career spanned no fewer than 15 seasons, during which he provided just about the only continuity (apart from the long-suffering supporters) amid seemingly unending changes in the dressing room, the manager's office and the boardroom. These years saw several periods of deep gloom in SW6, but without the courage and resilience of the huge centre-half the despair would have been even greater.

In his last full season in the first team, 1982/83, the Blues only narrowly avoided relegation to Division Three, and it was hard to remember that he had started his Chelsea career in a very different atmosphere, his third senior game being the home leg of the European Cup-Winners' Cup semi-final against Manchester City in April 1971. When Micky ran out onto the pitch for away games in those early days, his sheer size invariably drew murmurs of astonishment from the apprehensive home fans, and at 6ft 4in and 15$^1/_2$ stone he certainly presented an imposing sight.

Droy had learned his football in the non-League game, moving to Stamford Bridge from Slough Town at the age of 19 in October 1970, and in his first few seasons the rough edges were very apparent. He became established in the side only in the second half of 1973/74 when Dave Sexton decided that the club would have to battle its way out of trouble, and the presence of the unpolished stopper at the heart of the Blues' defence embodied the new mood of austerity at the Bridge. However, as Chelsea slipped towards the relegation trap-door the following winter, his courageous and aggressive displays were often inspirational, with a defiant performance at Upton Park outstanding. Although not entirely fit, having just recovered from injury, he headed away the stream of high balls sent in by West Ham and scored the decisive goal when he hurled himself at Peter Houseman's centre.

When Micky was ruled out by injuries for much of the second half of 1975/76, Steve Wicks was able to establish a firm grip on the number five shirt which he relinquished only briefly as Eddie McCreadie's team surged towards promotion, but Ken Shellito decided to use the two towering defenders together during the Blues' spirited fight for First Division survival the following season and the partnership proved surprisingly effective. Micky emerged as the fans' Player of the Year and his lengthy absences due to illness and then an ankle problem were undoubtedly a major factor in the side's lamentable efforts in 1978/79.

As his experience increased, 'Lurch' became more authoritative and, as his reading of the game improved, his lack of speed was rarely punished. He was now much more composed, his strength and reach making him irresistible in the tackle. He also showed increased poise on the ball, sometimes demonstrating quite remarkable finesse with his favoured left foot to dribble out of tight situations before making a searching forward pass. Although he was often sent upfield to remedy desperate situations, Droy didn't score too often, but his efforts certainly created chances for others.

Micky succeeded Ray Wilkins as club captain and his influence on a young side over the next four seasons was invaluable. He always played with total commitment, launching his mighty frame into challenges with utter fearlessness, and as a consequence he picked up a seemingly endless catalogue of niggling injuries which caused him to miss more than a quarter of the Blues' matches and affected his consistency. However, at his best – in other words, when he was fully fit – he was utterly dominant, particularly when the ball was in the air.

In the summer of 1983 John Neal recruited Joe McLaughlin and Droy started only one more first-team game for Chelsea, but he did a fine job for Crystal Palace following his move to Selhurst Park in March 1985.

BORN: Highbury, 7.5.51.
GAMES: 302 (11). GOALS: 19.
OTHER CLUBS: Luton Town *on loan* 84/5 (2, 0);
Crystal Palace 84/5-86/7 (49, 7);
Brentford 86/7 (19, 3).

1970/71-1984/85

TEDDY MAYBANK

Eddie McCreadie's decision to give 18-year-old Teddy Maybank his first-team debut in the crucial relegation battle with Tottenham at White Hart Lane in April 1975 was so daring that it deserved to succeed. However, the blond striker was unable to make much impression on a match more tense than any cup-tie, and hopes of a miraculous deliverance were dashed.

Strongly built and energetic, Maybank was at his most effective when running at defences with the ball, but in the 26 matches he played the following season he rarely produced his best form as the Blues struggled to adapt to the Second Division. Two fine headed goals at home to Carlisle in August confirmed that, despite his relative lack of inches, he was useful in the air, but for all his pace and skill he was unable to hit the target often enough and, following the fifth round Cup defeat at home to Crystal Palace, McCreadie turned to Steve Finnieston.

After joining Fulham on a one-month loan, Teddy became increasingly restless and, in spite of Chelsea's reluctance to lose a player of considerable potential, he was allowed to move to Craven Cottage permanently in a £65,000 deal in March 1977. Unhappily, injury problems meant that that early promise went unfulfilled.

BORN: Lambeth, 11.10.56.
GAMES: 32. GOALS: 6.
OTHER CLUBS: Fulham 76/7-77/8 (27, 14)
and 79/80 (19, 3);
Brighton and Hove Albion 77/8-79/80 (64, 16).

1974/75-1976/77

JOHN SISSONS

What would prove to be Dave Sexton's last major signing for Chelsea was uncharacteristically quixotic. In August 1974 he paid Norwich City £50,000 for John Sissons, the traditional left-winger who, as a slim, speedy 18-year-old, had played in West Ham's FA Cup-winning side ten years earlier. At Upton Park he became a victim of the tactical revolution which had forced his species to the brink of extinction, often finding himself held responsible for the shortcomings of the Hammers' defence, and he eventually moved on to Second Division Sheffield Wednesday. After four largely frustrating years with the sleeping giants of Hillsborough and a season in Norwich colours which had ended with the prospect of a return to the hurly-burly of Division Two, Sissons had not hesitated to accept the lifeline extended by Sexton.

In the first few games of the season the boyish-looking winger, no longer so slim or so speedy but still capable of advancing puposefully down the flank and putting over an accurate centre, looked sharp and eager but, with the team's confidence ebbing away, his form faded and after ten matches he was dropped. Sexton then departed and although Sissons played two further games, it soon became clear that he did not feature in the new regime's plans. He eventually departed for South Africa in March 1976, no doubt pondering what might have been.

BORN: Hayes, 30.9.45.
GAMES: 12 (1). GOALS: 0.
OTHER CLUBS: West Ham United 62/3-69/70 (213, 37);
Sheffield Wednesday 70/1-73/4 (115, 14);
Norwich City 73/4 (17, 2); Cape Town City.

1974/75

DAVID HAY

The signing of David Hay from Celtic in July 1974 was intended to signal the beginning of a new era at Chelsea. Chairman Brian Mears could not be accused of a lack of ambition, for the Scottish international had been outstanding in the recent World Cup, driving forward powerfully from midfield, and the fee of £225,000 made him London's most expensive footballer; but a cruel sequence of misfortunes meant that hopes of a Hay-inspired reversal of the club's decline were made to look foolish.

It took him some time to settle in his new surroundings and, as he searched in vain for his best form in a side lacking confidence, his own self-belief started to ebb away, the trickle turning into a flood when, following his return from a leg injury, the vision in his right eye became blurred. The widely admired Scotsman kept going until season's end with characteristic professionalism, but surgery was required for the removal of a cataract that summer.

David was still not sure of a place in the team the following season as the Blues failed to impress in the Second Division, but things began to improve when he was paired with Steve Wicks in the centre of the defence in February. He shackled Mick Channon ruthlessly when Southampton visited the Bridge, using his strength and intelligent positional play to great effect, and this partnership was to be the cornerstone of Chelsea's ultimately successful challenge for promotion in 1976/77.

Further problems with the same eye curtailed his season and threatened his career but, after no fewer than three operations to repair a detached retina, the steely Glaswegian made a courageous comeback 12 months later. However, the unkind fates had not yet finished with Hay and, as he fought to re-establish himself in the side in the autumn of 1978, he suffered a knee injury which would force his premature retirement a year later.

It was less than this fine player deserved.

BORN: Paisley, 29.1.48.
GAMES: 118 (2). GOALS: 3.
HONOURS: 27 Scotland caps (70-74).
OTHER CLUBS: Glasgow Celtic.
MANAGER: Motherwell; Glasgow Celtic; St Mirren.

1974/75-1978/79

STEVE SHERWOOD

When it was realised early on the morning of the home game against Ipswich on 27 December 1971 that injuries would rule out both Peter Bonetti and John Phillips, Steve Sherwood was asked to return urgently to Stamford Bridge to make his League debut, but the 18-year-old arrived just five minutes before kick-off and was not allowed to play, which was perhaps a foretaste of future disappointments. David Webb relinquished the 'keeper's jersey at Derby five days later and the 6ft 3in Yorkshireman performed valiantly, only to be beaten with seven minutes remaining when a shot from Archie Gemmill was deflected beyond his reach.

Sherwood's next opportunity came in November when he played three more League games, conceding seven goals, but he had to wait until the start of the 1975/76 season for his only extended run in the first team. A dropped corner which led to a 'Pop' Robson equaliser at Sunderland on the opening day was an unhappy beginning, and the blond giant's positioning sometimes looked suspect, so it was no surprise when, after a 4-1 defeat at Southampton in October, Eddie McCreadie turned to Peter Bonetti to steady the ship.

Steve, the younger brother of Olympic athlete John Sherwood, moved on to Watford the following November and stayed at Vicarage Road for more than ten years, playing for the Hornets in the 1984 FA Cup final.

BORN: Selby, 10.12.53. GAMES: 17. GOALS: 0.
OTHER CLUBS: Brighton and Hove Albion *on loan* (0, 0);
Millwall *on loan* 73/4 (1, 0); Brentford *on loan* 73/4-74/5 (62, 0);
Watford 76/7-86/7 (211, 1); Grimsby Town 87/8- (183, 0).

1971/72-1975/76

RAY LEWINGTON

To escape from what was the Second Division a side needs a player who can win the ball in midfield, and that was the role Ray Lewington performed for the Blues as they gained promotion on a tide of youthful enthusiasm in 1976/77. The red-haired terrier didn't miss a match and it was the platform provided by his biting tackles which allowed the more sophisticated talents of Ray Wilkins and Garry Stanley to flourish. The crucial game against Luton on Easter Saturday saw him at his best: he worked tirelessly throughout to give Chelsea control of the middle of the pitch, and crowned a stirring performance when he robbed Jimmy Husband and fed Steve Finnieston, who did the rest.

In the First Division the following season Lewington was unable to make the same impact, perhaps because he lacked the pace required at the higher level, and he was left out of the side for long spells. When Danny Blanchflower succeeded Ken Shellito in December 1978, he soon made up his mind that he had no use for what the chunky midfielder had to offer, and Ray was allowed to try his luck in Canada.

The rest of his career was spent in the lower divisions, including a successful spell as Fulham's player-manager, but he never quite recaptured the form he had produced under the influence of Eddie McCreadie.

BORN: Lambeth, 7.9.56. GAMES: 87 (5). GOALS: 4.
OTHER CLUBS: Vancouver Whitecaps;
Wimbledon 79/80 (23, 0); Fulham 79/80-84/5 (174, 20) and
86/7-89/90 (60, 1); Sheffield United 85/6 (36, 0).
MANAGER: Fulham (86-90).

1975/76-1978/79

JOHN PHILLIPS

Having been signed from Aston Villa for £25,000 to replace the injured Tommy Hughes as Peter Bonetti's deputy at the beginning of the season, 19-year-old John Phillips looked set to play in the 1971 European Cup-Winners' Cup final as Chelsea's first-choice goalkeeper. His chance to impress had come earlier than expected when the England international was sidelined for two months by a combination of a shoulder injury and pneumonia, but the ambitious youngster had seized it decisively, demonstrating courage, a safe pair of hands and growing poise as the Blues maintained a position in the top four and won through to the Athens final.

Had Dave Sexton shown faith in the highly motivated teenager at this crucial point, he might well have fulfilled the hopes raised by an assured performance in a rousing home win against Leeds and matured into a top-class performer. Instead Peter Bonetti was recalled and, while the cup was won, an opportunity was lost.

Although 'Sticks' made 31 appearances over the next two seasons, he was firmly cast in the role of understudy until New Year's Day 1974, when his rival was a victim of the purge that followed four successive defeats. He made a brilliant penalty save in the third round of the Cup against QPR four days later and, apart from two brief spells when the more experienced man was preferred, held the place for the next 18 months. However, he received scant protection from a porous defence and his form declined together with his confidence as the team slid ingloriously towards the drop.

A serious ankle injury meant that Phillips missed the start of the 1975/76 campaign, and thereafter he had only occasional spells in the first team. By the time he finally moved on to Brighton in March 1980 the cool certainty which had created such an impression nine years earlier had become little more than a memory.

BORN: Shrewsbury, 7.7.51.
GAMES: 149. GOALS: 0.
HONOURS: 4 Wales caps (73-77).
OTHER CLUBS: Shrewsbury Town 68/9-69/70 (51, 0); Aston Villa 69/70 (15, 0); Crewe Alexandra *on loan* 79/80 (6, 0); Brighton and Hove Albion 80/1 (1, 0); Charlton Athletic 81/2 (2, 0); Crystal Palace (0, 0).

1970/71-1978/79

GRAHAM WILKINS

Although his Chelsea first-team career spanned no fewer than ten seasons, Graham Wilkins made just 137 League appearances for the Blues and he was never certain of a place in the side. At his best the diminutive full-back was an accomplished performer, but competition from Gary Locke restricted his opportunities on the right flank, where he was more comfortable, and consistency always proved elusive.

Having made his senior debut as a 17-year-old on Boxing Day 1972, Graham had to wait until the following October for a second chance and his progress was interrupted when he broke his left leg at Old Trafford a week later. It took him some time to recover from that setback but he managed to establish himself at left-back in Eddie McCreadie's promotion-winning team in 1976/77, only to lose his place to John Sparrow in the closing weeks of the season.

While he was inevitably overshadowed by his gifted younger brother Ray, Graham had considerable natural ability and liked to play his way out of tight situations whenever possible. He looked impressive when moving forward with the ball but lacked composure and his defensive shortcomings were cruelly exposed on more than one occasion during the Blues' unhappy two-year sojourn in the First Division, most notably at Maine Road in November 1977 when he was run ragged by Manchester City's Peter Barnes and eventually sent off after his desperate attempts to halt the flying winger had incurred the displeasure of the referee.

Graham's approach was generally rather less aggressive, which led some simple-minded members of the Stamford Bridge crowd to question his commitment, but he could be a dogged defender, as he had demonstrated when he contained John Robertson of Nottingham Forest a few weeks earlier. However, his confidence was gradually eroded over the years and he became increasingly uncertain. The arrival of Dennis Rofe in February 1980 ended his chances of winning a regular place in the Blues' first team but he remained at the Bridge for two more, largely unproductive, seasons before moving to Brentford in the summer of 1982.

BORN: Hillingdon, 28.6.55.
GAMES: 148 (1). GOALS: 1.
OTHER CLUBS: Brentford 82/3-83/4 (38, 0);
Southend United *on loan* 83/4 (3, 0).

1972/73-1981/82

STEVE FINNIESTON

Every successful side needs at least one of its forwards to find the net regularly and Steve Finnieston will be remembered as the man who scored 24 League goals in 39 matches as Eddie McCreadie's energetic young side returned the Blues to the First Division. They included three penalties, a few gifts and plenty of close-range efforts, including the winner volleyed past an advancing 'keeper from eight yards in the vital home game against Nottingham Forest in April; but a reliable finisher who would punish the sort of mistakes that Second Division defences tend to make was precisely what McCreadie had been looking for when, in some desperation, he recalled the Edinburgh-born striker midway through the previous season. 'Jock', who had never doubted his ability to score goals, made no secret of the fact that he felt the opportunity was overdue, and responded by proving his point five times in a dozen appearances.

Although the strong and determined target man could shield the ball and lay it off to colleagues effectively – if not always very stylishly – and worked to improve other aspects of his game, it was his hunger for goals and coolness in the box that made him so important to the side. Finnieston rounded off the triumphant promotion season with a hat-trick in the last match against Hull but missed four months of the following campaign with Achilles tendon trouble, and when he returned – with a characteristic goal, banged home from a rebound, in the third round Cup win against Liverpool – a lot of the old sharpness seemed to have disappeared. However, when he was sold to Sheffield United for £90,000 that May, it confirmed the suspicion that many people at Stamford Bridge had never really believed in him and sadly another injury which forced Steve to give up League football denied him the chance to prove them wrong.

BORN: Edinburgh, 30.11.54.
GAMES: 86 (4). GOALS: 37.
OTHER CLUBS: Cardiff City *on loan* 74/5 (9, 2); Sheffield United 78/9 (23, 4).

1974/75-1977/78

KEN SWAIN

Although he subsequently enjoyed a long and distinguished career, winning Championship and European Cup medals with Aston Villa and continuing to play League football regularly until he was 39, Ken Swain's stay at Chelsea was relatively unspectacular and his contribution to the Blues' promotion in 1977 largely unremarked. Most of the plaudits went to players whose talent was destined to fade after a brief period in full blossom, while the unassuming Merseysider just kept on getting better . . .

This was only to be expected, perhaps, since Ken had come late to professional football, qualifying as a schoolteacher before moving to Stamford Bridge from Wycombe Wanderers in August 1973. A winger who was at home on either flank, he made a handful of senior appearances the following spring without making any lasting impact, but was not among the 25 players called into first-team action as the Blues lurched towards relegation in 1974/75. He was given another chance to prove his worth the following season and the injury which sadly ended Ian Hutchinson's career allowed the 24-year-old to establish himself as a striker in the closing months of the campaign.

The promising partnership he had formed with Steve Finnieston continued to develop as Eddie McCreadie's side set the pace at the top of the Second Division table the following winter, but Ken's thoughtful distribution, neat ball control and dogged persistence could not disguise the fact that, with only 13 goals in 36 League appearances, he was a profligate finisher, and Tommy Langley was preferred for the run-in.

The following August Ken Shellito announced that he intended to use Swain in midfield, feeling that his intelligent reading of the game would be put to better use in a deeper role, and the switch was immediately justified when the former winger capped an influential display at Old Trafford with a flighted centre that gave Bill Garner the winning goal. Ken continued to operate as a provider until November 1978 when, with the Blues struggling, he was dropped and asked for a transfer. Shortly afterwards he moved to Villa Park in a £100,000 deal – and discovered that his best position was full-back . . .

BORN: Birkenhead, 28.1.52.
GAMES: 127 (5). GOALS: 29.
OTHER CLUBS: Aston Villa 78/9-82/3 (148, 4);
Nottingham Forest 82/3-84/5 (112, 2);
Portsmouth 85/6-87/8 (113, 0); West Bromwich Albion *on loan* 87/8 (7, 1);
Crewe Alexandra 88/9-91/2 (126, 1).

1973/74-1978/79

BILL GARNER

A powerfully built, old-fashioned centre-forward, dangerous in the air but less happy when the ball was on the ground, Bill Garner was signed to provide Dave Sexton with an attacking option denied him by Ian Hutchinson's continuing fitness problems, but found difficulty in adapting to the demands of First Division football following his £100,000 move from humble Southend in September 1972. He was ineligible for League Cup ties, having played against the Blues in an early round of the competition, and this, combined with a series of minor injuries of the kind that were to dog him throughout his career with Chelsea, prevented him from staking an early claim to a regular first-team place.

His best performances that season were reserved for the FA Cup, two goals against Ipswich in round four – both with his feet – suggesting that the tall striker was progressing nicely, although an ugly clash with the Sheffield Wednesday captain in the next round at Hillsborough which resulted in both men being sent off revealed a suspect temperament. His heading prowess troubled the Arsenal defence in the quarter-final replay, creating a goal for Peter Houseman, but it was not enough to save the game.

Much of the following campaign was lost as a result of an unpleasant viral illness, and the remainder of Bill's stay at Stamford Bridge proved disheartening. Two thumping headers against QPR in February 1974 confirmed that he could still pose a considerable threat but, in common with Steve Kember and Chris Garland, he was a victim of inconsistent team selection, Sexton appearing to have little clear idea of the type of side he was attempting to construct to succeed his cup-winning teams. However, while they joined Keith Weller at Leicester when the Blues went down, Garner remained for another three, largely fruitless seasons, before joining Cambridge United on a free transfer in November 1978.

BORN: Leicester, 14.12.47.
GAMES: 105 (14). GOALS: 36.
OTHER CLUBS: Notts County 66/7 (2, 0);
Southend United 69/70-72/3 (102, 41);
Cambridge United 78/9-79/80 (24, 3);
Brentford 83/4 (3, 1).

1972/73-1978/79

GARY LOCKE

Following his League debut in September 1972, Gary Locke was Chelsea's first-choice right-back for almost a decade, but his career was plagued by a succession of injuries which gradually took their toll on his startling acceleration and drew much of the sting from his game. Only twice was he able to make more than 32 League appearances in a season, and the rich potential he had shown when he first broke into the side was never quite fulfilled.

Dave Sexton considered Locke's promise to be so exceptional that he was prepared to accept Crystal Palace's offer for the man in possession of the number two shirt, Paddy Mulligan, before the willowy 18-year-old had so much as kicked a ball in senior football, and his faith was rewarded when the England youth international performed impressively at Coventry the following Saturday. He seemed to have little difficulty in adapting to the demands of the First Division but at the end of March he suffered the first of the injuries that were to interrupt his progress, dislocating his right shoulder playing in goal in a practice match and missing the rest of the season. However, he had performed with admirable poise and assurance and quickly re-established himself in the first team the following autumn, winning the Player of the Year Trophy awarded by the Supporters Club.

Gary acknowledged that the Chelsea youth team manager, Ken Shellito, had been a major influence on his game and his polished displays certainly evoked memories of his distinguished predecessor. He had been well schooled in the mysteries of the full-back's art, his sound positional play and acute tactical awareness allowing him to dictate terms to the winger facing him. Elegant and composed, he timed his tackles with rare delicacy and as he gained experience he matured into a solid and reliable defender. Coming forward, Locke used the ball intelligently and his penetrating runs down the right wing in support of the attack regularly brought the Stamford Bridge crowd to life. A surging 50-yard burst which took him past three defenders deep into enemy territory and ended with a measured centre that offered an irresistible invitation to Ian Hutchinson in a 3-1 win against Birmingham in September 1973 was typical of his dashing, enterprising style.

Gary's consistently reliable form shone out like a beacon during the Blues' dismal slide towards relegation in 1974/75 and he was an ever-present member of the side which regained Chelsea's place in the First Division with such exuberance two years later. Although only 22 himself, he was more experienced than most of his team-mates and, as the tension which gripped Eddie McCreadie communicated itself to his young squad, his calming influence was invaluable.

Locke dislocated his troublesome right shoulder once again that summer and made only 18 League appearances the following season, while an ankle injury restricted him to just eight games in 1978/79, and it is tempting to conclude that Chelsea's stay in the First Division might have beeen rather more rewarding had they been able to call upon his services more often. A serious back problem in 1980 that threatened to cut short his career added to the tally of matches he had been forced to miss, and as the years went by the attacking forays became rarer and less effective. Inevitably, some of Gary's sprinting speed had been lost and he was no longer quite the formidable force he had once been.

When John Neal signed Joey Jones it was, in part, a reluctant acknowledgement that Locke's best days were behind him and, following a loan period, he was allowed to join Crystal Palace in February 1983. He stayed at Selhurst Park for four seasons, subsequently moving to New Zealand.

BORN: Kingsbury, 12.7.54.
GAMES: 315 (2). GOALS: 4.
OTHER CLUBS: Crystal Palace 82/3-85/6 (84, 1);
Napier City Rovers, New Zealand.

1972/73-1982/83

BRIAN BASON

Brian Bason appeared to be establishing himself in Eddie McCreadie's promotion-chasing team when he suffered a double fracture of the right shin in the 20th minute of a League Cup tie with Arsenal at Highbury in October 1976. Although he made a full recovery and was able to demonstrate his fitness with Vancouver Whitecaps that summer, there was little prospect of him breaking back into the side and, after spending a month on loan with Plymouth Argyle, he was transferred to the West Country club in January 1978.

A busy, industrious midfielder who generally played wide on the right, Bason made his first-team debut after his 17th birthday in a 2-1 defeat at Sheffield United in September 1972 and appeared in three further matches that season without placing any pressure on the men he had stood in for. His next appearance came more than two years later against Carlisle in the autumn of 1975 and although he did well, scoring with a thunderous drive, it was not enough to keep him in the side for long.

However, when he returned in 1976/77 in place of the injured Ian Britton, he gave the team a useful extra dimension, creating a number of goals, and looked set to stay until that fateful clash with Sammy Nelson.

BORN: Epsom, 3.9.55. GAMES: 20 (2). GOALS: 1.
OTHER CLUBS: Vancouver Whitecaps;
Plymouth Argyle 77/8-80/1 (129, 10);
Crystal Palace 80/1-81/2 (27, 0); Portsmouth *on loan* 81/2 (9, 0);
Reading 82/3 (41, 0).

1972/73-1976/77

DAVID STRIDE

When David Stride made his League debut at Birmingham in September 1978, it was already apparent that Chelsea would find it difficult to hang on to their place in the First Division, although few foresaw the humiliation that was to come. A total of 31 players were used during the season and frequent team changes were made in an unavailing effort to head off the inevitable, but in these unpromising circumstances the 20-year-old succeeded in making the left-back position his own.

A former winger, Stride was happiest when advancing down the flank in support of his attack but was developing into a sound defender when his run of 33 successive appearances was ended by a nasty head injury after ten minutes of the home game against Middlesbrough in April. He was taken to hospital where he was found to have suffered concussion and a hairline fracture of the skull, and missed the four matches that remained.

David had performed resourcefully in a side woefully short of confidence, but at the start of the following season Graham Wilkins was preferred and, with the club keen to reduce its playing staff to more manageable proportions, the former reserve team captain was sold to an American club, Memphis Rogues, in November 1979.

BORN: Lymington, 14.3.58. GAMES: 37. GOALS: 0.
OTHER CLUBS: Memphis Rogues; Minnesota Kicks;
Jacksonville Tea Men; Millwall 82/3-83/4 (55, 3);
Leyton Orient 84/5 (29, 0).

1978/79-1979/80

Standing alongside the mighty figure of Micky Droy, little Ian Britton looked like a sturdily built schoolboy, but during the course of a Chelsea first-team career spanning ten seasons the bustling midfielder proved conclusively that size isn't everything. He was only 5ft 5in tall and weighed just 9¹/₂ stone, but his tenacity enabled him to hold his own against opponents who, almost without exception, towered over him.

Ian had his first run in the side in the spring of 1973, but it was only when Ron Suart and Eddie McCreadie committed themselves to a youth policy in 1974/75 that his unspectacular promise showed signs of developing into something more than that. He played a leading role in a creditable 2-2 draw at Anfield in March and the following season he showed admirable consistency in an ever-changing team as the Blues came to terms with the shock of relegation. The key to the competitive Scot's game was a willingness to run for 90 minutes, allied to neat passing and the skill to beat an opponent. Playing on the left of midfield, he was one of the cornerstones of the promotion-winning team of 1976/77, his busy, purposeful style complementing the rather more eye-catching talents of Ray Wilkins.

Like most of his colleagues, Ian found the First Division something of an ordeal and his confidence took quite a battering, with the result that he became increasingly reluctant to attempt anything positive when in possession, preferring to play the safe ball to a colleague behind him. Back in Division Two, Britton made 41 League appearances as Chelsea came close to an immediate return under Geoff Hurst, but he gradually slipped from favour over the next two seasons, and in the summer of 1982 he was transferred to Dundee United, subsequently returning to England to play for Blackpool and Burnley.

BORN: Dundee, 19.5.54.
GAMES: 279 (10). GOALS: 34.
OTHER CLUBS: Dundee United;
Blackpool 83/4-85/6 (106, 15);
Burnley 86/7-88/9 (108, 10).

1972/73-1981/82

RAY WILKINS

For four seasons Ray Wilkins was hailed as Chelsea's saviour, the inspirational boy-genius who was going to guide the Blues away from the dark shadows cast by the threat of bankruptcy to the promised land of renewed success on the field. It was an intolerable burden for any one player to shoulder, no matter how outstanding his talent, and it was inevitable that the gifted midfielder would eventually sink beneath its weight.

Having made a handful of first-team appearances in 1973/74, Ray seemed to have established himself in the side the following season, his maturity and ice-cool nerve catching the eye in a sterling performance at Anfield in March, but four weeks later Ron Suart turned to his most experienced players in an effort to halt the Blues' alarming slide and Wilkins was out. However, when Eddie McCreadie took over as manager prior to the crucial match at White Hart Lane that would effectively decide whether the club returned to the Second Division after an interval of 12 years, he placed his faith in youth. Ray was recalled and, astonishingly, the 18-year-old was made captain. A born leader, he handled the pressure with remarkable assurance, and seemed to feel no embarrassment at chivying or encouraging men ten years his senior, but Spurs won the match and Chelsea went down.

The following season, as McCreadie searched frantically for a winning combination, 'Butch' was the fulcrum of the team, constantly involved and seeking to dictate every aspect of the game. His touch deserted him for a while but he recovered his form in time to win his first international cap against Italy in New York in May, embarking on what would prove to be a long and distinguished England career.

Ray confirmed his class in 1976/77, leading from the front in every game as the Blues stormed to promotion on a tide of emotion. Playing just behind the strikers, he had the freedom to exploit his creativity to the full, although the ploy proved less effective in the second half of the season when teams playing against Chelsea for the second time attempted to shackle him. Stylish and assured, the precocious midfield general produced a series of imperious displays illuminated by his remarkable awareness and pinpoint 40-yard passes. Even his greatest admirers would hesitate to describe Ray as quick or aggressive and he lacked the sharpness to go past an opponent, but his astute reading of the game and immaculate distribution enabled him to take command of matches as effectively as any scurrying workaholic. The perfectly angled through-ball that gave Tommy Langley the goal at Molineux which clinched promotion was typical, and he scored a few beauties as well, including a 25-yard volley in a 4-0 win against Sheffield United that dipped and swerved.

With Ken Shellito replacing McCreadie, Wilkins reverted to a more orthodox role the following winter but did not make the expected impression, partly because of a persistent groin strain that looked likely to end his season prematurely. However, his continuing value to the side was demonstrated when he returned for the last few matches to steer the Blues to safety after they had begun to drift into trouble during his absence.

Ray rarely produced his best form in 1978/79 and it is probably no coincidence that Chelsea spent most of the campaign propping up the table. Transfer speculation filled the back pages and he admitted that he was no longer enjoying his football. He was relieved of the captaincy by Danny Blanchflower in February but it was a season when nothing went right and he seemed to lose confidence as one defeat followed another. When the Blues were relegated it was inevitable that he would leave and he eventually rejoined Dave Sexton at Old Trafford, Manchester United paying £875,000 for his signature.

BORN: Hillingdon, 14.9.56.
GAMES: 193 (5). GOALS: 34.
HONOURS: 84 England caps (76-86).
OTHER CLUBS: Manchester United 79/80-83/4 (160, 7);
AC Milan; Paris St Germain; Glasgow Rangers;
Queens Park Rangers 89/90- (115, 6).

1973/74-1978/79

GARRY STANLEY

The comparisons with Bobby Charlton may have been a little fanciful, but there were certainly occasions during Chelsea's high-energy assault on the Second Division in 1976/77 when Garry Stanley showed at least as much promise as his highly rated colleague Ray Wilkins. However, while the England international went on to justify many of the extravagant claims made on his behalf during the course of that exciting season, the remainder of Stanley's career was to be something of an anti-climax.

At the age of 22, the midfielder was older than most of his team-mates, yet he had only made his debut at the start of the previous term, having sat on the bench without being called upon no fewer than eight times prior to that. The first question marks arose when, after a few indifferent games, he was left out of the side for the promotion run-in – because, Eddie McCreadie explained, the pressure was affecting him. But by that stage his powerful running on the right flank and neat, incisive passing had played a major part in bringing a return to the big time within the Blues' grasp. Strong and determined, 'Starsky' was also useful in the air and possessed a tremendous shot – the hardest in the country according to his manager – which brought him a memorable goal against Charlton at the Bridge in November.

Stanley had just a dozen games to measure himself against the best at the start of the 1977/78 season before a serious groin injury ruled him out until the following August and, although he played regularly on his return, the exuberance which had distinguished his performances two years earlier was no longer seen, as the status which had been fought for so passionately was surrendered with only token resistance. After spending the summer in America, Garry was transferred to Everton, but the fire which had made him effective had seemingly been extinguished.

BORN: Burton, 4.3.54.
GAMES: 115 (5). GOALS: 15.
OTHER CLUBS: Fort Lauderdale Strikers;
Everton 79/80-80/1 (52, 1); Swansea City 81/2-83/4 (72, 4);
Portsmouth 83/4-85/6 (47, 1); Wichita Wings;
Bristol City 88/9 (10, 0).

1975/76-1978/79

STEVE WICKS

It is seldom a good idea to return to the scene of past triumphs and Steve Wicks's second spell at Stamford Bridge could scarcely have been more disheartening. The powerfully built centre-half was signed from Queens Park Rangers for £470,000 – the biggest fee Chelsea had ever paid – in July 1986, seven years after he had been transferred to Derby County, but the new season was just three games old when John Hollins decided to revert to the established pairing of McLaughlin and Pates at the centre of the defence, leaving the 29-year-old to make occasional appearances as an understudy.

An injury to Pates gave Steve a chance to establish himself at the start of 1987/88, but he was soon sidelined by a serious back problem which required surgery and, despite making a courageous comeback and playing a characteristically determined role in the Blues' desperate struggle to avoid a return to Division Two, he was forced to announce his retirement in August 1988, when he was reportedly on the verge of joining Tottenham.

It was a sad end to an itinerant career that had begun when Ron Suart gave him his League debut against Ipswich in March 1975. The flaxen-haired giant was recalled to the first team when John Dempsey twisted his knee that December, and made spectacular progress, emerging as one of the key members of Eddie McCreadie's promotion-winning side the following season. Tall and strong, Wicks was rarely troubled when the ball was in the air and his tackling was resolute, but it was his mature professionalism that was most impressive, with a steady, assured display in an entertaining draw against Nottingham Forest at the City Ground in November outstanding.

The youngster's lack of experience was exposed when he faced First Division opposition the following winter but he learned quickly, benefiting from the presence of Micky Droy alongside him, and was developing into a highly accomplished defender when Danny Blanchflower agreed to let him move to the Baseball Ground in January 1979 to help finance his team rebuilding plans.

BORN: Reading, 3.10.56.
GAMES: 163 (1). GOALS: 8.
OTHER CLUBS: Derby County 78/9-79/80 (24, 0);
Queens Park Rangers 79/80-80/1 (73, 0) and 81/2-85/6 (116, 6);
Crystal Palace 81/2 (14 , 1).

1974/75-1978/79 & 1986/87-1987/88

DUNCAN McKENZIE

Chelsea's first major signing for four years demonstrated a faith in the value of gifted, crowd-pleasing forwards that was entirely in keeping with the club's colourful traditions; unhappily in this instance that faith proved to be misplaced. After a period of severe financial stringency, Duncan McKenzie was bought from Everton for £165,000 in September 1978 in the hope that, as well as adding a much-needed cutting edge to the Blues' attack, he would bring some self-belief to a side whose confidence had been visibly draining away over the previous 12 months.

An individual in a game increasingly dominated by the collective approach, he scored twice in his first three matches, producing glimpses of the audacity that had enchanted his admirers in the past as well as an appetite for the ball that some of his former managers might have viewed with a cynical eye. However, even the most talented forward is dependent upon the support and service he receives and, for all his apparent self-assurance, Duncan soon became as demoralised as his colleagues.

As the battle against the drop became more hopeless, he came to seem a costly irrelevance, a forlorn attempt to revive past glories amid present squalor, and in March he quietly moved on to Blackburn for less than half of what had been paid six months earlier.

BORN: Grimsby, 10.6.50. GAMES: 16. GOALS: 4.
OTHER CLUBS: Nottingham Forest 69/70-73/4 (111, 41); Mansfield Town *on loan* 69/70 (10, 3) and 72/3 (6, 7); Leeds United 74/5-75/6 (66, 27); Anderlecht; Everton 76/7-77/8 (48, 14); Blackburn Rovers 78/9-80/1 (74, 16); Tulsa Roughnecks; Chicago Sting; Hong Kong.

1978/79

JOHN SPARROW

When John Sparrow broke into the Chelsea side at the age of 16 in March 1974, it seemed that the club's wonderfully productive youth scheme had unearthed a natural successor to Eddie McCreadie, whose career was drawing to a close amid persistent fitness problems; but during the seven years he spent in contention for a first-team place, the East Ender never played more than a dozen League games in a season and, like many of his contemporaries, his early promise gradually faded away together with his self-belief.

Sparrow's lack of experience was exploited on a number of occasions during the Blues' melancholy slide into the Second Division, notably in the decisive defeat at White Hart Lane in April 1975, and this early exposure to the harsh realities of life at the bottom probably hindered the England youth international's progress. He was impressive coming forward, as he demonstrated when his centre gave Peter Houseman a goal on his debut, and possessed a dangerous long throw, but despite a useful turn of speed and firm tackle his defending was not sufficiently reliable to win him a regular place.

John did not have the best of luck with injuries and, with the arrival of Dennis Rofe finally ending his hopes of establishing himself, he moved on to Exeter City in January 1981.

BORN: Bethnal Green, 3.6.57.
GAMES: 68 (6). GOALS: 2.
OTHER CLUBS: Millwall *on loan* 78/9 (7, 0); Exeter City 80/1-82/3 (63, 3).

1973/74-1979/80

EAMONN BANNON

It was entirely characteristic of the somewhat romantic approach that Danny Blanchflower brought to the daunting task he faced that, when the departure of Ken Swain and Steve Wicks gave him the means to bring new players to Stamford Bridge, he opted to pay Hearts £200,000 for the services of Eamonn Bannon. A manager with a more conventional background would surely have preferred to recruit a battle-hardened veteran to bring organisation and resilience to a demoralised side, but the Irishman wanted to see his team play its way out of trouble.

The 20-year-old midfielder was certainly gifted, with the traditional Scottish talent for running with the ball and then threading through an imaginative pass. His stylish performances during the second half of the season made the ordeal of Chelsea's long-suffering supporters more bearable, but he was not able to bring about the transformation in the club's fortunes that the desperate situation demanded.

It was a pretty harrowing introduction to English football for the youngster and early the following season, with Geoff Hurst having moved into the manager's office, he became unsettled and decided to return to Scotland. His outstanding performances for Dundee United over the next few seasons confirmed his ability and made many of the Blues' fans regret that he hadn't come south in more favourable circumstances.

BORN: Edinburgh, 18.4.58.
GAMES: 27. GOALS: 1.
HONOURS: 11 Scotland caps (79-86).
OTHER CLUBS: Heart of Midlothian (twice);
Dundee United.

1978/79-1979/80

MICKY NUTTON

It looked as though Chelsea had discovered a defender of real promise when 19-year-old Micky Nutton combined with John Sitton to blot out the Liverpool attack at Stamford Bridge in March 1979. Micky had made just six previous first-team appearances (enough to make him a veteran compared with his colleague, who was playing only his second League game) but showed great composure, even finding time to go upfield and hit the post with a thumping header. However, some bad luck with injuries and stiff competition from Gary Chivers and Colin Pates meant that, despite his clear ability, the elegant centre-back was never able to command a regular first-team place.

Very quick but lacking authority in the air, Nutton was at his most effective when paired with Micky Droy in the middle of the defence, although he occasionally found himself at full-back or in midfield. He was comfortable in possession and his deceptive stride was the springboard of many attacks, but he was possibly a little too relaxed to prosper in the non-stop bustle of Second Division football.

As time went on, Micky appeared to lose his way and, after spending a month on loan at Reading, he was allowed to join Millwall in March 1983. However, that youthful potential was sadly never fully realised.

BORN: St John's Wood, 3.10.59.
GAMES: 81 (2). GOALS: 0.
OTHER CLUBS: Reading *on loan* 82/3 (6, 0);
Millwall 82/3-85/6 (82, 4).

1978/79-1982/83

COLIN VILJOEN

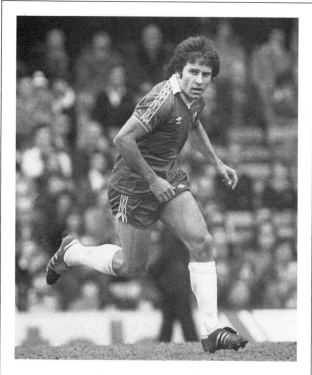

Like Colin Lee and Dennis Rofe, Colin Viljoen was signed by Geoff Hurst in the second half of 1979/80 in the hope that his experience and composure would help Chelsea clinch promotion, but the aristocratic midfielder appeared to find it difficult to adapt to the bustling style of Second Division football. Viljoen was an intelligent player whose measured passing could open up defences, but during his time with the Blues he only rarely produced the form that had made him such an influential member of the stylish Ipswich side of the early seventies. Nevertheless he remained a model professional who thought deeply about the game and was happy to offer advice to his younger colleagues.

The former England international's commanding performance at home to Shrewsbury in January 1981, when he was recalled after a four-month absence, suggested that the years had not eroded his talent, but his stay in the side was to be brief. The following winter, with John Neal now in charge, Colin appeared to have established himself at last and he played a large part in a memorable League Cup win over Southampton, but when injury sidelined him for several weeks he was unable to get back into the team and that summer he was released. It was a disappointing end to a distinguished League career.

BORN: Johannesburg, South Africa, 20.6.48.
GAMES: 22 (1). GOALS: 0.
HONOURS: 2 England caps (75).
OTHER CLUBS: South Transvaal;
Ipswich Town 66/7-77/8 (305, 45);
Manchester City 78/9-79/80 (27, 0).

1979/80-1981/82

TREVOR AYLOTT

After Trevor Aylott's first two matches for Chelsea it looked as though he might be the answer to Ken Shellito's prayers. Prior to the visit of Bristol City in October 1977 the team had failed to score in four matches and had managed only seven goals all season, prompting the anxious manager to invite the big, burly 19-year-old from Bermondsey to show that he could do what Bill Garner couldn't. Aylott battled away gamely, and his 55th-minute header from Charlie Cooke's beautifully weighted cross was enough to win the points.

Confidence soaring, the fans' new hero followed this up with an eager and aggressive performance against the League leaders, Nottingham Forest, at Stamford Bridge the following Saturday, thumping the only goal of the game past Peter Shilton after a powerful run. However, as the glow of this impressive beginning faded, Trevor's technical limitations became apparent and when no further goals followed Shellito looked elsewhere for the solution to his problems.

The heavyweight striker played another 13 games in 1978/79, but the hunger that had put him in the headlines a year earlier was missing and he failed to find the net. After five further appearances he was sold to Barnsley in November 1979 and began his extensive and generally fruitful travels.

BORN: Bermondsey, 26.11.57. GAMES: 29 (3). GOALS: 2.
OTHER CLUBS: Barnsley 79/80-81/2 (96, 26);
Millwall 82/3 (32, 5); Luton Town 82/3-83/4 (32, 10);
Crystal Palace 84/5-85/6 (53, 12); Barnsley *on loan* 85/6 (9, 0);
AFC Bournemouth 86/7-90/1 (147, 27);
Birmingham City 90/1-91/2 (27, 0); Oxford United 91/2 (37, 6);
Gillingham 92/3- (10, 2).

1977/78-1979/80

PETAR BOROTA

Petar Borota believed that, as a professional footballer, it was part of his job to entertain the people who paid to watch him, a heretical philosophy which led reporters to damn him with the tag 'eccentric'. The extrovert Yugoslav's colourful personality made him enormously popular with Chelsea's supporters, but in the press box his willingness to dash from his penalty area to clear the ball was held to embody unsound Continental attitudes towards goalkeeping. Nevertheless, the Player of the Year trophies he received in each of his two full seasons in the first team were evidence that at his best he was a spectacular but reliable performer.

Communication with his team-mates was not a problem, as he had a fair command of English, but his unpredictability was sometimes a little unsettling for his colleagues. In a cup-tie at Southampton, for example, he came out of the box and, instead of kicking the ball into the stand, back-heeled it to an astonished Micky Droy, explaining that he wanted to liven up the crowd as no goals had been scored.

Borota's adventurous style occasionally proved costly, as in a game against Orient when he completely missed the ball after another valiant sally beyond the 18-yard line, allowing the onrushing forward to score, but such errors were rare and he more than compensated for them with his outstanding shot-stopping. In 1980/81 his imposing physique, considerable agility and conspicuous bravery enabled him to break Peter Bonetti's club record of 16 League clean sheets in a season – and in the home game against Cardiff he went upfield for a corner in a memorable attempt to remedy a shortage of goals at the other end of the pitch.

A warm, likeable man, Petar was displaced by Steve Francis in November 1981 and the following summer John Neal allowed him to join Brentford, but his committed efforts will be remembered with gratitude by the people he put first – the fans.

BORN: Belgrade, Yugoslavia, 5.3.52.
GAMES: 114. GOALS: 0.
HONOURS: 14 Yugoslavia caps.
OTHER CLUBS: Belgrade Sporting; Partizan Belgrade;
Brentford (0, 0); Benfica; FC Porto.

1978/79-1981/82

CLIVE WALKER

Exciting, adventurous, unpredictable and hopelessly inconsistent, Clive Walker was the sort of player who is adored by the fans but makes exasperated managers yearn for some more secure form of employment. When the circumstances were right, the flying winger was capable of transforming a game single-handedly, but there were other days – too many – when he was largely ineffective.

Clive made his first appearance in the headlines when he scored twice at Molineux in December 1977, and became the darling of the Shed with a match-winning performance against Liverpool in the third round of the FA Cup a month later. The first of his two goals in Chelsea's epic 4-2 victory was typical of his thrillingly uncomplicated approach. Receiving the ball back from a team-mate after he had taken a throw-in, he sprinted past a bemused Joey Jones and hit a swerving shot into the top left-hand corner of the net from an acute angle.

After that game the European Champions' goalkeeper, Ray Clemence, suggested that Walker would find it increasingly difficult to make the same sort of impact as opponents became more familiar with his game, and to some extent that judgement was to be borne out in the years that followed. However, there was no denying the buzz of expectation that went round the ground whenever the flaxen-haired outside-left gained possession and set off towards goal.

Clive's ability to redeem even the most hopeless cause was never seen more clearly than when he came on as a substitute against Bolton Wanderers in October 1978 with 20 minutes remaining. The Blues were trailing 3-0 but the funereal mood of the crowd was replaced by mounting frenzy as the dashing 21-year-old's electrifying running inspired an irresistible fight-back, which was completed when his driven cross was sliced into his own net by the unfortunate Sam Allardyce to give Chelsea a victory that had been unthinkable before Walker was called from the bench.

Geoff Hurst sought to capitalise on Clive's startling pace and willingness to shoot at every opportunity by playing him in the centre of the attack, a strategy which yielded a rich harvest of spectacular goals, including a typical individual effort in a 4-0 win against Newcastle in January 1980. Employed in this role, he saw plenty of the ball and was less likely to fade from the game than when he was restricted to the flanks, and once he had broken clear of the defence in pursuit of a long through-pass, no one was going to catch him.

There were times when Walker seemed to be a luxury Chelsea could not afford in their reduced circumstances, and in John Neal's first two seasons in charge at the Bridge he was not certain of a place in an ever-changing team. However, the 25-yard drive at Bolton in May 1983 that spared the club the ignominy of Third Division football was a timely reminder that he could still conjure a goal out of nothing, and in the opening weeks of the following season he played as well as he had at any time in his career, scoring four times in eight appearances.

It seemed that the positive mood created by Neal's astute transfer dealings during the summer had given Clive renewed self-belief, but a broken jaw meant that the revival was sadly brief. Pat Nevin's rapid emergence prevented him from reclaiming his place on his return to fitness and in July he decided to make a fresh start at Roker Park, returning a few months later to score the goals that took Sunderland to the Milk Cup final at the Blues' expense.

BORN: Oxford, 26.5.57.
GAMES: 191 (33). GOALS: 65.
OTHER CLUBS: Sunderland 84/5-85/6 (50, 10);
Queens Park Rangers 85/6-86/7 (21, 1);
Fulham 87/8-89/90 (109, 29);
Brighton and Hove Albion 90/1- (106, 9).

1976/77-1983/84

GARY CHIVERS

It is always frustrating when a player fails to exploit his natural gifts, and there is no doubt that, had his talent been harnessed properly, Gary Chivers could have made a greater impact on the game than he has. Like his contemporaries Micky Nutton and Colin Pates, his best position was alongside the centre-half, although he filled in enthusiastically at full-back or in midfield on occasion.

Chelsea were already condemned to relegation to the Second Division when Gary made his first-team bow in April 1979, but the following season he was a regular member of Geoff Hurst's promotion-chasing team. He was not particularly strong in the air and would perhaps have benefited from a little more pace, but by the autumn of 1980 he had developed into one of the best young defenders in the Second Division. His inspirational displays were an influential factor in a sequence of eight wins in nine games that put the Blues firmly in contention for promotion, and a splendid goal in a 6-0 victory against Newcastle at Stamford Bridge was a fitting reward for an outstanding performance.

Always cool and unflustered, Chivers generally tried to play his way out of tight situations and Hurst encouraged his attacking instincts, but that relaxed style could help explain why he has not achieved the success that his first couple of years in League football led many people to expect. There were times when he seemed to lack urgency, and it is tempting to conclude that if Gary had shown more ambition and pushed himself harder he would have been more likely to maintain his early progress.

Instead, his form slumped over the next two seasons as Chelsea plumbed the depths of mediocrity, and he was not always sure of a place in the starting line-up. In the summer of 1983 John Neal decided that there was no room for him in his revamped team and he was allowed to join Swansea City.

BORN: Stockwell, 15.5.60.
GAMES: 143 (5). GOALS: 4.
OTHER CLUBS: Swansea City 83/4 (10, 0);
Queens Park Rangers 84/5-86/7 (60, 0); Watford 87/8 (14, 0);
Brighton and Hove Albion 87/8- (217, 13).

1978/79-1982/83

PHIL DRIVER

Geoff Hurst bought Phil Driver because he felt that the best way to overcome the well-organised defences of teams visiting Stamford Bridge was to get behind them on the flanks and, while Peter Rhoades-Brown and Clive Walker could perform this role on the left, he had no one to play on the right wing. Pencil-slim, with long, fragile-looking limbs, Driver played a starring role in the demolition of Newcastle in October 1980, his centres creating two of Colin Lee's three goals, but he found consistency hard to achieve and was often employed as a substitute, his arrival more than once sparking a dramatic improvement in the Blues' fortunes.

Direct and speedy, Phil was at his best when running at defenders, and his exciting style inevitably made him popular with Chelsea's dwindling support. An injury to Walker gave him an early opportunity to force his way into John Neal's team the following autumn and he did well, scoring three goals in as many games. Then, however, the former non-League player suffered serious damage to his knee at Cambridge which kept him out for the rest of the season. In 1982/83 he started another nine matches but was unable to rediscover his earlier sparkle and that summer he returned to Wimbledon before dropping out of League football.

BORN: Huddersfield, 10.8.59.
GAMES: 25 (21). GOALS: 4
OTHER CLUBS: Wimbledon 78/9-80/1 (16, 3)
and 83/4-84/5 (4, 0).

1980/81 - 1982/83

ALAN MAYES

Much was expected of Alan Mayes when he joined Chelsea from Third Division Swindon Town in December 1980. His goalscoring feats had attracted considerable publicity and the Stamford Bridge faithful hoped that his prowess in the penalty area would ensure that the club's promotion challenge did not falter. Unhappily, the 27-year-old striker was unable to give the fans what they wanted and, in their frustration at the almost total inability to put the ball in the net which wrecked the Blues' season, they turned on him.

Mayes certainly missed a few chances but the main reason for his lack of success was that he had come into a team whose self-belief was swiftly evaporating. He was a small, neat forward who liked the ball played in accurately to his feet so that he could twist and turn to lose his marker, but during his two and a half seasons at the Bridge he was obliged to survive on a diet of optimistic high balls that were of little use to a player of his physique or style. A determined and resilient character, Alan was able to savour a few moments of triumph such as his pair of well-taken goals against Leicester in March 1982, but in 1982/83 he was displaced by new recruits and that summer he became one of a number of players to move on as John Neal wielded the new broom with vigour.

BORN: Edmonton, 11.12.53.
GAMES: 71 (5). GOALS: 24.
OTHER CLUBS: Queens Park Rangers (0, 0);
Watford 74/5-78/9 (133, 31);
Northampton Town on loan 75/6 (10, 4);
Swindon Town 78/9-80/1 (89, 38) and 83/4-84/5 (62, 27);
Carlisle United 85/6 (10, 2); Newport County on loan 85/6 (3, 1);
Blackpool 86/7 (13, 6).

1980/81 - 1982/83

STEVE FRANCIS

Steve Francis seemed to have a long and distinguished career at Stamford Bridge ahead of him when he became Chelsea's first-choice 'keeper at the age of 17. He had shown remarkable maturity on his debut in a League Cup tie at Southampton and John Neal had no hesitation in turning to him a few weeks later when his patience with Petar Borota's erratic displays became exhausted. The youngster performed with impressive consistency and his exemplary handling indicated an exceptional natural talent.

However, Steve was a quiet, reserved lad and his lack of assertiveness on the pitch hindered his progress. The following season was a demoralising one for the Blues and, with the team slipping down the table, the young 'keeper's confidence was gradually eroded. After making 73 consecutive appearances he was replaced, albeit briefly, by Bob Iles, and that summer Eddie Niedzwiecki was recruited from Wrexham.

Francis now found himself in the role of understudy, but when the Welshman suffered a serious injury in March 1986 he failed to make the most of his opportunity, conceding 14 goals in four games (four of them in the Full Members' Cup final). That misfortune prompted John Hollins to look elsewhere, but Steve has enjoyed better luck since moving to Reading in February 1987.

BORN: Billericay, 29.5.64.
GAMES: 88. GOALS: 0.
HONOURS: Full-Members' Cup 85/6.
OTHER CLUBS: Reading 86/7- (216, 0).

1981/82-1985/86

DENNIS ROFE

Dennis Rofe was a perky, lively character with a huge amount of experience and it was these qualities as much as his ability as a left-back that prompted Geoff Hurst to sign him from Leicester City in February 1980 in an effort to consolidate Chelsea's promotion challenge. Aggressive and determined, the 29-year-old defender was a good organiser with a professional attitude to the game that some of his colleagues appeared to lack, and Hurst acknowledged the value of his influence by making him captain the following season.

By this stage of his career Rofe was perhaps a little short of pace, but he remained a rugged tackler with a good left foot who attacked enterprisingly. It took him a while to settle at Stamford Bridge, but towards the end of the 1980/81 campaign he began to produce the sort of form that had made him such a respected performer for more than a decade, with a polished display at home to Bolton standing out.

Dennis made 54 successive appearances after his arrival but when he limped out of a match against Charlton in September 1981 with a groin injury, his tenure in the first team was effectively at an end. He was unable to regain his place from Chris Hutchings and that summer he was allowed to move on to Southampton, where he subsequently embarked on a coaching career.

BORN: Epping, 1.6.50.
GAMES: 61 (2). GOALS: 0.
OTHER CLUBS: Leyton Orient 67/8-72/3 (171, 6);
Leicester City 72/3-79/80 (290, 6);
Southampton 82/3-83/4 (20, 0).
MANAGER: Bristol Rovers (92).

1979/80-1981/82

TOMMY LANGLEY

If international caps were awarded solely on the basis of effort and determination, Tommy Langley would have ended up with a cupboardful. However, the hard-working striker had the misfortune to establish himself in the Chelsea first team just as the Blues were setting out on what would prove to be a demoralising two-year stay in the First Division, and although he continued to show the boyish enthusiasm which had endeared him to the fans when he made his League debut as a bustling 16-year-old in November 1974, his game did not develop sufficiently for him to make a lasting impression at the highest level.

The England youth international had to wait until the closing weeks of the 1976/77 campaign before he was given much of a run in the team, replacing Ken Swain as Steve Finnieston's partner. He proved himself by running onto Ray Wilkins's pass at Molineux and shooting home off a post to clinch promotion, and was a regular the following season, emerging as top scorer with 13 goals from 46 appearances. The spirited youngster put the seemingly limitless energy that had earned him the nickname 'Lungs' to good use, constantly chasing lost causes and harrying defenders, but the highlights of his season were a splendid goal in a League victory over Liverpool at the Bridge and a hat-trick in a 5-4 win against Birmingham.

Tommy invariably put everything he had into his football – not least when acting as emergency 'keeper – and his eagerness meant that his finishing was not always as clinical as it might have been, but despite not being a great header of the ball he claimed more than a third of the meagre total of 44 League goals the Blues managed as they finished bottom of the table in 1978/79.

However, there were signs during the valiant promotion chase the following winter that he had ceased to make progress, tireless grafting almost becoming an end in itself, and in August 1980 he decided to switch to Queens Park Rangers. Geoff Hurst was sorry to see him go and the fee of £425,000 was an indication of the reputation he had built up, but he was unable to rediscover the momentum he had lost and became one of football's wanderers.

BORN: Lambeth, 8.2.58.
GAMES: 139 (13). GOALS: 43.
OTHER CLUBS: Queens Park Rangers 80/1 (25, 8);
Crystal Palace 80/1-82/3 (59, 8); AEK Athens; Coventry City 83/4 (2, 0);
Wolverhampton Wanderers 84/5 (23, 4); Aldershot *on loan* 84/5 (16, 4);
South China, Hong Kong; Aldershot 86/7-87/8 (81, 21); Exeter City 88/9 (21, 2).

1974/75-1979/80

PETER RHOADES-BROWN

Peter Rhoades-Brown was most effective when operating as a traditional left-winger and it was in this role that he first established himself in the side in the autumn of 1980. His pace and good close control usually enabled him to get the better of his marker and his accurate centres produced a stream of goals such as Colin Lee's equaliser against Preston at Stamford Bridge and Mike Fillery's diving header at Bolton. However, the youngster was unable to maintain this sparkling standard in the second half of the season as the Blues mysteriously forgot how to score.

When John Neal took over in the manager's office he asked 'PRB' to drop back into midfield. He was now expected to shuttle up and down the left flank, denying opponents space, but it was a game that was alien to him. He had plenty of stamina and had succeeded in making himself more aggressive, but he was not a natural defender and all too often his efforts to win the ball ended in clumsy or ill-timed tackles that incurred the referee's displeasure.

Peter was never able to achieve consistency and his crossing, in particular, tended to be erratic – perhaps because his evident enthusiasm was inclined to get the better of him. His finishing was also disappointing, but Chelsea fans will never forget his goal in a fifth round FA Cup tie against Liverpool when he ran with the ball from the halfway line before shooting coolly past Bruce Grobbelaar.

Hard-working and dependable, Rhoades-Brown appeared to lose confidence in his talent, and when the arrival of Mickey Thomas in January 1984 virtually ended his chances of regular first-team football he was allowed to move to Oxford. He played his part in his new club's climb from the Third Division to the First, but sadly fitness problems brought this popular player's career to a premature end.

BORN: Hampton, 2.1.62.
GAMES: 97 (12). GOALS: 5.
OTHER CLUBS: Oxford United 83/4-88/9 (112, 13).

1979/80-1983/84

CHRIS HUTCHINGS

Chris Hutchings was working as a bricklayer when Geoff Hurst brought him to Stamford Bridge from Harrow Borough of the Berger Isthmian League in July 1980. The 23-year-old made a handful of appearances in midfield that season, scoring the winning goal on his League debut at Cardiff in October eight minutes after replacing the injured Mike Fillery, but his real opportunity came when Dennis Rofe succumbed to a groin injury against Charlton the following September. Chris took over at left-back for the visit of Norwich the following Saturday and quickly made the position his own.

This was a difficult period for the Blues, the heroic fifth round FA Cup win against Liverpool in 1982 providing the only relief from the prevailing gloom, but Hutchings performed with admirable consistency in unpromising circumstances. A conscientious defender who used the ball sensibly and enjoyed getting forward at every opportunity, he was a member of John Neal's rebuilt team at the start of 1983/84, scoring against Derby on the opening day, but was unable to regain his place from Joey Jones after dropping out with a head injury. In November he was allowed to join Brighton, but he had proved himself as a League player and can have had few regrets about his decision to lay aside the pointing trowel.

BORN: Winchester, 5.7.57.
GAMES: 97 (4). GOALS: 3.
OTHER CLUBS: Brighton and Hove Albion 83/4-87/8 (153, 4); Huddersfield Town 87/8-89/90 (110, 10); Walsall 90/1 (40, 0); Rotherham United 91/2- (71, 4).

1980/81-1983/84

KEVIN HALES

After making eight first-team appearances in 1979/80, Kevin Hales was in the wilderness for more than a year before John Neal restored him to the starting line-up in November 1981. Second chances are no more common in football than they are elsewhere, and the 20-year-old midfielder did not waste his opportunity to persuade the new manager he deserved a regular place. In 14 appearances he was on the losing side only once, and his industrious and enthusiastic displays on the right flank – typified by a home game against Sheffield Wednesday in which he scored a splendid goal – made a significant contribution to a marked improvement in the Blues' results which saw them reach the FA Cup quarter-finals.

Small and slight, Hales occasionally appeared a little lightweight and may have lacked the sharpness to thrive at the highest level, but he was developing into a neat and reliable performer when his progress was cruelly interrupted by a serious knee injury sustained at Barnsley in March. He fought back courageously and returned to the side the following January, but the confidence that had been forming the previous season had inevitably disappeared. That summer he moved on to Orient and gave the East London club dependable service for a decade.

BORN: Dartford, 13.1.61.
GAMES: 25 (2). GOALS: 2.
OTHER CLUBS: Leyton Orient 83/4-92/3 (301, 23).

1979/80-1982/83

BRYAN ROBSON

The signing of 'Pop' Robson from Carlisle in August 1982 marked the beginning of the extensive rebuilding that was clearly essential if the Blues were to regain what their supporters regarded as their rightful place among the country's leading clubs. The hugely experienced striker had been a consistent goalscorer throughout a long and eventful career, but at the age of 36 his best days as a player were inevitably behind him. However, while his stay in the Chelsea first team seemed likely to be a short one, John Neal was confident that the example of his professionalism would help transform the spirit at the club.

Robson demonstrated the value of his cool finishing with an 87th-minute winner in the first match of the season at Cambridge but was unable to reproduce the neat, busy football which, together with his predator's eye for goal, had made him a popular hero at Newcastle and West Ham. In mid-September 'Pop' gave way to David Speedie and he made only a handful of appearances thereafter, a foot injury restricting his chances. After rejoining Carlisle on loan for a spell he was transferred to Sunderland in the summer, having failed to make the impact at Stamford Bridge that Neal had hoped for.

BORN: Sunderland, 11.11.45. GAMES: 12 (5). GOALS: 5.
OTHER CLUBS: Newcastle United 64/5-70/1 (206, 82);
West Ham United 70/1-73/4 (120, 47) and 76/7-78/9 (107, 47);
Sunderland 74/5-76/7 (90, 34), 79/80-80/1 (52, 23)
and 83/4 (12, 3); Carlisle United 80/1-81/2 (48, 21)
and 84/5-85/6 (13, 1); Carlisle United *on loan* 82/3 (11, 4).

1982/83

PAUL CANOVILLE

When he was in the mood, Paul Canoville could transform a game. That was never seen more clearly than in the fifth round Milk Cup replay at Hillsborough in January 1985, when he came on for the injured Colin Lee at half-time with the Blues three goals down and inspired an irresistible fight-back. The tall, leggy winger scored with his first touch, after about ten seconds, and his second goal appeared to have put Chelsea into the semi-finals, only for Wednesday to make it 4-4 from the penalty spot in the dying seconds.

A natural athlete with pace and great stamina, Canoville demonstrated his rich potential during the desperate battle against relegation in the closing weeks of 1982/83 and looked set to build on the foothold he had gained in the side the following season. His exciting, unpredictable style soon had the morons who had jeered him when he first appeared in the team singing his praises, but he was infuriatingly inconsistent and a hat-trick against Swansea ironically served as a reminder that his finishing generally lacked composure.

The arrival of Mickey Thomas in January blocked Paul's progress and thereafter his exuberant skills were seen to best effect when he was used as a substitute. In August 1986 he was transferred to Reading, having started just five matches the previous season, but injury sadly prevented him from proving his worth at Elm Park.

BORN: Hillingdon, 4.3.62. GAMES: 67 (36). GOALS: 15.
OTHER CLUBS: Reading 86/7-87/8 (16, 4).

1981/82-1985/86

MIKE FILLERY

Nothing is more certain to promote groans among the devotees of pure football than the tendency of some League managers to stress the importance of 'commitment', 'effort' and 'competitiveness', while omitting to mention the desirability of being able to pass the ball to a player wearing the same colour shirt; but it cannot be denied that if Mike Fillery had possessed these mundane qualities in greater abundance, his outstanding natural talent would have made him one of the most highly regarded creative midfield players in the country. Instead, dispiritingly, his gifts were largely wasted.

Fillery's nonchalant, languid manner infuriated those members of the dwindling Stamford Bridge crowd who had never learned to appreciate the finer things in life and even his most devoted admirers were regularly driven to despair by his disappearance for long periods from games that his ability should have allowed him to dominate. He was an established member of the Chelsea first team for four seasons, having had his first taste of senior football during the closing weeks of the wretched drift towards relegation in 1978/79, but consistency proved elusive. The hurly-burly of Second Division football was scarcely suited to his champagne style but, like his friend Gary Chivers, he appeared to lack drive and motivation.

Mike's cultured left foot was capable of great delicacy, the superb swerving free-kick that gave the Blues the lead in the sixth round FA Cup tie against Spurs in March 1982 being the best-remembered example, but could also hit the ball with startling power, as a screaming 35-yard match-winner at Orient in 1980/81 confirmed. In addition, the stylish midfielder had good close control and used possession intelligently, while his healthy scoring record included a number of well-judged headers.

John Neal kept faith with Fillery even when his influence declined alarmingly during the miserable 1982/83 season, but that summer he was transferred to Queens Park Rangers, where he impressed for a while before his career once again appeared to run out of steam, partly as a result of fitness problems.

BORN: Mitcham, 17.9.60.
GAMES: 176 (5). GOALS: 41.
OTHER CLUBS: Queens Park Rangers 83/4-86/7 (97, 9);
Portsmouth 87/8-90/1 (67, 6); Oldham Athletic 90/1 (2, 0); Millwall *on loan* 90/1 (1, 0);
Torquay United *on loan* 91/2 (4, 0).

1978/79-1982/83

TONY McANDREW

Tony McAndrew's Chelsea career was wrecked by injury when it had scarcely begun. A robust, combative midfielder who could also play in the centre of the defence, he had been John Neal's captain at Middlesbrough and was brought to Stamford Bridge in September 1982 to add resilience and determination to a side conspicuously lacking those fundamental qualities. However, after he had made just nine appearances he was laid low by a nasty back problem which required surgery.

During a lengthy and painful fight to regain fitness Tony demonstrated the courage and professionalism that Neal had hoped would benefit the club on the field, but at the start of the following season he was unable to force his way into the dramatically reconstructed side. He was recalled in December and when John Hollins stood down he took over as captain, which suggested that Neal felt he still had a major contribution to make, but he was unable to recapture his old drive, the injury appearing to have taken its toll on his mobility.

McAndrew demonstrated the value of experience by assuming the role of penalty-taker, coolly solving what had become an exasperating problem, but when everyone was fit he returned to the sidelines and the following September he returned to Ayresome Park as part of the deal that brought Darren Wood to London.

BORN: Glasgow, 11.4.56.
GAMES: 23. GOALS: 4.
OTHER CLUBS: Middlesbrough 73/4-81/2 (247, 13) and 84/5-85/6 (66, 2);
Darlington 88/9 (11, 0); Hartlepool United 88/9 (4, 0).

1982/83-1983/84

GORDON DAVIES

Gordon Davies was a schoolteacher until he joined Fulham from Merthyr Tydfil, but in his six full seasons at Craven Cottage he earned a reputation as an outstanding marksman. Then in November 1984 Chelsea gave him the chance he had been waiting for to prove himself in the First Division.

'Ivor' knew that he would not find it easy to force his way into the team, but he was given an early opportunity to stake his claim when David Speedie missed three games through suspension shortly after his arrival. Judged purely as a goalscorer, Davies could scarcely have done better, heading home a Pat Nevin cross on his debut at Hillsborough and following that up two weeks later with a hat-trick in a 4-3 win at Goodison that was a model of cool finishing.

Small and quick, Gordon was an opportunist who tended to disappear from games until a half-chance came along, and in terms of overall contribution to the team he could not replace Speedie, who returned to the starting line-up after two games on the bench. There were further openings for the cheerful Welsh international later in the season when 'Speedo' was again absent through suspension, but he was never more than an understudy and the following October, now aged 30, he decided to make a fresh start with Manchester City.

BORN: Merthyr Tydfil, 8.8.55.
GAMES: 13 (2). GOALS: 6.
HONOURS: 16 Wales caps (79-86).
OTHER CLUBS: Fulham 77/8-84/5 (247, 114) and 86/7-90/1 (147, 45); Manchester City 85/6-86/7 (31, 9);
Wrexham 91/2 (22, 4). MANAGER: Tornado, Norway.

1984/85-1985/86

JOEY JONES

The arrival of Joey Jones from Wrexham in October 1982 did much to disperse the dark clouds that had gathered over Stamford Bridge. Fans who had lost all hope that the club would ever shake off the shabby mediocrity that had engulfed it found themselves cheering enthusiastically in response to the effervescent Welsh international's defiant clenched fist or cheery thumbs-up. His positive attitude lifted spirits in the dressing room in equally dramatic fashion and by the end of the season a team which had seemed to be prostrated by self-pity had summoned sufficient pride to scramble clear of relegation. It was exactly the response John Neal had hoped for when he signed the former Liverpool full-back, whose career he had launched during his time in charge at the Racecourse Ground.

Although Jones had quickly become Chelsea's first-choice number two, it had taken him some time to discover his touch. He could not be described as a polished defender and his distribution was often disappointing, but his uncompromising tackling, total commitment and refusal to concede the possibility of defeat until the final whistle ensured that he was adored by the lads in the Shed, who came to think of him as one of their own. The following season Joey switched to the left and played a leading part in Chelsea's successful pursuit of the Second Division Championship, but the signing of Doug Rougvie that summer relegated him to the role of understudy. He made a total of 21 appearances in all four defensive positions in 1984/85, but when John Hollins became manager it was decided that the absences from training that were the inevitable consequence of Joey's reluctance to move to the south-east were no longer acceptable. In August 1985 he was sold to Huddersfield, to the regret of all those who remembered the part he had played in inspiring Chelsea's revival.

BORN: Llandudno, 4.3.55.
GAMES: 89 (2). GOALS: 2.
HONOURS: Second Division Championship 83/4. 72 Wales caps (75-86).
OTHER CLUBS: Wrexham 72/3-74/5 (98, 2), 78/9-82/3 (146, 6) and 87/8-91/2 (132, 11);
Liverpool 75/6-77/8 (72, 3); Huddersfield Town 85/6-86/7 (68, 3).

1982/83-1984/85

COLIN PATES

When it was revealed in October 1988 that Colin Pates had moved to Charlton on loan with a view to a permanent transfer, many Chelsea fans greeted the news with disbelief. Although he was only 27, the polished defender had come to seem an indispensable part of the Stamford Bridge scene over the previous nine years. Changes to the playing staff during that period had been as unceasing as alterations to the club's change strip, but Pates had survived the repeated purges and it had somehow been taken for granted that he would remain with the Blues for the rest of his career.

Colin made his first-team debut as a gangling 18-year-old centre-half in a remarkable 7-3 win at Orient in November 1979 and Micky Droy's frequent absences through injury meant that he had plenty of opportunity to demonstrate his ability over the next couple of seasons, but he was not really sufficiently dominant when the ball was in the air to develop into a top-class number five. The appointment of John Neal prompted an upturn in the youngster's fortunes and he played in every League game in 1981/82, establishing himself as Droy's regular partner at the back before moving forward into midfield in the second half of the season when a spate of serious injuries depleted the squad.

As Neal acknowledged, Pates had by no means been born to the role, as he lacked mobility and his distribution was no more than adequate, but he threw himself into the task in characteristically wholehearted style, and was one of the few players to emerge with credit from the Blues' inglorious struggle to stave off relegation to Division Three the following season, invariably giving his all whatever position he was asked to fill.

Colin's efforts were sufficient to earn him a place alongside Joe McLaughlin in the centre of the defence when Neal's dramatically reshaped team was revealed at the start of the next campaign and they proved to be a well-matched pair, the Scot dealing with most of the high balls while Pates, more composed and rather more constructive, tidied up the loose ends. They provided a solid foundation for the Blues' successful assault on the Second Division Championship, steadily gaining confidence and conceding less than a goal a game.

Although he was one of the youngest members of the side, 'Sharky' was handed the captaincy towards the end of the season and seemed to thrive on the additional responsibility, producing a series of assured, authoritative displays as the club chased honours over the next two years. Calm and professional yet aggressive in the tackle, Colin had matured into a solid, reliable defender who read the game well and used the ball thoughtfully whenever circumstances permitted, his commanding display in a 3-1 win against Liverpool in December 1984 confirming that he had become one of the best young centre-backs in the country.

However, disharmony in the dressing room was beginning to undermine the Blues' performances and, after an unhappy season during which he had had to overcome a challenge for his place from new signing Steve Wicks, Colin surrendered the skipper's armband at the beginning of 1987/88. A cartilage operation sidelined him until mid-October and he managed only 17 League appearances that season, although he was recalled for the vital game against Charlton and the tense play-off matches.

At the start of the new season Pates was back in favour and, with Joe McLaughlin out of the side, he became established as Graham Roberts's partner in the middle of the back four. But then came the phone call from Charlton manager Lennie Lawrence and Bobby Campbell's unexpected decision to accept his offer of £400,000 for a player who still had a lot to offer at Stamford Bridge . . .

BORN: Carshalton, 10.8.61.
GAMES: 345 (1). GOALS: 10.
HONOURS: Second Division Championship 83/4; Full Members' Cup 85/6.
OTHER CLUBS: Charlton Athletic 88/9-89/90 (38, 0);
Arsenal 89/90-92/3 (21, 0);
Brighton and Hove Albion *on loan* 90/1 (17, 0).

1979/80-1988/89

DOUG ROUGVIE

During eight seasons with Aberdeen Doug Rougvie had won two Scottish League Championship medals, three Scottish Cup winner's medals and a Scottish cap, and had been a member of the European Cup-Winners' Cup-winning side in 1983, so when he joined Chelsea in a £150,000 deal in August 1984 there seemed to be no doubt about his class. The 28-year-old defender had been signed to replace Joey Jones at left-back and his arrival was regarded as an indication that the Blues would not be content simply to make up the numbers in the First Division.

Ferocious in the tackle and strong in the air, Dougie soon took over the Welshman's role as the Stamford Bridge folk-hero, his rampaging style endearing him to the fans. He was a robust, battling player, quick to lose his temper but with an equally ready smile, who always seemed to bring passion and enthusiasm to his football. However, his performances during his three years with the Blues were disappointing, his impulsiveness making him vulnerable whenever forwards ran at him with the ball, a weakness that became painfully apparent at White Hart Lane that November when Tottenham's elusive winger, John Chiedozie, tormented him mercilessly.

Dougie seemed to be unable to adapt to the demands of English football and in the second half of the season he was displaced by Keith Dublin. Although he fought his way back into the side at the beginning of 1985/86, he then lost his place once again and was rarely a first choice thereafter. However, he proved a valuable stand-in, his height making him particularly effective when taking the place of one of the regular centre-backs, and he performed with his usual commitment whenever called upon. Nevertheless it was clear that he had no part to play in John Hollins's long-term plans and in the summer of 1987 he was transferred to Brighton.

BORN: Ballingry, 24.5.56.
GAMES: 100. GOALS: 3.
HONOURS: Full Members' Cup 85/6. 1 Scotland cap (83).
OTHER CLUBS: Aberdeen; Brighton and Hove Albion 87/8 (35, 2);
Shrewsbury Town 88/9 (21, 3); Fulham 88/9 (18, 1);
Dunfermline Athletic.

1984/85-1986/87

COLIN LEE

Once Bill Garner had dropped out of the first-team reckoning, Chelsea found themselves without a big, traditional centre-forward and it was to rectify this weakness in his promotion-chasing squad that Geoff Hurst signed Colin Lee from Tottenham in January 1980. The athletic striker was prevented from making an immediate impact by a persistent hamstring problem but the first few months of the following season saw Lee at his most effective. By the end of November he had scored no fewer than 14 times, his ability 'upstairs' ensuring that the service provided from the flanks was turned into goals, but that golden spell was forgotten when the Blues failed to find the net in all but three of their last 22 League matches.

John Neal's wholesale rebuilding in the summer of 1983 gave new impetus to Lee's career and, in his role as the link between the attack and midfield, he showed skill and subtlety as well as strength. A stirring 5-3 win at Fulham demonstrated the potential of his partnership with Kerry Dixon, but illness unluckily cost Colin his place and in his absence David Speedie established himself as the rampaging number nine's provider.

Wholehearted and professional, Lee fought back from this setback by slotting in at right-back when John Hollins bowed out; his power in the air and composure made a major contribution to Chelsea's march to the Second Division Championship, but the arrival of Darren Wood that autumn cast renewed doubt over his future. A series of niggling injuries hampered Colin over the next couple of years and he was rarely certain of a first-team place. Two goals when standing in for Dixon in the 1986 Full Members' Cup final and a match-winning pass to Colin West against Arsenal the following season confirmed that the talent was still there but his troublesome hamstrings were continuing to bother him and in July 1987 he moved to Brentford to pursue his interest in coaching.

BORN: Torquay, 12.6.56.
GAMES: 200 (23). GOALS: 41.
HONOURS: Second Division Championship 83/4; Full Members' Cup 85/6.
OTHER CLUBS: Bristol City; Hereford United *on loan* 74/5 (9, 0);
Torquay United 76/7-77/8 (35, 14);
Tottenham Hotspur 77/8-79/80 (62, 18); Brentford 87/8-88/9 (24, 1).
MANAGER: Watford (90).

1979/80-1986/87

JOHN BUMSTEAD

For thirteen seasons a succession of Chelsea managers knew that they could rely on John Bumstead to do a solid job of work for them. The embodiment of selfless professionalism, the industrious midfielder would produce the same performance, week in, week out, with the consistency of a carefully maintained machine – totally dependable, and therefore easily taken for granted.

A career dedicated to stifling the talents of more gifted players began when John was given his first-team debut at Leeds in November 1978, the tenacious 19-year-old rarely straying more than a couple of yards from the side of Tony Currie throughout the game. It was a difficult time for a youngster to try and make his mark: Chelsea were second from bottom in the First Division and within weeks Ken Shellito had been replaced as manager by Danny Blanchflower. The following season Geoff Hurst succeeded the amiable Ulsterman and under his tutelage John's career blossomed. He was quite outstanding as the Blues mounted an exciting promotion charge but a tackle from behind against Shrewsbury in February left him with a dislocated ankle, and during his ten-week absence the Blues' assault faltered.

It took Bumstead a long time to recover his bite but his battling displays during John Neal's first two seasons at Stamford Bridge confirmed that the dogged Londoner possessed the sort of spirit that was going to be needed if Chelsea were to restore their faded fortunes. A quiet, modest man who carried out the task assigned to him without fuss and seemingly without emotion, John was a highly effective destroyer, as difficult to shake off as a dog with its jaws clamped round a postman's leg, but there was more to his game than that. He passed the ball tidily and made a valuable contribution as a goalscorer, a stunning 35-yard drive at the Valley in November 1981 demonstrating that he had a superb shot which he used all too rarely.

When Neal's reconstructed side was revealed at the start of 1983/84, John was paired with Nigel Spackman in the engine room and performed with his usual understated efficiency, although a number of well-struck goals from free-kicks ensured that his efforts were not totally overlooked. When back trouble sidelined him for a month he had difficulty dislodging Tony McAndrew, but he was recalled towards the end of the campaign and shared in the Blues' thrilling Championship triumph.

Bumstead's committed style meant he collected injuries with disheartening regularity but he remained a member of Chelsea's first-choice line-up until 1988/89, when it seemed that he might be leaving Stamford Bridge. However, the departure of Darren Wood gave him the chance to reclaim his place and he had the satisfaction of scoring the goal against Leeds that clinched another Second Division Championship medal, turning the ball past Mervyn Day from close range after good work by Kerry Dixon.

John started the following season on the substitute's bench – his ability to fill in at right-back or in the middle of the defence made him a useful player to have in reserve – but once again he fought back to prove that the passing years had not diminished his effectiveness. He made only a handful of appearances in 1990/91, but when Aston Villa visited the Bridge in November he shackled David Platt in the same relentless style that he had subdued Tony Currie more than a decade earlier. At the end of the campaign, with his 33rd birthday in sight, this unassuming and highly regarded professional was given a free transfer and joined Charlton, serving the Valiants dependably for two years before back problems forced his retirement in 1993.

BORN: Rotherhithe, 27.11.58.
GAMES: 379 (30). GOALS: 44.
HONOURS: Second Division Championship 83/4, 88/9;
Full Members' Cup 85/6, 89/90.
OTHER CLUBS: Charlton Athletic 91/2-92/3 (56, 3).

1978/79-1990/91

JOE McLAUGHLIN

While the Stamford Bridge faithful were savouring the skills of Nevin, Speedie and Dixon, Joe McLaughlin was getting on with the job . . . coolly, professionally, dependably – and largely unnoticed. He was Chelsea's first-choice centre-half throughout his six years with the club and his importance to the side was only too apparent whenever he was sidelined by injury, but he seldom received the recognition his doughty efforts deserved.

The athletic Scot was signed from Morton for £95,000 during John Neal's spectacular swoop on some of the less well illuminated corners of British football in the summer of 1983 and immediately formed an impressive partnership in the centre of the defence with Colin Pates, missing just one game as the Blues stormed to the Second Division title. Although he was not the tallest of number fives, his timing and determination meant that he was rarely troubled in the air, while his fearless tackling and mobility ensured that forwards enjoyed little respite when the ball was on the floor.

When Peter Withe scored twice in a 4-2 defeat at Aston Villa in September 1984, it seemed that 'Big Joe' might find life in the top flight more difficult, but those fears proved unfounded and by the spring he had made such progress that the experienced striker posed little threat in the return fixture at the Bridge. McLaughlin was appointed captain at the start of 1987/88, but these were difficult times for the Blues and the burdens of office appeared to affect his form. He had always favoured a 'safety first' approach but now his distribution became decidedly erratic and, with the crowd turning on him, he surrendered the armband to Graham Roberts in August 1988. He bounced back with characteristic courage to win his second Division Two Championship medal but had decided that he needed a change of environment and was allowed to join Charlton in a £600,000 deal in the summer of 1989.

BORN: Greenock, 2.6.60.
GAMES: 268. GOALS: 7.
HONOURS: Second Division Championship 83/4, 88/9; Full Members' Cup 85/6.
OTHER CLUBS: Morton; Charlton Athletic 89/90 (31, 0);
Watford 90/1-91/2 (46, 2); Falkirk.

1983/84-1988/89

EDDIE NIEDZWIECKI

If a team is to achieve sustained success, a dependable goalkeeper is essential. The signing of Eddie Niedzwiecki from Third Division Wrexham in June 1983 played an important part in Chelsea's return to the limelight over the next three years and the injury which tragically cut short his career was surely one reason the Blues' sojourn in the First Division proved to be surprisingly brief.

The Welshman with the Polish name grew in confidence during his first season at Stamford Bridge and was soon dominating his penalty area, coming for crosses with authority and calling decisively, but it was his bravery and agility that made Niedzwiecki exceptional. Both were called upon in a Milk Cup replay at Craven Cottage in November 1985: Fulham deserved to win comfortably but he stopped everything that was thrown at him and a Dixon goal at the other end was enough to put Chelsea through.

Only the brilliance of Everton's Neville Southall prevented Eddie winning a string of Welsh caps before the fateful night in March 1986 when his left knee was badly damaged in a League game against Queens Park Rangers. Major surgery was required but he battled his way back to fitness with characteristic courage and returned to League action at Aston Villa in November. He was not able to move with his old freedom, however, and after a dozen more appearances he was back in hospital. He returned to the side at the start of the following season and seemed to be approaching his best when the knee let him down once again against Oxford in October. This time there was to be no comeback.

Eddie faced his new challenge with the determination that had made him so popular with Chelsea's supporters and threw himself into a career in management. After a season and a half learning the trade in charge of the Blues' youth side he moved to Reading as Ian Porterfield's assistant, and returned to Stamford Bridge when the Scot succeeded Bobby Campbell in 1991.

BORN: Bangor, 3.5.59.
GAMES: 175. GOALS: 0.
HONOURS: Second Division Championship 83/4.
2 Wales caps (85-87).
OTHER CLUBS: Wrexham 77/8-82/3 (111, 0).

1983/84-1987/88

DAVID SPEEDIE

A fire burned within David Speedie that made him abrasive, argumentative – and a player of rare inspiration. He had come up the hard way, earning his living at the bottom of a coal mine for ten months before Barnsley gave him a contract, and the ferocity with which the little striker celebrated his goals gave the impression that he had a point to prove to those who had doubted him as a youngster. A relentless competitor, he thrived on conflict, and his unfailing belligerence made him a hero of the Stamford Bridge crowd, which was still chanting his name with affection when he returned with Coventry City more than three years after his departure.

Signed by John Neal from Darlington for £80,000 in May 1982, Speedie won a regular first-team place after scoring twice on his debut against Oldham in September, his courage and tenacity bringing some much-needed zest to a team chronically short of confidence. He found himself relegated to the bench when Neal's rebuilt side was unveiled at the start of the following season, but he seized the opportunity presented by an illness which sidelined Colin Lee with characteristic determination, and rapidly became a pivotal member of the side which won the Second Division Championship in electrifying style and went on to challenge for further honours over the next two years.

Although he was only 5ft 6½in tall, 'Speedo' was an outstanding header of the ball, his timing and sheer ebullience enabling him to outjump defenders who towered over him. The first of his three goals in the Full Members' Cup final against Manchester City at Wembley in 1986 was typical, but in general his finishing lacked the ruthlessness expected of a top marksman. Always eager to get behind the defence, Dave was caught offside with frustrating regularity and when he did succeed in breaking clear with only the goalkeeper to beat he often appeared indecisive; but he could be highly effective at close range, as he demonstrated when he coolly lobbed a last-minute equaliser past Arsenal's John Lukic at Stamford Bridge in January 1985.

A dependable target man, Speedie frequently dropped back into midfield to find space and much of his best work was done there, shielding the ball, turning and laying it precisely into the path of Mickey Thomas or Pat Nevin as they surged towards goal. He supplied Kerry Dixon with many of his openings and they came to be regarded as one of the most dangerous pairings in English football, Dixon's speed and strength complementing his partner's fine close control and eye for a penetrating through-ball.

Never one to keep his feelings to himself, Dave reacted venomously if an opponent was so rash as to try to intimidate him, and team-mates who failed to deliver the ball in the way he required could expect to receive a tongue-lashing, as could referees whose interpretation of incidents on the field was at variance with the fiery Yorkshireman's. His ceaseless aggression earned him a string of bookings, and as a consequence he was regularly unavailable for selection, which did little to endear him to his employers . . .

The industrious striker won his first international cap for Scotland in May 1985 but the rich promise the Blues had shown since their return to the First Division was to remain unfulfilled. Amid the turmoil that engulfed the club in 1986/87, Speedie's form slumped and it seemed that, once again, Chelsea had found it impossible to sustain a working relationship with a volatile but enormously gifted player. He made just 22 League appearances that season and was sold to Coventry City for £750,000 in July, subsequently moving to Liverpool in February 1991 to add a little zip to the Anfield giants' annual title challenge.

BORN: Glenrothes, 20.2.60.
GAMES: 197 (8). GOALS: 64.
HONOURS: Second Division Championship 83/4; Full Members' Cup 85/6.
10 Scotland caps (85-89).
OTHER CLUBS: Barnsley 78/9-79/80 (23, 0); Darlington 80/1-81/2 (88, 21);
Coventry City 87/8-90/1 (122, 31); Liverpool 90/1 (12, 6);
Blackburn Rovers 91/2 (36, 23); Southampton 92/3- (11, 0);
Birmingham City *on loan* 92/3 (10, 2); West Bromwich Albion *on loan* 92/3 (7, 2);
West Ham United *on loan* 92/3 (11, 4).

1982/83-1986/87

KERRY DIXON

There were times when Kerry Dixon looked pedestrian, even lethargic, but when he had the goal in his sights he was instantly transformed. A superbly athletic striker, he seemed to live for the satisfaction of putting the ball in the net and his dashing exploits inevitably made him the hero of the Stamford Bridge faithful.

Kerry was signed from Reading in August 1983 as part of John Neal's extensive rebuilding plans and began to repay the £175,000 fee at once with two goals on the opening day of the season. He would never be the most elegant of players and at first he looked a little cumbersome, but he finished the campaign as the Second Division's leading scorer.

The big number nine was fortunate that the players around him complemented his single-minded style so well. He was majestic in the air and thrived on a seemingly unending supply of inch-perfect crosses from Pat Nevin on the right flank, like the one from which he headed the goal at Grimsby that clinched the Championship. However, his greatest asset was his blistering pace, and he quickly established a partnership with David Speedie that was to become one of the most respected in the country, the fiery Yorkshireman's selfless work ensuring that his partner had plenty of enticing through-balls to run onto. Strange as it might seem, Dixon was not an outstanding finisher – his record from the penalty spot was abysmal – but his splendid anticipation meant that he could afford to be profligate.

Kerry earned his first full international caps during the summer tour of North America in 1985, but his career suffered a major blow when he sustained torn stomach muscles in a fourth round FA Cup tie against Liverpool the following January. He missed only a handful of matches but he was hampered by the injury for some time and many observers concluded that it must have had a permanent effect on him since he was never to find goals so easy to come by again. However, it should be remembered that the exciting team Neal had assembled was starting to disintegrate, with the result that Kerry was no longer getting the reliable service he needed.

Two splendid goals at Old Trafford earned Dixon a place in the England party for the 1986 World Cup, but the next two seasons proved largely frustrating and in the early part of 1988 it seemed that he was likely to join Arsenal or West Ham in a £1 million transfer. In the event he stayed at Stamford Bridge and his 25 goals were a major factor in the Blues' storming Second Division Championship triumph in 1988/89.

Dixon had never been a player who wasted too much energy chasing hopeless causes but under the influence of Bobby Campbell his game developed and he became much more of a creator, using his pace and enormously improved close control to go past defenders on the flanks. His overall contribution was greater than ever but his effectiveness as a marksman was inevitably compromised. He scored regularly on the Blues' return to the First Division, but over the next couple of years the flow gradually dried up once more. The electrifying pace had begun to fade and once again the supply of ammunition was fitful at best. It was clear that a move would be in the interests of all concerned and in July 1992 Dixon was transferred to Southampton for £575,000. Bobby Tambling's scoring record which had been his target for so long would remain unbroken, but Kerry left behind him a store of golden memories which Chelsea fans will cherish for many years to come.

BORN: Luton, 24.7.61.
GAMES: 413 (7). GOALS: 193.
HONOURS: Second Division Championship 83/4, 88/9;
Full Members' Cup 89/90.
8 England caps (85-86).
OTHER CLUBS: Tottenham Hotspur (0, 0);
Reading 80/1-82/3 (116, 51); Southampton 92/3- (9, 2);
Luton Town *on loan* 92/3 (17, 3).

1983/84-1991/92

MICKEY THOMAS

For the match at Derby on 14 January 1984 John Neal made two changes to his side which transformed Chelsea from exciting but unpredictable promotion hopefuls into worthy Second Division Champions: Colin Lee came in for John Hollins at right-back; and, decisively, Mickey Thomas, who had recently arrived from Stoke City, took over the number eleven shirt from the orthodox left-wingers who had previously occupied it. A player of prodigious energy and boundless enthusiasm, the 29-year-old Welsh international did the work of two men, combining the roles of industrious midfielder and enterprising outside-left in one all-action package, and the Blues remained undefeated for the rest of the season.

Since his departure from Old Trafford in August 1981, Thomas had somehow lost his way and his reputation had inevitably suffered, but during his season and a half in the Chelsea team he was a model of consistency, becoming a favourite of the fans, just as John Neal (who had guided his career in its formative years at Wrexham) had predicted. He made an immediate impact with an influential performance and two well-taken goals on his home debut against the leaders, Sheffield Wednesday, and continued to play a leading role in the Stamford Bridge revival the following season, despite some bad luck with injuries. Once again Mickey responded to the challenge presented by the Owls' combative style, this time in the Milk Cup, and his irresistible displays in the three matches needed to settle the tie typified the indomitable spirit that carried the Blues into the semi-finals.

When John Hollins succeeded Neal that summer he signed Jerry Murphy, followed a few weeks later by Mick Hazard. Thomas, who missed the start of the season with a broken jaw, evidently had no place in his vision of the club's future and was sold to West Bromwich Albion in September – to the dismay of those who had taken the mercurial Welshman to their hearts.

BORN: Newtown, 7.7.54.
GAMES: 53 (1). GOALS: 11.
HONOURS: Second Division Championship 83/4. 51 Wales caps (76-86).
OTHER CLUBS: Wrexham 71/2-78/9 (230, 33) and 91/2-92/3 (34, 2); Manchester United 78/9-80/1 (90, 11);
Everton 81/2 (10, 0); Brighton and Hove Albion 81/2 (20, 0); Stoke City 82/3-83/4 (57, 14) and 89/90-90/1 (46, 7);
West Bromwich Albion 85/6 (20, 0); Derby County *on loan* 85/6 (9, 0);
Wichita Wings; Shrewsbury Town 88/9 (40, 1); Leeds United 89/90 (3, 0).

1983/84-1984/85

NIGEL SPACKMAN

Nigel Spackman's economical style may have lacked the adornments that set the terraces roaring and prompt journalists to unleash their eloquence, but his influential displays in midfield made a huge contribution to Chelsea's renaissance in the mid-eighties. He was signed from Third Division Bournemouth for £40,000 in June 1983 and immediately formed a highly effective partnership with John Bumstead at the heart of John Neal's remodelled side, missing only two games as the Blues stormed to the Second Division title. Nigel's biting tackle and seemingly inexhaustible reserves of energy made him a formidable ball-winner and his passing, if unambitious, was painstaking in its accuracy. Although he possessed a powerful shot, a Spackman goal was a rare event, but he invariably showed enterprise and intelligence when the opportunity arose to break forward in search of an opening.

A thoughtful, purposeful player, 'Spackers' had little difficulty in adapting to the demands of top-flight football the following season, and his performance at White Hart Lane in November was simply magnificent. He totally overshadowed his immediate adversary, Glenn Hoddle, and in the last twenty minutes took command of the middle of the pitch as Spurs wilted in the face of his relentless aggression.

Spackman's determination and professionalism typified the spirit of the new Chelsea, but when John Hollins moved into the manager's office in the summer of 1985 his place in the team became less secure. As disharmony once again took hold of the dressing room with the inevitable effect on results, there were persistent stories that he was unsettled and in February 1987 he was allowed to join Liverpool in a £400,000 deal.

After spells at QPR and Glasgow Rangers, Nigel returned to Stamford Bridge in September 1992 to operate in a holding role in front of the back four, but after a handful of games he suffered a serious back injury that kept him on the sidelines for much of the season, frustrating hopes that he would be able to spark a Chelsea revival as he had nearly a decade earlier.

BORN: Romsey, 2.12.60.
GAMES: 184 (3). GOALS: 14.
HONOURS: Second Division Championship 83/4;
Full Members' Cup 85/6.
OTHER CLUBS: AFC Bournemouth 80/1-82/3 (119, 10);
Liverpool 86/7-88/9 (51, 0); Queens Park Rangers 88/9-89/90 (29, 1);
Glasgow Rangers.

1983/84-1986/87 & 1992/93-

PAT NEVIN

It is an accepted part of football wisdom that small, tricky wingers with delicate skills are like the decorations on a Christmas tree: pretty to look at but of no practical value, and apt to disintegrate when anyone touches them. However, that unflattering comparison could not be applied to Pat Nevin during his five seasons at Stamford Bridge. The artistry that made the tiny Scottish sorcerer the idol of the terraces was put to work, harnessed to the needs of the team, and he was rarely guilty of self-indulgence. Intelligent and hard-working, he became Chelsea's most dependable source of goal-scoring opportunities, and a key member of a rousing side that looked set to challenge the best.

Signed from Clyde of the Scottish First Division for £95,000 in May 1983, Nevin was not in the starting line-up when John Neal's remodelled side was unveiled at the beginning of the new season, but when he made his first-team debut as a substitute in a Milk Cup tie against Gillingham in September it was immediately apparent that he possessed breathtaking ball control allied to delightful audacity. He didn't miss a game for the rest of the season and it is a measure of his contribution to the Blues' exhilarating Second Division Championship triumph that the manager's most frequently repeated tactical advice to his men was a simple exhortation to 'give it to Pat'.

Nevin seemed to be able to hold the ball for ever, even when he was surrounded by opponents bent on taking it from him, and a mesmerising 80-yard dribble against Newcastle in November reinforced the impression that he could beat defenders as he pleased. Although he usually played on the right, he was equally at home on his left foot and a fruitful ploy was to cut inside, drawing the centre-back, before slipping the ball through for the rampaging Dixon to run onto. Pat also contributed 14 valuable goals that season, the best of them an exquisite, curling free-kick that helped the Blues to a 6-1 win against Swansea in December.

The 'wee man' maintained his high standards in the First Division the following winter. His looping, curling crosses played invitingly into the box from near the corner flag provided Kerry Dixon and David Speedie with a steady stream of chances, but it was Pat's remarkable awareness that was most impressive. Just when it seemed that he was weaving his way into an impenetrable maze, he would release the ball with the precision of a rapier thrust, just as he did to make Chelsea's third and fourth goals in the epic 4-4 draw at Hillsborough in the Milk Cup.

The thoughtful Scot, a devotee of obscure rock bands and Russian literature, was inevitably subjected to some wild tackling but he had an uncanny ability to ride even the most agricultural assault and was certainly not lacking in courage. However, as time went by he became less effective. He won his first Scottish cap against Romania in March 1986 but as Chelsea lost their way he saw less of the ball and was usually closely marked, often by two or three men. He continued to work diligently for the side but became an increasingly forlorn figure, waiting in vain for the service he needed if he was to make an impression.

It was therefore no surprise that, when defeat at the hands of Middlesbrough in the play-offs in May 1988 consigned Chelsea to the Second Division once more, Nevin exercised his right to move on and joined Everton, a transfer tribunal setting the fee at £925,000. Shortly afterwards Bobby Campbell signed Peter Nicholas and Graham Roberts to give the side the hard-edged pragmatism it had undeniably lacked, but they could scarcely be expected to replace this peerless entertainer and goal-maker in the hearts of the Stamford Bridge faithful.

BORN: Glasgow, 6.9.63.
GAMES: 237 (5). GOALS: 45.
HONOURS: Second Division Championship 83/4; Full Members' Cup 85/6.
16 Scotland caps (86-93).
OTHER CLUBS: Clyde; Everton 88/9-91/2 (109, 16);
Tranmere Rovers *on loan* 91/2 (8, 0);
Tranmere Rovers 92/3- (43, 13).

1983/84-1987/88

KEITH DUBLIN

Whether racing forward from left-back to link with the attack or testing his pace against some speedy winger, Keith Dublin moved with the lithe grace of a natural athlete. A cultured player who always tried to use the ball constructively, the composed England youth international's tackling was crisp and decisive, yet somehow his defending lacked authority, perhaps because his confidence in his exceptional sprinting ability had led him to neglect the niceties of positional play as a youngster.

Having made his debut in the final home game of the triumphant 1983/84 season only to miss the Championship decider at Grimsby through injury, Keith was given his First Division baptism after the Milk Cup semi-final defeat in March 1985 and showed great promise, his polished display against Spurs earning rave reviews. After a three-month spell in the first team the following winter, he finally won possession of the number three shirt from Doug Rougvie in 1986/87, forming an impressive partnership with Steve Clarke in the second half of the campaign. However, the signing of Clive Wilson and Tony Dorigo made it clear that John Hollins had lost faith in Dublin and in August 1987 he joined the growing colony of Stamford Bridge exiles at Brighton.

BORN: High Wycombe, 29.1.66.
GAMES: 66 (2). GOALS: 0.
HONOURS: Full Members' Cup 85/6.
OTHER CLUBS: Brighton and Hove Albion 87/8-89/90 (132, 5);
Watford 90/1- (135, 1).

1983/84-1986/87

KEITH JONES

Keith Jones appeared to have all the qualities required by the modern midfielder. He could win the ball in the tackle and use it effectively, either playing a simple pass to a nearby colleague or a more ambitious defence-splitter, and wasn't afraid to get into the box and score a few himself.

The England youth international looked like winning a regular place in the side in the autumn of 1984 with a series of thoughtful performances, the best of which was against Manchester City in the Milk Cup, when he notched up his fourth goal in ten full appearances after pouncing on Paul Canoville's mishit shot. However, when an aggressive Manchester United side put him under pressure a few weeks later, Keith was unable to impose himself on the game and was replaced at half-time by David Speedie. That chastening experience took its toll on his fragile confidence and he returned to the shadows for the next 18 months, playing only occasionally.

In 1986/87 'KJ' was given an extended run which represented his make-or-break opportunity, but in an ever-changing side he failed to produce his best form and it became clear that he had little future at Stamford Bridge. The following September he was transferred to Brentford, where he emerged as one of the most influential midfield generals in the lower divisions before moving to Southend.

BORN: Dulwich, 14.10.65.
GAMES: 57 (12). GOALS: 10.
OTHER CLUBS: Brentford 87/8-91/2 (169, 13);
Southend United 91/2- (63, 6).

1982/83-1986/87

DALE JASPER

Dale Jasper's natural ability was highly regarded in the Chelsea dressing room and John Neal was convinced that he would play an important part in the club's future, but a sequence of misfortunes prevented him from translating that talent into a regular first-team place. Cool and elegant, he made his League debut at centre-half, emerging with credit as the Blues salvaged a point with three goals in the last six minutes at Cardiff in March 1984, and confirmed his adaptability by playing at left-back in the 1-0 win at Grimsby which clinched the Second Division title.

However, Dale's best position was in midfield and that is where he started the following season, showing considerable promise until a foot injury allowed John Bumstead to regain his place. His next opportunity came when he was called from the bench to replace Joe McLaughlin after 11 minutes of the first leg of the Milk Cup semi-final against Sunderland in February, but it was not Chelsea's night and the 21-year-old conceded two unlucky penalties which were to prove decisive. It was a setback from which Jasper's career never really recovered. He made only one full appearance in 1985/86 and before the season was out the club had reluctantly taken the decision to give him a free transfer. Unhappily, his spells with Brighton and Crewe brought him little better fortune.

BORN: Croydon, 14.1.64.
GAMES: 13 (2). GOALS: 0.
OTHER CLUBS: Brighton and Hove Albion 86/7-87/8 (49, 6);
Crewe Alexandra 88/9-91/2 (111, 2).

1983/84-1985/86

TONY GODDEN

It is a fact of football life that one man's misfortune represents another's opportunity. After ten seasons with West Bromwich Albion during which he had had his fair share of ups and downs, Tony Godden was signed on loan following Eddie Niedzwiecki's injury in March 1986 to provide cover for the Welshman's deputy, Steve Francis. However, when the goals-against tally started mounting alarmingly, Godden was given a chance to relaunch his career with the team that was fourth in the First Division. His authority and experience helped steady the ship and the transfer was made permanent that summer.

Tony had the ability to be a match-winning goalkeeper, as he demonstrated at Old Trafford in September when he saved two penalties to ensure that Kerry Dixon's second-minute goal was enough to give the Blues the points. However, there were other days when he looked less convincing, although it should be said that the protection he was given was sometimes scanty.

Godden's efforts to make himself an indispensable part of the Chelsea team were ultimately undermined by illness and injury. With Roger Freestone arriving to understudy Niedzwiecki, he was no longer needed at Stamford Bridge and was allowed to join Birmingham in July 1987, but he had done a valuable job for the club at a difficult time.

BORN: Gillingham, 2.8.55. GAMES: 38. GOALS: 0.
OTHER CLUBS: West Bromwich Albion 76/7-85/6 (267, 0);
Preston North End *on loan* (0, 0); Luton Town *on loan* 82/3 (12, 0);
Walsall *on loan* 83/4 (19, 0); Birmingham City 87/8-88/9 (29, 0);
Bury *on loan* 88/9 (1, 0); Sheffield Wednesday *on loan* (0, 0);
Peterborough United 89/90 (24, 0).

1985/86-1986/87

GORDON DURIE

There are few more stirring sights in football than that of a big, powerful forward heading straight for goal, defying the burly defenders who stand in his path to stop him. When he was at the pinnacle of his form, Gordon Durie looked utterly irresistible, a potent combination of pace and surprising delicacy leaving opponents helpless in his wake, but his dramatic, uncompromising style inevitably exacted its dues. The muscular Scot was injured with heartbreaking regularity and, in the end, it came to seem that his spells in the first team were little more than brief interludes between extended periods on the treatment table.

It took Gordon a little time to make his mark at Stamford Bridge following his £380,000 move from Hibernian at the end of 1985/86. He started the new campaign on the flank but that proved to be one of John Hollins's less successful ideas and after three games the new arrival was relegated to the substitute's bench. A knee operation interrupted his progress and the only real highlight of a frustrating first season in London was a rousing display against Aston Villa in the FA Cup.

The departure of David Speedie that summer allowed Gordon to prove his worth in the middle of the attack, a flurry of goals at the start of the campaign earning him his first full Scottish cap. The knee trouble that sidelined him for three months was a major factor in the Blues' wretched slide towards relegation, but in the long term his career may well have benefited from a season of Second Division football. Durie relished the space he was given by weaker defences and his confidence visibly blossomed. He developed a streak of arrogance that made him all the more effective, and his five goals at Walsall in January were plundered with a crowd-pleasing swagger.

Largely as a result of his continuing fitness problems, Gordon was infuriatingly inconsistent, but when the mood took him he could win games single-handedly. He was essentially a lone raider and his partnership with Kerry Dixon never really fulfilled its obvious potential. The Scot had a thunderous shot – as he demonstrated when he rifled a quite unstoppable free-kick past Liverpool's Bruce Grobbelaar in December 1989 – and was sometimes tempted to go for glory when a measured pass to a colleague would have resulted in a clear-cut opening. Often spurning the simple chances that came his way, he scored a number of magnificent individual goals, with a classically direct effort in a 6-4 win at the Baseball Ground the following season typifying his rousing style. Receiving the ball from a Dave Beasant throw near the halfway line, Gordon set off towards the Derby goal in characteristically single-minded fashion, swept into the penalty area, then bamboozled a couple of hapless defenders before steering his shot past Peter Shilton.

A recurrent groin problem restricted 'Juke Box' to 14 League appearances in 1989/90 but his late-season form gained him a place in the Scottish party for the World Cup in Italy, and the following campaign was probably the best of his five-year stay at Stamford Bridge. Injuries handicapped him once again but his powerful running always posed a threat and against Manchester United he scored a goal that was truly breathtaking, battering the ball past Les Sealey after the Reds' back four had retreated in the face of his onslaught.

It had been reported for some time that Gordon was keen to move back to Scotland so that he and his wife could be closer to their families, so it was no real surprise when he was involved in a £2.2 million transfer on the eve of the following season. However, the fans who had once idolised the charismatic striker made no attempt to conceal their bitterness when it was announced that he was moving no further north than White Hart Lane.

BORN: Paisley, 6.12.65.
GAMES: 145 (8). GOALS: 63.
HONOURS: Second Division Championship 88/9; Full Members' Cup 89/90.
23 Scotland caps (87-92).
OTHER CLUBS: East Fife; Hibernian;
Tottenham Hotspur 91/2- (48, 10).

1985/86-1990/91

DEREK JOHNSTONE

ROBERT ISAAC

DUNCAN SHEARER

DEREK JOHNSTONE 1983/84-1984/85

Forward. BORN: Dundee, 4.11.53.
GAMES: 1 (3). GOALS: 0.
HONOURS: 14 Scotland caps (73-79).
OTHER CLUBS: Glasgow Rangers (twice);
Dundee United *on loan*. MANAGER: Partick Thistle.

TERRY HOWARD 1984/85-1986/87

Full-back. BORN: Stepney, 26.2.66.
GAMES: 6. GOALS: 0.
OTHER CLUBS: Crystal Palace *on loan* 85/6 (4, 0);
Chester City *on loan* 86/7 (2, 0); Leyton Orient 86/7- (276, 28).

ROBERT ISAAC 1984/85-1986/87

Defender. BORN: Hackney, 30.11.65.
GAMES: 13. GOALS: 0.
OTHER CLUBS: Brighton and Hove Albion 86/7-88/9 (30, 0).

JOHN MILLAR 1985/86-1986/87

Full-back. BORN: Coatbridge, 8.12.66.
GAMES: 11. GOALS: 0.
OTHER CLUBS: Hamilton Academical *on loan*;
Northampton Town *on loan* 86/7 (1, 0);
Blackburn Rovers 87/8-90/1 (126, 2); Heart of Midlothian.

DUNCAN SHEARER 1985/86

Forward. BORN: Fort William, 28.8.62.
GAMES: 2. GOALS: 1.
OTHER CLUBS: Huddersfield Town 85/6-87/8 (83, 38);
Swindon Town 88/9-91/2 (159, 78);
Blackburn Rovers 91/2 (6, 1); Aberdeen.

LES FRIDGE 1985/86

Goalkeeper. BORN: Inverness, 27.8.68.
GAMES: 1. GOALS: 0.
OTHER CLUBS: St Mirren.

TERRY HOWARD

JOHN MILLAR

LES FRIDGE

JOHN McNAUGHT

JOHN COADY

MICKY BODLEY

JOHN McNAUGHT 1985/86-1987/88

Midfielder. BORN: Glasgow, 19.6.64.
GAMES: 12 (1). GOALS: 2.
OTHER CLUBS: Hamilton Academical; Partick Thistle.

COLIN WEST 1986/87-1987/88

Forward. BORN: Middlesbrough, 19.9.67.
GAMES: 8 (8). GOALS: 4.
OTHER CLUBS: Partick Thistle *on loan*;
Swansea City *on loan* 88/9 (14, 3); Dundee.

JOHN COADY 1986/87-1987/88

Full-back/midfielder. BORN: Dublin, 25.8.60.
GAMES: 10 (9). GOALS: 3.
OTHER CLUBS: Shamrock Rovers; Derry City.

BILLY DODDS 1986/87-1988/89

Forward. BORN: New Cumnock, 5.2.69.
GAMES: 0 (5). GOALS: 0.
OTHER CLUBS: Partick Thistle *on loan*; Dundee.

MICKY BODLEY 1987/88

Central defender. BORN: Hayes, 14.9.67.
GAMES: 8. GOALS: 1.
OTHER CLUBS: Northampton Town 88/9 (20, 0);
Barnet 91/2- (69, 3).

PERRY DIGWEED 1987/88

Goalkeeper. BORN: Westminster, 26.10.59.
GAMES: 3 (*on loan* from Brighton and Hove Albion). GOALS: 0.
OTHER CLUBS: Fulham 76/7-80/1 (15, 0);
Brighton and Hove Albion 80/1- (179, 0);
West Bromwich Albion *on loan* (0, 0);
Charlton Athletic *on loan* (0, 0);
Newcastle United *on loan* (0, 0); Wimbledon *on loan* (0, 0).

COLIN WEST

BILLY DODDS

PERRY DIGWEED

DARREN WOOD

During his four and a half seasons at Stamford Bridge, Darren Wood maintained the standard he had achieved with admirable consistency and was seldom out of the first team for long. A hard-working, adaptable player with the ingrained pragmatism of a true Yorkshireman, he offered a model of professionalism at a time when the Blues' fortunes were fluctuating with the unpredictability of the Stock Exchange, but the suspicion remains that he was capable of rather more.

A £50,000 signing from Middlesbrough in September 1984, Darren had gained considerable experience during a brief but eventful senior career at Ayresome Park, and the 20-year-old's glowing reputation suggested that he would have little difficulty in establishing himself as the Blues' first-choice right-back at the expense of Colin Lee. However, it was not until the following autumn that he earned a secure place in the side, and although he played his part in the Blues' many achievements that season, it was clear that, like so many modern full-backs, he was more impressive coming forward than in defence. Enthusiastic and energetic, he used the ball intelligently and relished every opportunity to attack, but although his tackling had bite he often looked uncertain when faced by a tricky winger.

The arrival of Steve Clarke from St Mirren in January 1987 appeared to cast a deep shadow over Wood's future, but after four games as substitute he was recalled in midfield and revelled in his new role, working tirelessly and throwing himself into every challenge with quite awe-inspiring bravery. Showing an aggression that had previously seemed alien to him, Darren continued to impress during Chelsea's feckless slide into Division Two in 1987/88, and a cartilage operation which caused him to miss the last few weeks of the season undoubtedly hindered the Blues' struggle for survival.

Wood returned to the fray with his passion undiminished and it was a considerable surprise when he was transferred to Sheffield Wednesday in January 1989. Unhappily, his return to Yorkshire was to be blighted by injuries.

BORN: Scarborough, 9.6.64.
GAMES: 167 (11). GOALS: 4.
HONOURS: Second Division Championship 88/9; Full Members' Cup 85/6.
OTHER CLUBS: Middlesbrough 81/2-84/5 (101, 6);
Sheffield Wednesday 88/9-89/90 (11, 0).

1984/85-1988/89

JERRY MURPHY

Jerry Murphy became John Hollins's first signing when he joined Chelsea from Crystal Palace on a free transfer in August 1985. He had been a member of Terry Venables's exciting young side in the late seventies and made more than 200 appearances during the course of nine seasons at Selhurst Park, but terrible luck with injuries prevented him from winning a regular first-team place at Stamford Bridge.

Murphy made an encouraging start to his career with the Blues, playing in the first seven matches of the new campaign on the left of midfield and impressing on his home debut against Coventry. His calm and measured style was easily mistaken for a lack of urgency but, although he was a little short of pace, his perceptive and accurate passing promised to give the side a more cultured look. The London-born Irish international then lost his place through injury but he played his part in a richly merited 1-1 draw at Anfield on his return to the side in November.

Competition from Kevin McAllister and Mick Hazard restricted Jerry's opportunities during the remainder of the campaign, and during the next two seasons he made just 13 appearances, fitness problems continuing to frustrate his efforts to establish himself. He left the club in the summer of 1988 and dropped out of League football, no doubt wondering what he had done to deserve such misfortune.

BORN: Stepney, 23.9.59.
GAMES: 39. GOALS: 3
HONOURS: 3 Ireland caps.
OTHER CLUBS: Crystal Palace 76/7-84/5 (229, 20).

1985/86-1987/88

ROY WEGERLE

The road that led Roy Wegerle to Stamford Bridge was unusually tortuous. Born in South Africa, he went to college in America and became a professional with the Tampa Bay Rowdies (who were managed by Rodney Marsh, the former Queens Park Rangers star) but was unable to pursue his career in Europe until his father discovered that he was entitled to a West German passport. He finally signed for Chelsea in June 1986, having spent two months with the Blues 'on trial' the previous season.

Roy could do things with the ball that took the breath away, but never succeeded in harnessing his abundant skill to the needs of the team, with the result that he made only occasional appearances, often as a substitute. He usually played on the wing or in midfield, but his ability to lose his marker would surely have been employed to greater effect in a central striking role. He confirmed his talent with a magnificent goal in the third round of the FA Cup at Derby in January 1988, running from the halfway line before beating Peter Shilton, but when Bobby Campbell succeeded John Hollins he quickly decided that he had no use for Roy's intermittent inventiveness. That summer he was sold to Luton for £75,000 but by December 1989 he had made such startling progress that QPR paid £1 million to take him to Loftus Road . . .

BORN: Johannesburg, South Africa, 19.3.64.
GAMES: 18 (10). GOALS: 4. HONOURS: USA caps.
OTHER CLUBS: Tampa Bay Rowdies;
Swindon Town *on loan* 87/8 (7, 1); Luton Town 88/9-89/90 (45, 10); Queens Park Rangers 89/90-91/2 (75, 29); Blackburn Rovers 91/2-92/3 (34, 6); Coventry City 92/3- (6, 0).

1986/87-1987/88

MICK HAZARD

Mick Hazard was something of an anachronism in modern English football: a cultured midfield general who relied upon his audacious skills to justify his selection. He would do his best to 'close down' opponents and win the ball, but he was often a helpless civilian in the war of attrition which has come to dominate the middle of the pitch in so many matches. That didn't worry the purists among Chelsea's supporters, however, who appreciated that one moment of magic from the little maestro might be enough to win a game. Hazard could create space for himself with such ease that his lack of pace was seldom a handicap, and his thoughtful distribution was capable of prising open even the most securely locked defence, the beautifully disguised pass which presented Kevin Wilson with his second goal at White Hart Lane in September 1989 typifying his subtlety.

Mick's arrival at Stamford Bridge in September 1985 from Tottenham appeared to indicate that John Hollins intended to modify the direct style that had brought the Blues such success over the previous two seasons in favour of a more considered build-up, yet during his four and a half years with the club Hazard was never certain of a place in the starting line-up. This was partly because he rarely received the steady supply of possession he needed to thrive, but it must be admitted that he was apt to disappear from the game for long periods, seemingly unable to get involved. He was often at his most effective as a substitute, and hardly ever stamped his authority on a game for the full 90 minutes.

Hazard made just four appearances during the Blues' irresistible surge to the Second Division title in 1988/89, but seemed to be back in favour the following autumn. However, he had been unsettled for some time and, having been consigned to the reserves once more following the crashing defeats by Wimbledon and Queens Park Rangers that put an end to any thoughts of a serious challenge for the Championship by Bobby Campbell's men, he decided to try his luck with Second Division Portsmouth.

BORN: Sunderland, 5.2.60.
GAMES: 94 (9). GOALS: 12.
HONOURS: Full Members' Cup 85/6.
OTHER CLUBS: Tottenham Hotspur 79/80-85/6 (91, 13);
Portsmouth 89/90 (8, 1);
Swindon Town 90/1- (110, 17).

1985/86-1989/90

CLIVE WILSON

When he was running at defences, Clive Wilson looked irresistible. Nimble and well balanced, he was blessed with pace and the sort of tantalising ball skills that put a smile on the faces of the fans, but all too often he would take the easy option and pass the responsibility for opening a way to goal to a colleague. It was partly a question of tactics, no doubt. Clive was generally employed on the left of midfield and was not free to push forward without heed of the consequences, but his stay at Stamford Bridge would surely have proved more rewarding had he placed greater faith in his exceptional natural talent.

Wilson was signed from Manchester City in March 1987 but it was agreed that he would remain at Maine Road on loan for the rest of the season to help City's unavailing battle against relegation. He made a bright start to his Chelsea career, his cool head and thoughtful distribution attracting favourable comment, but before long the Blues were sliding down the table with gathering momentum and by mid-January Clive had been consigned to the substitute's bench.

Equally at home in the centre of midfield, Wilson was nothing if not versatile. Many of his appearances for his previous club had been at left-back, and when Tony Dorigo was sidelined at the start of the following campaign the cheerful Mancunian was the obvious deputy. His assured, enterprising performances suggested that he would benefit from a permanent switch to the number three shirt, but with Dorigo fit again he had to resume his frustrating fight for a place in midfield. Consistency remained elusive and he played only a supporting role in the Blues' march to the Second Division Championship.

Clive started just a dozen League games in 1989/90, but a vibrant display when he came on as a substitute at Loftus Road in December provided a reminder of his ability to terrorise defences when in the mood. Although he remained a valuable member of Bobby Campbell's squad, he wanted regular first-team football and in the summer, resisting attempts to persuade him to sign a new contract, he joined Queens Park Rangers for £450,000.

BORN: Manchester, 13.11.61.
GAMES: 85 (18). GOALS: 5.
HONOURS: Second Division Championship 88/9; Full Members' Cup 89/90.
OTHER CLUBS: Manchester City 81/2-86/7 (109, 9);
Chester City *on loan* 82/3 (21, 2);
Queens Park Rangers 90/1- (94, 7).

1987/88-1989/90

KEVIN WILSON

Kevin Wilson was a busy, industrious striker with neat control and a sharp eye for a half-chance, but even his greatest admirers would have to concede that he lacked the explosive virtuosity of Gordon Durie, his rival for a place alongside Kerry Dixon in the Blues' attack. As a result, for most of his stay at Stamford Bridge the Northern Ireland international was cast in a supporting role, moving to centre-stage only when one of the big-name stars was indisposed.

A £335,000 signing from Ipswich in June 1987, Kevin started his Chelsea career on the substitute's bench and Christmas was looming by the time he had scored his first goal for his new club. His confidence had gradually leaked away and for a time it seemed that even the basic skills were beyond his desperate grasp, but the following season he was to make an influential contribution to the Blues' irresistible assault on the Second Division Championship. Once Dixon and Durie had renewed their injury-blighted partnership in attack, Wilson was switched to midfield and his eager foraging, initially on the right flank, then on the left, helped ensure that his better-known colleagues were supplied with a steady flow of chances.

The Scot's absence for much of 1989/90 allowed Wilson to renew his credentials as a striker. The first of his two goals in a splendid 4-1 win at White Hart Lane confirmed his opportunism, the second the coolness of his finishing, but it was his deft touch and the composure with which he linked with the players around him that really caught the eye. With Durie restored to full vigour 'Willo' reverted to midfield, but the opening weeks of the following season presented another opportunity to try his luck up front and he responded in style, with five goals in eight outings.

Thereafter Wilson dropped out of the reckoning but his rival's departure in the summer of 1991 presented him with the chance to earn a secure first-team place that he had been waiting for for so long. When he failed to deliver the goods Ian Porterfield turned to Clive Allen, and on transfer deadline day Kevin joined Notts County to boost their fight against relegation.

BORN: Banbury, 18.4.61.
GAMES: 155 (36). GOALS: 55.
HONOURS: Second Division Championship 88/9; Full Members' Cup 89/90.
31 Northern Ireland caps (87-93)
OTHER CLUBS: Derby County 79/80-84/5 (122, 30);
Ipswich Town 84/5-86/7 (98, 34);
Notts County 91/2- (40, 2).

1987/88-1991/92

STEVE CLARKE

When he is on song, Steve Clarke is probably the most exciting right-back in the country. However, partly as a result of an unfortunate sequence of injuries, the Scottish international has failed to produce his best form with the consistency expected of a player of such abundant ability.

Steve moved to Stamford Bridge from St Mirren in January 1987 and it was immediately apparent that John Hollins had signed a player of genuine class. The 23-year-old lost no time in taking possession of the number two shirt and his performances during the Blues' inept drift towards relegation the following season were sufficiently impressive to win him five full caps, although, somewhat mysteriously, he has been overlooked since.

Quick and aggressive, Clarke is a sound defender with a biting tackle, but it is his rampaging bursts down the right flank that mark him out as a man to watch. All too often the opening he has carved is squandered by a hasty final pass or a shot dragged wide of the target, but the sight of the tall, lithe full-back exchanging passes with a team-mate and racing into the penalty box is guaranteed to bring Stamford Bridge to its feet. During the Blues' imperious conquest of the Second Division Championship, Clarke was able to give free rein to his attacking instincts, and he maintained that form the following season, a brilliantly worked goal at White Hart Lane crowning a satisfying team performance, but there were clouds on the horizon.

A back injury sustained during training with the Scottish squad in preparation for the World Cup cost Steve his place in the Chelsea team – and in Italy. Dismayed by the frustration of his international ambitions, he asked for a transfer but after nine months on the list he agreed to put the past behind him. The arrival of Ian Porterfield in the summer of 1991 gave Clarke a chance to make a new start and he responded with the best football of his career, only for a groin injury to sideline him for two months. Further fitness problems hampered him in 1992/93, but he was recalled to the first team by David Webb in March and quickly confirmed that his ability remained undimmed.

BORN: Saltcoats, 29.8.63.
GAMES: 215 (4). GOALS: 9.
HONOURS: Second Division Championship 88/9.
5 Scotland caps (87-88).
OTHER CLUBS: St Mirren.

1986/87-

DAVID LEE

If David Lee were playing his football on the Continent, he would be employed as a creative centre-back, a sweeper in the tradition of Franz Beckenbauer and Ronald Koeman who is expected to bring the ball out of defence and initiate attacks. It is a role he is equipped to perform with distinction and he would surely be hailed as a young defender of rare promise. In Britain, however, the idea of a spare man at the back has never really caught on and few managers are interested in a measured build-up. As a result, Lee's ability has been shamefully under-utilised.

When the gangling Bristolian was introduced to senior football during the Blues' relentless drive to the Second Division Championship in 1988/89 his efforts were notable more for their enthusiasm than their elegance, although he showed a happy knack for scoring important goals, but he started the following season alongside Graham Roberts and Ken Monkou in the middle of a five-man defence and his assured displays were soon earning rave reviews. Revelling in the freedom to get forward the system allowed him, David displayed remarkable confidence, picking his way around opponents with a deftness that seemed at odds with his somewhat ungainly appearance, but shortly before Christmas the bubble burst and he spent the second half of the campaign on the bench.

Lee spent nearly two years in the wilderness, attempting to revive his fading career with spells on loan at Reading and Plymouth, but when Paul Elliott was sidelined in September 1992 'Rodney' seized his chance in splendid style, establishing a well-balanced partnership with Frank Sinclair that provided a solid foundation for the Blues' rise up the table. Largely as a result of the tall defender's cultured promptings, Chelsea started to play with a fluency they had not shown for some time, but once again the honeymoon was over all too soon. Following a disastrous sequence of results, David Webb was called in to replace Ian Porterfield and, with the emphasis switching from freewheeling creativity to watertight defence, Lee seemed to have little future at Stamford Bridge.

BORN: Kingswood, 26.11.69.
GAMES: 95 (28). GOALS: 10.
HONOURS: Second Division Championship 88/9; Full Members' Cup 89/90.
OTHER CLUBS: Reading *on loan* 91/2 (5, 5);
Plymouth Argyle *on loan* 91/2 (9, 1).

1988/89-

GRAHAM ROBERTS

Graham Roberts was 29 when he joined Chelsea from Glasgow Rangers in August 1988, but his greying hair, rugged features and aura of total self-assurance gave him the air of a battle-hardened veteran who did not expect to be unduly troubled by the callow conscripts facing him. Bobby Campbell signed him in the hope that, together with Peter Nicholas, who had arrived from Aberdeen five days earlier, he would give the Blues the resilience and aggression that would be required if they were to gain promotion at the first attempt, and the £475,000 transfer fee proved to be money well spent.

'Robbo' was a born leader and it seemed natural that he should assume both the captaincy and the ticklish role of penalty-taker, a task he performed with such aplomb that 12 of his 15 League goals came from the spot. He didn't miss a game during Chelsea's record-breaking march to the Second Division Championship, imperiously conducting operations from his position at centre-back, and if his progress around the pitch was decidedly stately, his reading of the game was so good that he was rarely inconvenienced. The former England international's tackling was ferocious and he seemed to relish his 'hard man' image, putting the eager young heroes who tried to fluster him in their place with disdain.

Roberts was joined by David Lee and Ken Monkou in a three-man central defensive unit the following season and at first the new tactics worked splendidly, the Blues leading the table after 13 matches. But then Campbell's assistant, Ian Porterfield, moved to Reading, Roberts joined the coaching staff and suddenly huge holes started appearing at the back, although the relationship between these three circumstances is uncertain. Within a few weeks Graham had resigned his new post and requested a transfer. He remained with the club until November 1990, when he joined West Bromwich Albion, but did not play in the first team again, to the dismay of the fans who had seen him as the symbol of a new beginning.

BORN: Southampton, 3.7.59.
GAMES: 83. GOALS: 22.
HONOURS: Second Division Championship 88/9.
6 England caps (83-84).
OTHER CLUBS: Portsmouth (0, 0);
Tottenham Hotspur 80/1-86/7 (209, 23);
Glasgow Rangers; West Bromwich Albion 90/1-91/2 (39, 6).

1988/89-1989/90

TONY DORIGO

Inevitably there were those stern critics who preferred to dwell on Tony Dorigo's shortcomings. Lamenting the continuing porosity of the Blues' rearguard, they maintained that the stylish left-back was not a sound defender; he lacked aggression, and his fondness for attack meant that his true responsibilities were sometimes neglected. However, such mean-spirited criticism was not typical. Most Chelsea fans were only too well aware that they were enjoying a rare privilege: the sight of a player out of the very top drawer wearing a blue shirt.

Dorigo had an unusual background, to say the least. An Australian who retained a rich Antipodean accent that would have seemed more natural at Lord's or the Oval, he had travelled to England as a teenager to build a career with Aston Villa, the only club which had deigned to reply to his letter asking for a trial. When Villa were relegated at the end of 1986/87, the ambitious youngster decided to move on, joining Chelsea in a £475,000 deal, but his first season at Stamford Bridge was to prove no less disappointing.

Tony lost no time in demonstrating his class. He possessed electrifying pace that enabled him to win the ball with the delicacy of a pickpocket when others might have had to rely on smash and grab tactics, and his cultured partnership with Steve Clarke seemed certain to banish memories of the Blues' perennial weakness at full-back. Dorigo was occasionally caught out of position – generally after one of his thrilling forays upfield had come to nought – but, like a Grand Prix car slicing through the rush-hour traffic, he was usually able to overhaul his hapless opponent and dispossess him. The 22-year-old's immaculate performances caught the imagination of the Stamford Bridge crowd and he was voted the fans' Player of the Year, but it was a season when little went right for Chelsea and once again he was faced with the unattractive prospect of Second Division football.

A groin injury prevented Dorigo from earning his first full England cap during the European Championships that summer and caused him to miss the start of the new season, but of greater concern to the Chelsea management was his desire to leave Stamford Bridge in order to safeguard his international prospects. Tony made three written transfer requests but Bobby Campbell was adamant that he would not be allowed to go, and in April Dorigo announced that he was prepared to honour his four-year contract. By that time the Blues were on the threshold of the First Division, and the polished defender had played a starring role in their triumph.

Tony was simply majestic when he was coming forward with the ball, his speed and close control taking him past defenders with apparent ease. He produced a steady stream of inviting crosses from the left flank and scored a number of important goals, none better than a superb individual effort against Manchester City at Maine Road in March 1989 when he collected the ball in his own half and raced into the City penalty area before rounding the 'keeper and stroking it home. He was also a master of the flighted free-kick, as he demonstrated with the superbly placed strike that won the ZDS Cup final against Middlesbrough at Wembley in 1990.

Stuart Pearce's consistency meant that Dorigo's international ambitions remained largely unfulfilled but he finally won his first full cap in December 1989 and deputised for the Nottingham Forest stalwart when England met Italy to decide third place in the 1990 World Cup. However, during the course of the following season it gradually became clear that, despite Chelsea's efforts to keep him at the Bridge, he would not be staying when his contract expired in the summer. He eventually opted for Leeds United, a transfer tribunal setting the fee at £1.3 million. No amount of cash could adequately compensate the Blues for the loss of a player of Dorigo's quality, and the fans' gloom was intensified when their former favourite helped the Yorkshire club to the Championship.

BORN: Melbourne, Australia, 31.12.65.
GAMES: 180. GOALS: 12.
HONOURS: Second Division Championship 88/9; Full Members' Cup 89/90.
11 England caps (89-93).
OTHER CLUBS: Aston Villa 83/4-86/7 (111, 1); Leeds United 91/2- (71, 4).

1987/88-1990/91

KEN MONKOU

Few Continental players have adapted to the special demands of English football more effectively than Ken Monkou. The tall Dutchman was quick to appreciate that the enterprising style that immediately endeared him to the Stamford Bridge crowd was less likely to find favour with the coaching staff nursing their anxiety on the touchline, and he tightened up his natural game to emerge as one of the most dependable central defenders in the country.

Signed from Feyenoord for the bargain-basement fee of £100,000 in March 1989, Monkou was given time to settle into his new surroundings and when he made his full debut at the start of the following season it was in a five-man defence that had apparently been devised to give free rein to his creative abilities. With Graham Roberts and David Lee available to cover him, Ken was given a licence to drive forward in search of an opening and his slightly ungainly, long-legged forays soon had the terraces roaring with approval. For a while the Blues were riding high in the table, but this glimpse of foreign exoticism – a flash of rich colour amid the West London grime – was not destined to last.

In the new year Ken settled down to form a steady partnership with Erland Johnsen in a conventional back four and now it was his defensive abilities that caught the eye. Tall and athletic, he was exceptional in the air and his tackling had bite and authority. He became the first black player to be voted the fans' Player of the Year and the following season the combination of Dutch panache with the homely virtues of Wimbledon-born Jason Cundy gave the Blues' rearguard a reassuringly solid look, Monkou's inspirational display against Manchester United at Stamford Bridge typifying his commanding form.

The arrival of Paul Elliott increased the competition for places in 1991/92 and after a few shaky performances – notably a nightmare against Everton – Ken was the odd man out. An attempt to use him at left-back proved unsuccessful and in August 1992 the popular Dutchman moved on to Southampton in search of a fresh challenge.

BORN: Necare, Surinam, 29.11.64.
GAMES: 117 (2). GOALS: 2.
HONOURS: Full Members' Cup 89/90.
OTHER CLUBS: Feyenoord;
Southampton 92/3- (33, 1).

1988/89-1991/92

KEVIN McALLISTER

An old-fashioned winger who looked truly comfortable only when the ball was at his feet and he could run at his full-back, Kevin McAllister made valiant efforts to conform to the mould imposed by modern football. Scurrying up and down the right flank like an eager schoolboy, the tiny Scot strove courageously to involve himself in the frantic midfield battle but most of the time he found himself excluded from the action, almost as if the bigger boys had refused to let him join in their game.

Signed from Falkirk by John Neal shortly before he handed over the reins to John Hollins, Kevin spent his first three seasons at Stamford Bridge in the shadow of Pat Nevin, and his first-team opportunities were frustratingly limited. He played in the Full Members' Cup final at Wembley in March 1986, but that seemed likely to be the highlight of his Chelsea career when he started the 1987/88 season on a weekly contract and ended it back at Falkirk on loan.

However, the departure of Nevin that summer presented McAllister with an open door and, after some initial hesitation, he strode through it, earning a regular place in the side that swept irresistibly to the Second Division Championship. Kevin may have lacked his compatriot's extensive repertoire of ball skills and exceptional vision, but his persistence and spirit made him quite a handful, as he showed against Hull when he surged outside two defenders before sending over a high centre which was despatched with relish by Kerry Dixon.

However, McAllister's evident enthusiasm sometimes resulted in over-excitement, to the detriment of his finishing and final ball into the box, and he found himself back on the substitute's bench in the first half of the following season. He regained his place at Christmas, but rarely made much impression on the well-organised defences he faced in the First Division and spent long spells ineffectually chasing shadows. His confidence visibly fading, Kevin made only a handful of appearances in 1990/91 and returned to Falkirk that summer for a fee of £225,000.

BORN: Falkirk, 8.11.62.
GAMES: 101 (39). GOALS: 13.
HONOURS: Second Division Championship 88/9;
Full Members' Cup 85/6, 89/90.
OTHER CLUBS: Falkirk (twice); Falkirk *on loan*.

1985/86-1990/91

ROGER FREESTONE

It takes time for a goalkeeper to ripen to full maturity. Roger Freestone was thrown into battle before he was ready to meet the challenge and his career has suffered as a result.

Signed from Newport County for £90,000 in March 1987, the young Welshman played in the last few games of the season after injury had sidelined Tony Godden and found himself promoted to first-choice when Eddie Niedzwiecki was confined to the treatment room by a recurrence of his knee injury the following autumn. A strapping six-footer, Freestone displayed superb reactions and impressive agility, but he was rather less convincing when the ball was crossed into the penalty area and his positioning occasionally revealed his inexperience. His recall coincided with a disastrous slump in the Blues' form, and after he had made 15 League appearances behind a wobbling defence without collecting a single win bonus, John Hollins turned in desperation to Perry Digweed.

New signing Kevin Hitchcock's fitness problems gave Freestone another chance in 1988/89, but his confidence had taken a battering and he rarely looked assured or commanding. Although Chelsea were enjoying an impressive unbeaten run, Bobby Campbell decided to recruit Dave Beasant in January and Freestone found himself out in the cold, eventually moving to Swansea City in September 1991.

BORN: Caerleon, 19.8.68. GAMES: 53. GOALS: 0.
HONOURS: Second Division Championship 88/9.
OTHER CLUBS: Newport County 86/7 (13, 0);
Swansea City *on loan* 89/90 (14, 0); Hereford United *on loan* 89/90 (8, 0); Swansea City 91/2- (88, 0).

1986/87-1988/89

JASON CUNDY

During his two seasons in the Chelsea first team Jason Cundy became a firm favourite with the Stamford Bridge crowd and the club's decision to sell him to Tottenham prompted a wave of angry protests. The burly centre-back was not a player of great delicacy or refinement but he threw himself into every tackle with undisguised relish, and it was this air of playing for the hell of it, as if he were a Sunday morning footballer testing his mettle with his mates, that made him so popular.

Jason was not far short of his 21st birthday when he was finally given his League debut in September 1990, but he soon made up for lost time, earning a regular place alongside Ken Monkou in the second half of the season. He was still a bit raw and clumsy-looking, but he had a physique that brooked no argument and covered the ground with impressive speed for such a big man. A defiant performance in the Rumbelows Cup quarter-final replay confirmed that Cundy was developing into a defender to be respected, but a series of frustrating injuries prevented him from maintaining his progress the following autumn. Fit once more, he regained his place in the new year and his partnership with Paul Elliott was a key factor in the Blues' dogged progress to the quarter-final of the FA Cup, but when defeat at Roker Park effectively ended Chelsea's season Ian Porterfield decided to make changes to his squad, and on transfer deadline day Cundy moved to Spurs on loan in anticipation of the completion of an £800,000 deal in the summer.

BORN: Tooting, 12.11.69. GAMES: 56 (1). GOALS: 2.
OTHER CLUBS: Tottenham Hotspur 91/2- (25, 1).

1990/91-1991/92

PETER NICHOLAS

When Peter Nicholas moved on to Watford in March 1991, he could look back with considerable satisfaction on the job he had done for Chelsea during his two and a half years at Stamford Bridge. The experienced midfielder had arrived from Aberdeen on the eve of the 1988/89 season and, together with Graham Roberts, the other seasoned campaigner recruited from Scottish football by Bobby Campbell to give the side extra bite and composure, had steered the Blues to the Second Division title by a comfortable margin.

A highly encouraging start to the following campaign suggested that the Welsh international's robust pragmatism would prove equally effective among football's aristocracy, but he was never really accepted by the fans, who grudgingly acknowledged the value of his professionalism but reserved their affection for players with rather more verve and dash. Although 'Nicho' was primarily a ball-winner, he was capable of producing passes of exquisite delicacy, such as the perfectly weighted through-ball that presented Kevin McAllister with a goal in a 4-0 win against Sheffield Wednesday in August, and his flighted corners created a number of goalscoring opportunities. Unfortunately, a lack of mobility hampered his efforts and his distribution was sometimes frustratingly wayward, failings that made him the target of the spiteful jeers of a section of the crowd.

Resolute and courageous, Peter succeeded Graham Roberts as captain and became only the second Chelsea skipper to lift a trophy at Wembley in peacetime when Middlesbrough were defeated in the Full Members' Cup final in March 1990. However, when Campbell decided to give youth its chance at Old Trafford the following autumn it was clear that, at the age of 31, Nicholas had no place in his long-term plans and, his task complete, the former Crystal Palace star made the journey to Vicarage Road to help the Hornets in their fight against relegation. However, little more than a year later he was back at Stamford Bridge, having been given the crucial role of supervising the development of Chelsea's youngsters.

BORN: Newport, 10.11.59.
GAMES: 92 (1). GOALS: 2.
HONOURS: Second Division Championship 88/9; Full Members' Cup 89/90.
73 Wales caps (79-91).
OTHER CLUBS: Crystal Palace 77/8-80/1 (127, 7) and 83/4-84/5 (47, 7);
Arsenal 80/1-82/3 (60, 1); Luton Town 84/5-86/7 (102, 1);
Aberdeen; Watford 90/1-91/2 (40, 1).

1988/89-1990/91

ALAN DICKENS

If ever confirmation were needed that in modern football simple ability is no guarantee of success, it is provided by the dizzying plunge in the fortunes of Alan Dickens during his four seasons at Stamford Bridge. A cultured midfielder whose forte was the acutely angled through-ball, he was signed from newly relegated West Ham in August 1989 to add some guile to a side which had taken a fairly direct route to the Second Division title. A transfer tribunal set the fee at £635,000, the second-highest Chelsea had ever paid, but the move to West London seemed to rob him of the poise and assurance that had distinguished his performances for the Hammers.

With the Blues riding high in the table, Alan held his place until mid-December, even though he often found himself a spectator as the action swirled frantically around him, but after three heavy defeats he was out. He languished on the fringes of the first team for more than a year, but his professionalism and loyalty remained irreproachable and when he was finally recalled he battled away with the grim determination of a man aware that he belonged to a species facing extinction. However, Dickens never seemed to have the space he needed to exploit his unquestioned skill, largely because he lacked acceleration, and the arrival of Vinnie Jones early the following season marked the end of his chances at the Bridge. After another year in the shadows Alan was given a free transfer, joining Brentford in February 1993.

BORN: Plaistow, 3.9.64.
GAMES: 46 (9). GOALS: 4.
OTHER CLUBS: West Ham United 82/3-88/9 (192, 23);
West Bromwich Albion *on loan* 92/3 (3, 1);
Brentford 92/3 (15, 1).

1989/90-1991/92

ERLAND JOHNSEN

David Webb's return to Stamford Bridge appears to have revived Erland Johnsen's moribund Chelsea career. The big Norwegian international is a strong, resolute defender with an ice-cold temperament that has served him well in the hurly-burly of the English game. Although he looks polished in possession, this Viking has no taste for adventure; he is content to win the ball and clear it without taking any silly risks. Anxious to tighten up the Blues' defence, the new manager evidently found this somewhat dour pragmatism appealing, for he restored Johnsen to the first team and the Scandinavian's dependable form played a significant part in a welcome late-season recovery.

Erland joined the Blues from Bayern Munich in December 1989 and his assured performances in the new year suggested that he had had little difficulty adjusting to the pace of English football, the 22-year-old forging a central defensive partnership with Ken Monkou that helped the Blues clinch fifth place in the First Division. However, he lost his place at the start of the following season and by the time he had recovered from a broken wrist he found it impossible to dislodge Jason Cundy. When an outstanding display at White Hart Lane in August 1991 proved insufficient to earn him an extended run in the side, Johnsen understandably concluded that he had no future with Chelsea, but he remained at Stamford Bridge, making occasional appearances as an understudy, until, at last, a manager arrived who wanted what he had to offer.

BORN: Frederikstad, Norway, 5.4.67.
GAMES: 51 (1). GOALS: 0.
HONOURS: Full Members' Cup 89/90. 18 Norway caps.
OTHER CLUBS: Moss FK, Norway; Bayern Munich.

1989/90-

DAVE BEASANT

A goalkeeper's mistakes are almost always costly and there is little he can do to redeem himself: perfection is included in the job description. When the assured form that had earned Dave Beasant international recognition deserted him, he found himself in a downward spiral from which there appears to be no escape.

Beasant joined the Blues from Newcastle in January 1989 for £725,000 – a club record – to reinforce a promotion drive that had already built up seemingly irresistible momentum. Famed for his habit of dribbling out of his penalty area before launching a thunderous kick down the field, Dave could not be truthfully described as a stylist, his goalkeeping resembling the unruly mop of hair that crowned his mighty frame, but the courage with which he would dive in among the flailing boots to retrieve a ball he had only parried at the first attempt could not be faulted. For a year or so he made a valuable contribution to the Blues' success, pulling off a number of match-winning saves with spectacular agility, but then the goals started to flow, his confidence leaked away and the muttering began.

A cracked bone in a finger ended an uninterrupted run of senior appearances stretching back nine years in the autumn of 1990, and the following season a series of niggling injuries allowed Kevin Hitchcock to mount a serious challenge for the goalkeeper's jersey. Dave's increasingly erratic performances drew mounting hostility from the unsympathetic Stamford Bridge crowd, and when he gifted Norwich victory in September 1992 Ian Porterfield made it clear that the big goalkeeper would have to find himself alternative employment. Beasant had spells on loan at Grimsby and Wolves, but ironically it was to be the manager who departed and not the player he had castigated.

When David Webb took over he promptly decided that he wanted the former Wimbledon stalwart back in the first team, and an amazing reversal of fortunes was complete. Beasant repaid the new manager's faith with a number of valiant displays but rarely looked entirely at ease and before the season was out he had been displaced by Dimitri Kharin.

BORN: Willesden, 20.3.59.
GAMES: 157. GOALS: 0.
HONOURS: Second Division Championship 88/9; Full Members' Cup 89/90. 2 England caps (89).
OTHER CLUBS: Wimbledon 79/80-87/8 (340, 0);
Newcastle United 88/9 (20, 0); Grimsby Town *on loan* 92/3 (6, 0);
Wolverhampton Wanderers *on loan* 92/3 (4, 0).

1988/89-

VINNIE JONES

There was the Vinnie Jones of popular legend: the tattooed, shaven-headed monster created by the sensation-hungry press, a wild, vicious degenerate who revelled in violence and regarded a football match as an opportunity to settle old scores and open some new ones; and then there was the Vinnie that the Stamford Bridge crowd came to adore: a strong, aggressive midfielder with more talent than his critics were prepared to admit who always gave the punters their money's worth.

From the moment he completed his £575,000 transfer from Sheffield United in August 1991 it was clear that Vinnie's drive and competitiveness would have a significant role to play in Ian Porterfield's rebuilding plans. Exhorting his colleagues to greater efforts with a clenched fist, offering advice and encouragement to his younger team-mates, his influence on the pitch was invaluable and he struck up an immediate rapport with the fans, who warmed to his cheerful defiance and refusal to concede a thing.

Tall and muscular, the former hod-carrier was a formidable tackler and his forbidding presence in front of the back four gave Andy Townsend the freedom to get forward and threaten defences. Vinnie's uncompromising lunges were occasionally a source of embarrassment to his more faint-hearted admirers, and his abrasive style inevitably reaped a harvest of bookings. His absence from the FA Cup quarter-final against Sunderland through suspension was to prove costly, but it would be wrong to lose sight of his creative contribution, since to the surprise of many he turned out to be a more than capable passer of the ball.

Vinnie's height posed a threat at every set piece and his long throws produced a string of goalscoring opportunities, but his best all-round performance came at Anfield in February when his thunderous 25-yard volley helped the Blues to a memorable triumph. Jones could not truthfully be described as an elegant or subtle player but he was undeniably effective, and it was therefore a considerable surprise when he was transferred to Wimbledon the following September, Porterfield apparently feeling that Nigel Spackman could perform the same role with rather more finesse.

BORN: Watford, 5.1.65.
GAMES: 52. GOALS: 7.
OTHER CLUBS: Wimbledon 86/7-88/9 (77, 9) and 92/3- (27, 1);
Leeds United 89/90-90/1 (46, 5);
Sheffield United 90/1-91/2 (35, 2).

1991/92-1992/93

PAUL ELLIOTT

Ian Porterfield's efforts to build a Chelsea side capable of challenging for honours suffered a savage blow when Paul Elliott was carried from the pitch at Anfield in September 1992 following a sickening collision with Liverpool's Dean Saunders. The towering centre-half had suffered severe damage to the ligaments of his right knee that would sideline him for the rest of the campaign and cast a shadow over his career, and his commanding presence was to be sorely missed as the Blues endured another frustrating season.

Chelsea had been trailing Paul for some time when they finally clinched the £1.4 million deal with Celtic that brought him back to London in July 1991, and it was soon apparent that he would lend poise and authority to a defence that had been woefully inconsistent for too long. His height, imposing physique and impressive athleticism enabled him to dominate the penalty area and he was quite superb in the air, attacking the ball with confidence and aggression.

Cool under pressure, Elliott's tackling was crisp and decisive, and his performance against Sheffield United in the FA Cup was nothing less than heroic as he dealt calmly with everything the Yorkshiremen could throw at him. His measured distribution reflected the experience he had gained during his time in Italy, where defenders are expected to be able to use the ball constructively, and he could be equally effective at the opposite end of the pitch, as he demonstrated on his Chelsea debut against Wimbledon, when he scored the Blues' first goal of the season with a thumping header from a Dennis Wise corner.

Resolute and defiant, the big defender was regularly to be seen encouraging his team-mates with a clenched fist, and he quickly became a firm favourite with the Stamford Bridge crowd. The following season he was joined in the middle of the back four by Mal Donaghy and it seemed that the Blues had a solid foundation on which to build a winning team, but then came the fateful clash at Anfield. A thoughtful, compassionate man, Paul faces a long fight to regain fitness, but it is a battle he has the courage and strength of character to win.

BORN: Lewisham, 18.3.64.
GAMES: 54. GOALS: 3.
OTHER CLUBS: Charlton Athletic 81/2-82/3 (63, 1);
Luton Town 82/3-85/6 (66, 4);
Aston Villa 85/6-86/7 (57, 7);
Pisa; Glasgow Celtic.

1991/92-

GARETH HALL

When he ran onto the pitch at Plough Lane to make his senior debut in May 1987, Gareth Hall's immediate ambition was clear: he wanted to be Chelsea's first-choice right-back; and to achieve that he would have to dislodge the man in possession, Steve Clarke. Six years later, little had changed. Managers had come and gone, and all the other faces in the dressing room were different; but Gareth was still battling to loosen the Scot's grip on the shirt they both coveted.

Inevitably, the intervening period has seen enough ups and downs – or rather ins and outs – to sustain a thrice-weekly soap opera, but it is a little hard to understand why the Stamford Bridge coaching staff should have experienced such apparent difficulty in choosing between the merits of the two candidates. Gareth is an eager, hard-working player who makes the fullest possible use of the modest gifts that have been bestowed upon him; a solid, reliable defender, he covers assiduously and throws himself into tackles with evident enthusiasm, but no one could honestly claim that he possesses Clarke's abundant class.

Following that first outing at Wimbledon, Hall made occasional appearances as an understudy in 1987/88 (his robust displays earning him a place in the Welsh team that faced Yugoslavia), but he produced his best performances in the play-off matches against Blackburn, when he was used as a midfield ball-winner and proved highly effective. Bafflingly, he was dropped for the decisive matches against Middlesbrough. He had a decent run at right-back the following season when Clarke was injured, but the real breakthrough came in February 1990 when he finally managed to secure a regular place in the side at his rival's expense. Gareth remained the first choice for much of the following campaign but Clarke was restored at the start of 1991/92 and Hall, understandably frustrated, asked for a move.

The Scot's injury problems gave Gareth the chance to fight back, and in 1992/93 he appeared to regain the upper hand, a dogged display at Everton typifying his splendid form. However, a suspension allowed Clarke to prove his pedigree once more, and their long-running battle for supremacy seems set to continue . . .

BORN: Croydon, 20.3.69.
GAMES: 133 (16). GOALS: 4.
HONOURS: Second Division Championship 88/9; Full Members' Cup 89/90.
9 Wales caps (88-92).

1986/87-

KEVIN HITCHCOCK

A series of disheartening setbacks have frustrated Kevin Hitchcock's efforts to secure a firm grasp on the goalkeeper's jersey since his arrival at Stamford Bridge, but every time he has been knocked down he has picked himself up from the canvas and made another attempt. However, as the 1992/93 season drew to a close, it seemed that the enthusiastic East Ender had finally been counted out.

Kevin was signed from Third Division Mansfield Town hours before the transfer deadline in March 1988 in a desperate bid to arrest the Blues' wretched slide towards the Second Division, and the 25-year-old's confidence immediately transmitted itself to a defence that had appeared to be on the verge of collapse. His assured handling and agility suggested a bright future but a catalogue of injuries prevented him from building on that promising start the following season, and the purchase of Dave Beasant meant that when he regained fitness Kevin found himself contesting a place in the reserves with Roger Freestone.

Hitchcock enjoyed a brief taste of first-team action when Beasant damaged a finger in the autumn of 1990, but shortly afterwards he joined Northampton on loan and it seemed that he was unlikely to remain a Chelsea player for long. However, the following season it was the former Wimbledon hero's turn to struggle for fitness and Kevin finally managed to re-establish himself as Chelsea's first-choice goalkeeper, a brilliant penalty save in the fourth round of the Cup against Everton erasing the memory of a schoolboy howler against Luton.

Beasant was recalled towards the end of the campaign but when the Stamford Bridge crowd finally lost patience with his fallibility the following autumn Hitchcock's position seemed unassailable. An exceptional shot-stopper but less secure when the ball was crossed into the box, Kevin proved his worth with a brilliant performance at Middlesbrough in December, but an unconvincing display at Blackburn two months later proved fatal to his prospects. New manager David Webb decided on a change and shortly afterwards Hitchcock moved to West Ham on loan, his hopes of making the grade at the Bridge in tatters.

BORN: Custom House, 5.10.62.
GAMES: 77. GOALS: 0.
OTHER CLUBS: Nottingham Forest (0, 0);
Mansfield Town 83/4-87/8 (182, 0);
Northampton Town *on loan* 90/1 (17, 0);
West Ham United *on loan* (0, 0).

1987/88-

FRANK SINCLAIR

If he maintains the spectacular progress he made in 1992/93, Frank Sinclair seems sure to develop into a centre-back of the highest class. Although he is not particularly tall, the young Londoner is seldom beaten in the air and his startling pace ensures that no forward can escape his clutches for long. Strong and very determined, he uses the ball thoughtfully and defends with the poise and authority of a battle-hardened veteran.

Frank had his first taste of senior football in April 1991, playing at left-back; his verve was readily apparent, but it was equally obvious that he would have been better employed on the other flank. A spell on loan at West Bromwich Albion the following season earned him brief notoriety when he allowed a difference of opinion with a referee to get out of hand and collected a nine-match suspension, but his form on his return to the Chelsea side at the end of the campaign created an altogether more favourable impression.

An ankle problem prevented Sinclair from pressing his claim at the start of the new season but, in the wake of the horrific injury which sidelined Paul Elliott, he was recalled at Maine Road to subdue David White, Manchester City's flying winger, and his assured performance was instrumental in a timely victory. He then switched to the middle of the back four alongside David Lee and cemented his place in the side with a series of masterly displays that bode well for the future.

BORN: Lambeth, 3.12.71.
GAMES: 52. GOALS: 2.
OTHER CLUBS: West Bromwich Albion *on loan* 91/2 (6, 1).

1990/91 -

ANDY MYERS

If it is true, as some cynical observers have suggested, that football in the nineties has become primarily a test of strength and speed, Andy Myers has little to fear. His bulging thighs and muscular neck suggest that he is not going to be knocked off the ball too often, and his powerful running is likely to trouble most defences. But there is more to Myers – a graduate of the FA School of Excellence – than simple physical prowess, for he possesses a generous measure of natural ability and a fierce desire to win that will serve him well.

Andy was still a month short of his 18th birthday when he was given his full debut against Liverpool in October 1991, playing on the left wing, but he emerged from a stern test with credit, marking the occasion with a goal. However, it was an outstanding performance at left-back against Southampton four months later that really launched his career. Filling in for the recently departed Tom Boyd, Myers contained Matthew Le Tissier with the aplomb of a veteran, but it was the eager teenager's spirited attacking that had the crowd cheering. He retained his place for the tense Cup-ties against Sheffield United and Sunderland, and looked set to make a concerted bid for the number three shirt at the start of 1992/93. A serious ankle injury frustrated his immediate ambitions, but there seems little doubt that this gifted youngster's time will come.

BORN: Isleworth, 3.11.73.
GAMES: 16 (6). GOALS: 1.

1990/91 -

GRAHAM STUART

Graham Stuart's magnificent goal at Hillsborough in August 1992 surely banished any lingering doubts about his talent. Collecting the ball in the left-back position, he ran half the length of the pitch, jinked his way past two bewildered defenders on the edge of the Sheffield Wednesday penalty area, then coolly slipped the ball past Chris Woods, evoking memories of Peter Osgood's brilliant dribble at Burnley more than a quarter of a century before. All that remains is for Stuart to produce that kind of match-winning virtuosity with rather more consistency.

Graham's ability to go past opponents is probably the strongest part of his game, and most of his first-team appearances have been made on the right wing. He is quick and well-balanced with good close control, but he has yet to master the art of delivering the ball accurately to the men in the middle and it may be that he would be more effective in a central striking role.

Having scored on his debut against Crystal Palace in April 1990, Graham was recalled to the side at Old Trafford the following November and missed only a handful of games thereafter, but the 20-year-old never had a shirt to call his own and was unable to settle down in one position. 'Bobby' (the nickname is a constant reminder that he is a graduate of the FA School of Excellence established during Bobby Robson's reign as England manager) was troubled for much of the season by what proved to be a stress fracture of the shin and he missed the first three months of the following campaign while the problem was sorted out. A splendid performance against Nottingham Forest in November demonstrated his potential as a striker but in the event the only goal he managed all season was a brilliant individual effort in the fifth round of the Cup against Sheffield United.

Fully fit once more, Graham earned a regular place in 1992/93 and as the season progressed it became clear that he was gradually coming to terms with the demands of League football. Increasingly influential, he saw a lot of the ball and scored a healthy ration of goals, but the feeling persists that we have yet to see the best of him.

BORN: Tooting, 24.10.70.
GAMES: 89 (21). GOALS: 18.

1989/90-

ANDY TOWNSEND

There are any number of players who can win the ball in midfield and deny their opponents space. A handful of them are capable of opening up a defence with a precisely weighted pass, but those who also have the mobility to drive forward and take a crack at goal are as rare as trustworthy politicians – which is sufficient to explain the high esteem in which Andy Townsend is held by his fellow-professionals.

Townsend joined the Blues in the summer of 1990, a transfer fee of £1.2 million having been agreed with Norwich City before he boosted his growing reputation with some stirring performances for the Republic of Ireland in the World Cup finals in Italy (he qualifies for Jack Charlton's cosmopolitan team through his grandmother). After a quiet start he enjoyed a splendid first season at Stamford Bridge, his tigerish tackling and powerful running making him a firm favourite with the fans, who voted him their Player of the Year.

A fierce competitor who still seems to enjoy his football as much as he did when he was playing as a part-timer with Welling United and Weymouth, Andy is an instinctive leader, constantly encouraging and advising the men around him. His infectious enthusiasm and bubbly personality have proved an invaluable influence in the dressing room, and when Peter Nicholas dropped out of the side it was natural that he should take over the captaincy. One criticism that could possibly be made is that Townsend appears to reserve his best performances for the big occasion, but it would be fairer to say that he responds to the passionate atmosphere generated by a large crowd.

When he is in the mood, Andy is capable of totally dominating the middle of the pitch. A real terrier who allows his adversary no peace, he covers a huge amount of ground during the course of a match and uses the ball with precision and imagination, although his right foot is by no means a match for his left. He also possesses a thunderous shot – which he makes too little use of – but the most exciting part of his game is his surging bursts towards goal, his strength carrying him past defenders who are seemingly powerless to stop him. Perhaps the greatest testimony to Townsend's ability is the way he totally overshadowed Paul Gascoigne in the Rumbelows Cup quarter-final replay at White Hart Lane in 1991, scoring the first goal when he ran onto a flick from Kerry Dixon then presenting the big striker with the second when his well-struck drive came back off a post.

Andy made a flying start to the following season, scoring five goals before the end of September, one of them a quite superb 30-yard screamer at Queens Park Rangers. The arrival of Vinnie Jones to stand guard in front of the defence gave him the freedom to press forward more often, but he was struggling with a groin injury and it eventually became impossible to delay surgery any longer. He was out of action for just five weeks – which says much for his determination – but never quite recaptured the fizz he had shown before the lay-off.

Townsend was back to his best in 1992/93, with a brilliant individual goal against Crystal Palace in the quarter-final of the Coca-Cola Cup adding weight to the extravagant claims that there is no more effective midfielder in Europe. However, it was not enough to win the tie and Andy's evident dismay was understandable. He clearly finds it intensely frustrating that, despite his immense personal contribution, he is not a member of a winning side, and there has been constant speculation that other clubs are keen to secure his services. Chelsea have declared that they have no intention of weakening their team by parting with such an influential player. Instead, their aim must be to help him fulfil his ambitions at Stamford Bridge.

BORN: Maidstone, 23.7.63.
GAMES: 138. GOALS: 19.
HONOURS: 36 Ireland caps.
OTHER CLUBS: Southampton 84/5-87/8 (83, 5);
Norwich City 88/9-89/90 (71, 8).

1990/91-

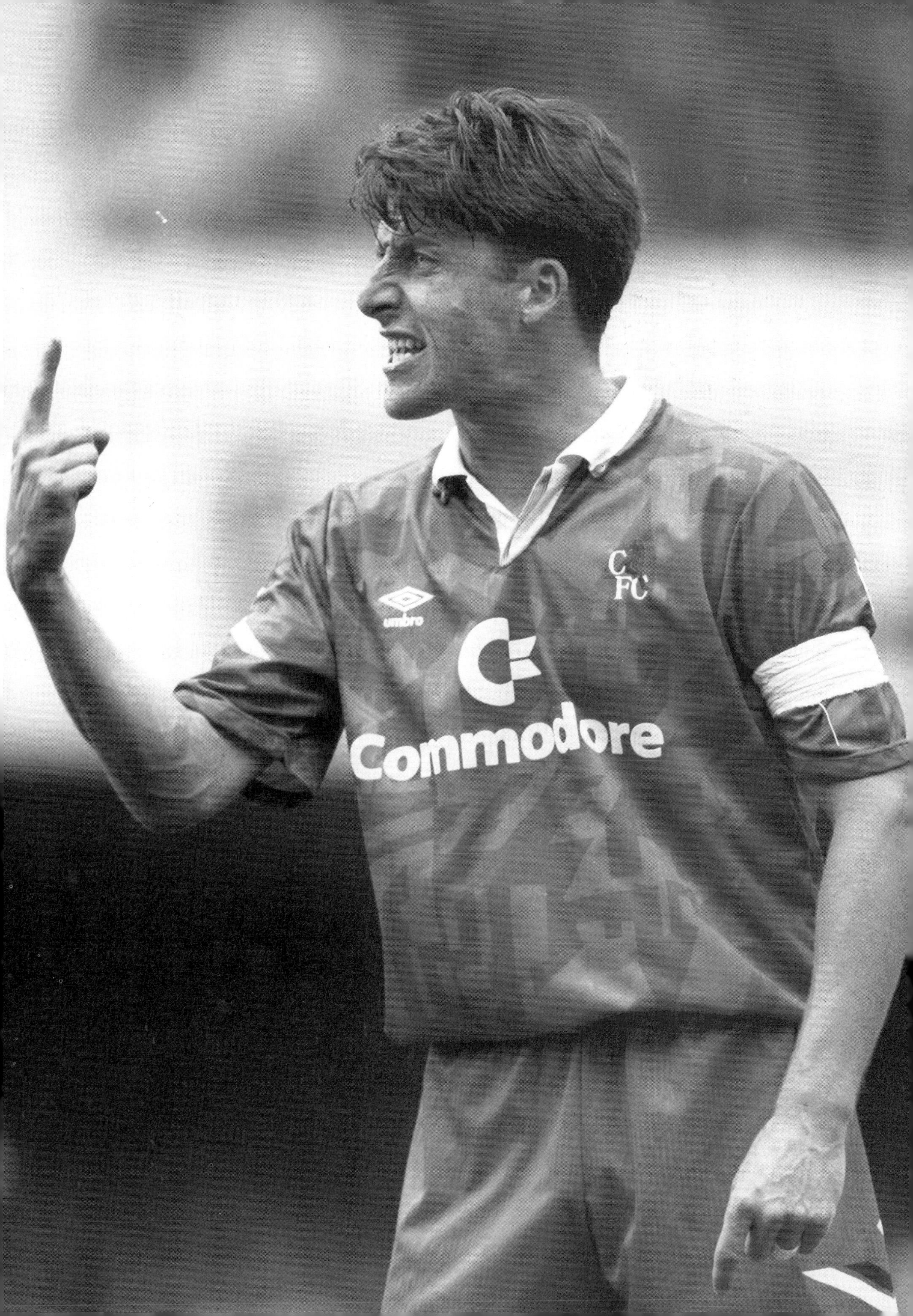

CFC
umbro
Commodore

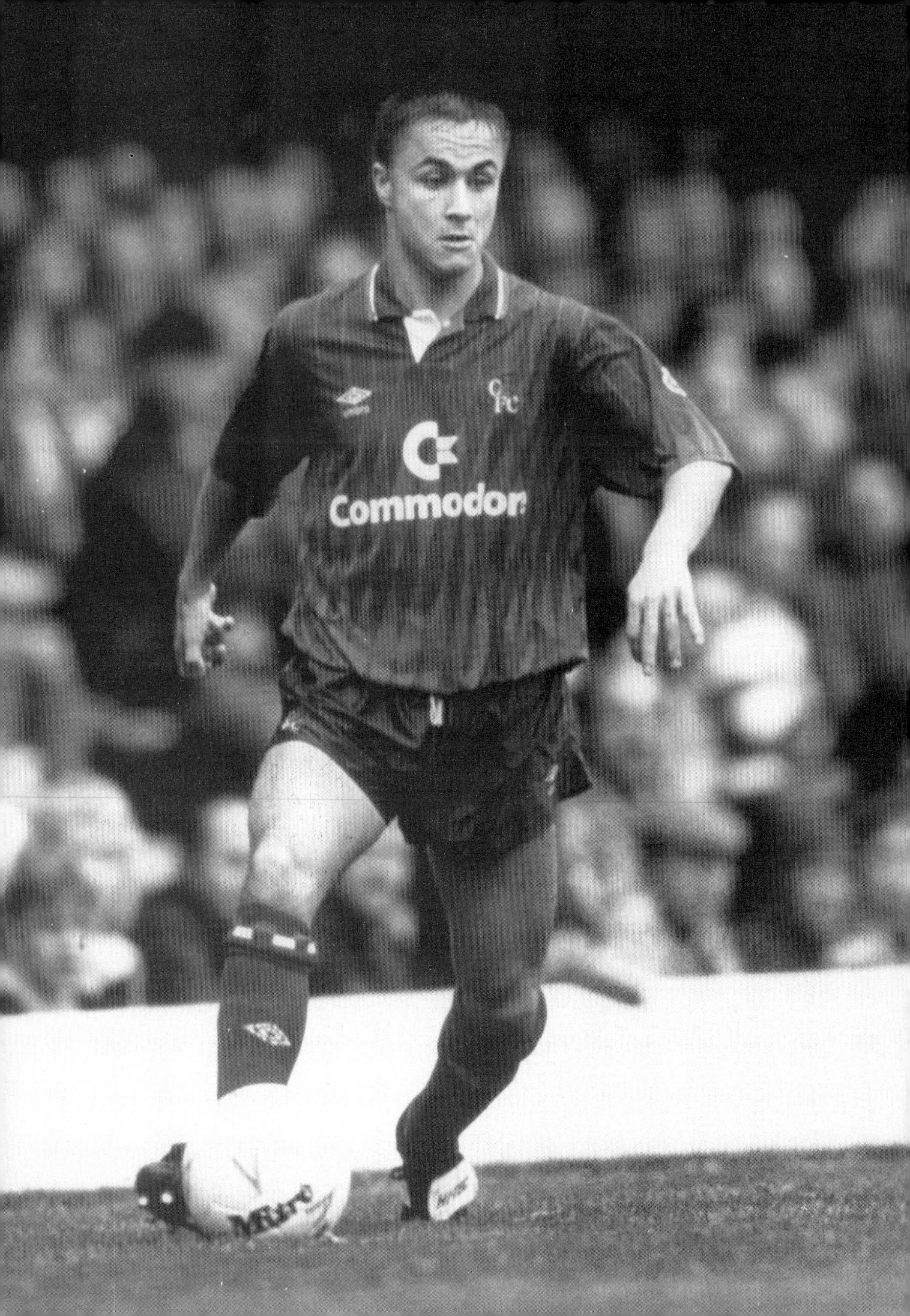
Commodore

DENNIS WISE

After three eventful seasons at Stamford Bridge, Dennis Wise now enjoys star billing. His teasing centres are the source of most of the Blues' goals and the feisty little winger is acknowledged as their most creative player, the one man capable of rescuing lost causes. However, his style is not especially eye-catching, and while his talent is beyond question his relationship with the Stamford Bridge crowd has not always been an easy one.

When Dennis was signed from Wimbledon in July 1990 – shortly after the transfer of Andy Townsend from Norwich had been agreed – it seemed that Chelsea were gearing up for a serious Championship challenge in the wake of their fifth-place finish the previous season. The £1.6 million fee was a club record and the spirited Londoner's influential display in the Dons' 5-2 win at the Bridge the previous December suggested that he would be a real asset.

An eager, cheerful character with the grin of a cheeky schoolboy, Dennis made a spectacular home debut on the opening day of the new campaign, teasing and tormenting the Derby defence before strong-arm tactics finally subdued him. It was an enormously impressive beginning and the fans looked forward to further wizardry from the impish winger with undisguised relish. However, in the next game he was sent off after a clash with Andy Gray of Crystal Palace, and as the season progressed he was seldom able to recapture that irresistible mood, his efforts to curb his temper seeming to take their toll on the natural aggression which was the key to his game.

Wise emerged as a reliable penalty-taker and his pinpoint corners produced a number of goals such as Ken Monkou's match-winning header against Manchester United, but too often he found himself dropping back in search of the ball, unable to make much impression. He was briefly left out of the side and the crowd, their hopes turned to ashes, became increasingly hostile, but at the end of the season he was surprisingly called into the England party for a European Championship qualifying match in Turkey and had the satisfaction of silencing those who had ridiculed his selection with the winning goal.

Seemingly cheered by the arrival of his old Wimbledon sparring partner, Vinnie Jones, Dennis gradually recaptured his touch the following season. His disciplinary record continued to be a source of embarrassment, and regular absences from the side through suspension came to seem inevitable, but he was nevertheless the Blues' top scorer with 14 goals, none more spectacular than the bicycle kick that earned a point in the last minute at Queens Park Rangers.

Equally at home on either wing, Dennis is the epitome of the modern flank player: he works tirelessly covering and chasing, and is rarely to be seen taking on defenders in the manner traditionally expected of a winger. His greatest strength is his ability to deliver the ball into the penalty area with the accuracy of a laser-guided missile, and he has an uncanny knack of curling it around the man facing him with the minimum of backlift that makes him difficult to contain.

Significantly, Dennis produced his best performances when he was used in midfield, operating immediately behind the strikers in a free role that allowed him to see plenty of the ball and make full use of his perceptive passing. He had a magnificent game there in the Blues' rousing victory at Anfield in February, and looked highly impressive when he moved inside once again in December 1992 while Mick Harford was sidelined. However, Wise was then ruled out for two months by a training injury and during his lay-off the Blues' season was shattered by Cup defeats at Crystal Palace and Middlesbrough. In his absence it became painfully clear just how much Chelsea had come to rely on him, and there is no doubt that he will be central to their plans in the years to come.

BORN: Kensington, 15.12.66.
GAMES: 121 (1). GOALS: 31.
HONOURS: 5 England caps (91).
OTHER CLUBS: Wimbledon 84/5-89/90 (135, 27).

1990/91-

TOM BOYD

Replacing a player of the class of Tony Dorigo was never going to be easy, but it would be fair to say that during his eight months at Stamford Bridge Tom Boyd failed to make much of an impression. The timing of his move from Motherwell probably didn't help: the completion of the Scottish international's £800,000 transfer was delayed to allow him to lead the Fir Park club to victory in the Scottish Cup final, and by the time he reported for pre-season training with Chelsea the Blues had a new manager.

The first indication of Ian Porterfield's doubts about Boyd's effectiveness at left-back came when Tom started the opening game of the season in midfield. That experiment was short-lived and he quickly settled down in a conventional role on the left of the back four, but it seemed significant that when the manager wanted to make a tactical substitution it was often the number three board that was held aloft.

Boyd was a neat, tidy player who used the ball sensibly, but there was no area of the game at which he excelled: he was not particularly quick or aggressive, and he certainly lacked Dorigo's attacking flair. It looked as though he might have been happier on the right flank but Chelsea were already well provided for in that position, and when an injury to Kerry Dixon left the Blues in urgent need of a big centre-forward Porterfield lost no time in agreeing an exchange deal involving Celtic's Tony Cascarino.

BORN: Glasgow, 24.11.65.
GAMES: 31 (1). GOALS: 0.
HONOURS: 15 Scotland caps (90-93).
OTHER CLUBS: Motherwell;
Glasgow Celtic.

1991/92

CLIVE ALLEN

Clive Allen was the wrong side of thirty when he arrived at Stamford Bridge in December 1991 and largely barren spells with Bordeaux and Manchester City had tarnished the reputation for deadly finishing he had earned at Tottenham, but over the next four months the well-travelled striker confirmed that goalscoring is a gift that time cannot erode. The £250,000 deal that had brought the nomad back to London was hailed as the bargain of the season, but then, just as suddenly as he had appeared, he was gone . . .

Clive had never had too much pace and chasing long through-balls was not really his game, but he was certainly quick-witted and his sharp reactions, anticipation and immaculate control made him a constant threat in the penalty box. A spectacular volley against Everton in the fourth round of the Cup will linger in the memory of all those who witnessed it, but when Sheffield United came to the Bridge in the next round Clive showed that he was more than a goalscorer, holding the ball and laying it off with the finesse of a master craftsman. A typical close-range effort against Sunderland opened the way to the semi-finals, but then Allen seemed to fall from favour. When defeat in the replay at Roker Park had effectively ended the Blues' season, Ian Porterfield decided to prune his squad in preparation for further signings in the summer and on transfer deadline day Clive was sold to West Ham.

BORN: Stepney, 20.5.61. GAMES: 22 (2). GOALS: 9.
HONOURS: 5 England caps (84-88).
OTHER CLUBS: Queens Park Rangers 78/9-79/80 (49, 32) and 81/2-83/4 (87, 40); Arsenal (0, 0); Crystal Palace 80/1 (25, 9); Tottenham Hotspur 84/5-87/8 (105, 60); Bordeaux; Manchester City 89/90-91/2 (53, 16); West Ham United 91/2- (31, 15).

1991/92

MAL DONAGHY

Although Mick Harford's spectacular goalscoring exploits inevitably attracted most of the back-page headlines, the consistent form of the other battle-hardened veteran recruited by Ian Porterfield on the eve of the 1992/93 season provided an even more impressive demonstration of the unfortunate Scot's acumen in the transfer market. Mal Donaghy was fast approaching his 35th birthday when he arrived at Stamford Bridge from Manchester United, but the Northern Ireland international proved to be such a tower of strength during a difficult campaign that he retained his place in the starting line-up long after the manager who had signed him had departed.

Donaghy started the season alongside Paul Elliott in the middle of the back four – an indication of Porterfield's laudable desire to play constructive football from the back, for Mal is not a man to kick the ball anywhere – and produced a series of immaculate displays, his polished defending offering a welcome contrast to the frenzy all around him. When the big centre-half was sidelined by injury, Mal switched to left-back, where he performed with equal assurance, his reading of the game more than compensating for his lack of sprinting speed. Elegant and unhurried in his every action, the former Luton stalwart provided invaluable guidance to the youngsters who played alongside him, and the opportunity to learn from such a craftsman can only have advanced their football education.

BORN: Belfast, 13.9.57.
GAMES: 45 (1). GOALS: 2.
HONOURS: 82 Northern Ireland caps (80-93).
OTHER CLUBS: Luton Town 78/9-88/9 (410, 16);
Manchester United 88/9-91/2 (89, 0);
Luton Town *on loan* 89/90 (5, 0).

1992/93-

EDDIE NEWTON

To commend a player's versatility is often to acknowledge his mediocrity; the jack of all trades is commonly the master of none. In the case of Eddie Newton, however, there is nothing back-handed about the compliment. During his first season in the Chelsea team the 20-year-old played in four different positions and excelled in each of them, displaying a poise and panache that delighted the Stamford Bridge crowd.

A hand injury picked up in the reserves cost Eddie his planned debut in April 1991, but the following season he spent three months on loan at Cardiff City and the experience he gained playing in midfield for the Fourth Division side proved invaluable when he was finally given his chance in the Blues' last match of the campaign at Everton. A second-half substitute for Graeme Le Saux, Newton capped an assured display at left-back with a well-struck goal from 20 yards and in 1992/93 he was rarely out of the side. Having started on the right flank, he briefly reverted to full-back before settling down as Andy Townsend's partner in the middle of the pitch, but at Spurs he was pushed up front as a lone striker in the closing stages and – inevitably – won the game with two late goals. An elegant, stylish player who makes the game look deceptively easy, Eddie is happiest in midfield where he can attempt to dictate the shape of the match with his delicate skills and incisive passing. But wherever he is playing it is a joy to watch a footballer of such natural finesse.

BORN: Hammersmith, 13.12.71.
GAMES: 39 (3). GOALS: 7.
OTHER CLUBS: Cardiff City *on loan* 91/2 (18, 4).

1991/92-

GRAEME LE SAUX

Graeme Le Saux came into the professional game later than most, but when he finally forced his way into the Blues' first team it was quickly apparent that the energetic midfielder had the ability to become a real match-winner. Sadly, he failed to maintain his initial progress and it came as no surprise when David Webb decided that the Channel Islander's career would benefit from a change of scene.

Le Saux was 19 when he arrived at Stamford Bridge from Jersey club St Paul's in December 1987 and he had to wait two years for a real chance to impress, but a thrilling display at left-back in an otherwise forgettable Full Members' Cup match against West Ham left no doubt about his potential. He crowned an eventful First Division baptism as a substitute at Crystal Palace on Boxing Day with an injury-time equaliser, and the following season the enthusiastic youngster earned a regular place in the starting line-up, his evident commitment and all-action style delighting the Stamford Bridge crowd.

Playing wide on the left of midfield, 'Bergerac' had the pace and tenacity to trouble all but the most resolute defences, and a scintillating performance against Tottenham in the quarter-final of the Rumbelows Cup, when his direct running left poor Terry Fenwick totally bemused, provided ample confirmation of his ability to turn the course of a match. He still had much to learn – all too often his exciting bursts down the flank produced no tangible result, a wayward final pass marring all that had gone before – but there was no doubt that he possessed a spark that coaching could not supply.

Although he continued to forage tirelessly, Graeme's form in 1991/92 was generally less spectacular. Some impressive performances at full-back at the end of the campaign suggested that he would enjoy considerable success in that role, but he seemed reluctant to make the switch a permanent one. When he was sidelined by an ankle injury at the start of the following season Graham Stuart was able to stake his claim, and Le Saux found it impossible to regain his place. His career appeared to have lost momentum, and shortly before transfer deadline day he joined Blackburn, with Steve Livingstone moving in the opposite direction.

BORN: Jersey, 17.10.68.
GAMES: 99 (21). GOALS: 9.
OTHER CLUBS: Blackburn Rovers 92/3- (9, 0).

1988/89-1992/93

TONY CASCARINO

No one who remembers Tony Cascarino's swashbuckling performances for Millwall can doubt that, if he could recapture that sort of form, he would add real menace to the Chelsea attack. However, unhappy spells at Aston Villa and Celtic appear to have sapped the Irish international's confidence, and since his return to London he has rarely been fully fit.

Cascarino was signed from the Glasgow club – with Tom Boyd moving back to Scotland – in February 1992 as a short-term insurance policy. With the Blues drawn to face Sheffield United in the fifth round of the Cup and Kerry Dixon struggling with an injury, Ian Porterfield felt that it was essential to add a big target man to his armoury. Tony was short of match practice and looked a little cumbersome at times, but his ability to soar above his marker to win the ball in the air was immensely encouraging. He did not enjoy the best of luck over the next few weeks – he seemed to strike the woodwork at regular intervals – but a brilliant far-post header against West Ham left no doubt about his potential.

Summer knee surgery followed by a second operation ruled the tall striker out for much of 1992/93, but when David Webb took over in February Cascarino was immediately given his chance to impress and, with Mick Harford having moved on, there is no reason why he should not take permanent possession of the number nine shirt.

BORN: St Paul's Cray, 1.9.62.
GAMES: 21 (1). GOALS: 4.
HONOURS: 41 Ireland caps.
OTHER CLUBS: Gillingham 81/2-86/7 (219, 78);
Millwall 87/8-89/90 (105, 42);
Aston Villa 89/90-90/1 (46, 11);
Glasgow Celtic.

1991/92-

MICK HARFORD

An abrasive, awkward centre-forward, all sharp edges and aggression, Mick Harford was 33 when he joined the Blues from newly relegated Luton on the eve of the 1992/93 season, so there was never any doubt that his stay at Stamford Bridge would be relatively brief. In the event, the lugubrious Wearsider was a Chelsea player for just eight months, but during that time he confirmed that he had forgotten none of the lessons he had learned during a long and honourable career in the number nine shirt.

Although Mick was justly famed for his ability with his head, it was the deftness with which he controlled the ball before bringing the midfield men into the game that was most impressive. He was not the quickest of movers but he had the strength to resist the attentions of the eager youths attempting to contain him and, to the surprise of many, he proved to be a clinical finisher, a spectacular 25-yard drive on his debut against Oldham paving the way for a steady stream of well-taken goals in the first half of the season.

Harford was suspended for three matches in December, his combative style having earned him a flurry of yellow cards, and then he picked up a calf injury. When he returned to the side the bite that had helped Chelsea climb the table before Christmas had gone and, with the Blues' season in ruins, the former England international was sold to Sunderland shortly before transfer deadline day. But it had been fun while it lasted.

BORN: Sunderland, 12.2.59. GAMES: 33 (1). GOALS: 11.
HONOURS: 2 England caps (88).
OTHER CLUBS: Lincoln City 77/8-80/1 (115, 41);
Newcastle United 80/1 (19, 4); Bristol City 81/2 (30, 11);
Birmingham City 81/2-84/5 (92, 25);
Luton Town 84/5-89/90 (139, 57) and 91/2 (29, 12);
Derby County 89/90-91/2 (58, 15); Sunderland 92/3- (11, 2).

1992/93

JOHN SPENCER

John Spencer may have failed to make the grade at Glasgow Rangers, but his livewire performances for Chelsea in the second half of 1992/93 suggested that the Blues had picked up a real bargain. The tiny Scottish striker – at 5ft 6in he doesn't win the ball in the air too often – was signed shortly before the start of the season for £450,000. Injuries prevented him from making much of an impression before Christmas, although he had the odd outing as a substitute, but a superb goal against Manchester City in January – crashed past Tony Coton from 15 yards – set him on his way and his bubbling enthusiasm quickly endeared him to the Stamford Bridge crowd.

A lively, bustling player with good close control and plenty of confidence, Spencer is an instinctive goalscorer who thrives on half-chances at close quarters. He has a powerful shot which he isn't afraid to use, but a neat interchange with Graham Stuart against Arsenal confirmed that he can be an effective provider as well. In the closing weeks of the campaign he appeared to have displaced Robert Fleck, but it remains to be seen whether his contribution outside the box will be considered sufficient to justify his inclusion when he encounters the inevitable dry spell.

BORN: Glasgow, 11.9.70.
GAMES: 13 (13). GOALS: 7.
OTHER CLUBS: Glasgow Rangers;
Morton *on loan*; Liasun,
Hong Kong *on loan*.

1992/93-

DAMIAN MATTHEW

It is tempting to speculate how Damian Matthew might have fared had he been born ten or twenty years earlier. A cultured play-maker who likes to hold the ball and weigh up his options before finding his man with a carefully weighted pass, he cuts a forlorn figure amid the relentless bustle of the modern game. His undisputed talent has proved sufficient to earn him a stack of England under-21 caps, but at club level it has been glimpsed only intermittently. Denied the time and space he needs if he is to be effective, Matthew's influence has usually been peripheral, and his valiant efforts to turn himself into a midfield workhorse have been largely unavailing.

Damian had his first experience of the frenzied pace of first-team football as long ago as April 1990, but he has had only one realistic opportunity to come to terms with it – a run of six successive matches the following season. He helped the Blues to a memorable Rumbelows Cup victory at White Hart Lane, but after an ineffectual display in the first leg of the semi-final he dropped out of contention. A long-term injury sidelined him for much of the next campaign, and when he was recalled to the side at the start of 1992/93 he lost his place to Eddie Newton after just two matches. In a team playing measured, passing football with three men in midfield, Matthew might shine, but it now seems unlikely that he will make his mark at Stamford Bridge.

BORN: Islington, 23.9.70.
GAMES: 19 (8). GOALS: 0.
OTHER CLUBS: Luton Town *on loan* 92/3 (5, 0).

1989/90-

ROBERT FLECK

When protracted negotiations with Norwich City for the transfer of Robert Fleck were finally concluded a few days before the opening fixture of the 1992/93 season and a fee of £2.1 million – a club record – agreed, the satisfaction of the Chelsea management team was undisguised. Nine months earlier Fleck had reduced Stamford Bridge to stunned silence with a quite magnificent goal smashed over Dave Beasant in the Canaries' comprehensive 3-0 win, and there seemed little doubt that the fiery striker's imperious style would delight the Blues' supporters, who have always demanded that their heroes should perform with panache.

Unhappily, Fleck's first season at Stamford Bridge was to prove largely frustrating. He is an unselfish player who works tirelessly for the team and he created a steady stream of chances for others – an intelligent run that made space for Graham Stuart at Hillsborough, a neat one-two with Eddie Newton at Aston Villa and an inviting cross for Mick Harford at Oldham come to mind – but he didn't score goals in anything like the numbers expected.

Robert is at his most effective when running onto a through-ball down the middle, as he did to score that memorable goal for Norwich, but at Chelsea that sort of service has rarely been forthcoming. He is quick and strong but his record confirms that he is not a particularly predatory finisher in the box. In the first half of the season Mick Harford's goals kept the pressure off the Scottish international's shoulders, but when a spell as the lone striker failed to yield the anticipated rewards his place came under threat from John Spencer. Fleck persevered, but his confidence had gradually drained away and by the end of the campaign it was hard to see where his next goal was coming from.

Robert certainly has the ability to succeed at Stamford Bridge; it will be easier for him if Chelsea start playing to his strengths.

BORN: Glasgow, 11.8.65.
GAMES: 35 (3). GOALS: 3.
HONOURS: 4 Scotland caps (90-91).
OTHER CLUBS: Partick Thistle;
Glasgow Rangers;
Norwich City 87/8-91/2 (143, 40).

1992/93-

DAVE MITCHELL

IAN PEARCE

DARREN BARNARD

DAVE MITCHELL 1988/89-1990/91

Forward. BORN: Glasgow, 13.6.62.
GAMES: 8. GOALS: 0.
HONOURS: Australia caps.
OTHER CLUBS: Glasgow Rangers; Eintracht Frankfurt;
Feyenoord; NEC Nijmegen *on loan*;
Newcastle United *on loan* 90/1 (2, 1);
Swindon Town 91/2- (69, 17).

CRAIG BURLEY 1990/91-

Midfielder. BORN: Cumnock, 24.9.71.
GAMES: 9 (6). GOALS: 0.

IAN PEARCE 1990/91-

Forward/central defender. BORN: Bury St Edmunds, 7.5.74.
GAMES: 0 (5). GOALS: 0.

JOE ALLON 1991/92-1992/93

Forward. BORN: Gateshead, 12.11.66.
GAMES: 4 (14). GOALS: 3.
OTHER CLUBS: Newcastle United 84/5-86/7 (9, 2);
Swansea City 87/8-88/9 (34, 11);
Hartlepool United 88/9-90/1 (112, 50);
Port Vale *on loan* 91/2 (6, 0);
Brentford 92/3- (24, 6).

DARREN BARNARD 1991/92-

Left-winger. BORN: Rinteln, Germany, 30.11.71.
GAMES: 9 (9). GOALS: 1.

MICHAEL GILKES 1991/92

Winger. BORN: Hackney, 20.7.65.
GAMES: 0 (2) (*on loan* from Reading). GOALS: 0.
OTHER CLUBS: Reading 84/5- (238, 32);
Southampton *on loan* 91/2 (6, 0).

CRAIG BURLEY

JOE ALLON

MICHAEL GILKES

ANTHONY BARNESS

DIMITRI KHARIN

NEIL SHIPPERLEY

ANTHONY BARNESS 1992/93-

Full-back. BORN: Lewisham, 25.2.73.
GAMES: 2. GOALS: 0.
OTHER CLUBS: Charlton Athletic 91/2-92/3 (27, 1).

GERRY PEYTON 1992/93

Goalkeeper. BORN: Birmingham, 20.5.56.
HONOURS: 33 Ireland caps.
GAMES: 0 (1) (*on loan* from Everton). GOALS: 0.
OTHER CLUBS: Burnley 75/6-76/7 (30, 0);
Fulham 76/7-85/6 (345, 0);
Southend United *on loan* 83/4 (10, 0);
AFC Bournemouth 86/7-90/1 (202, 0); Everton (0, 0);
Bolton Wanderers *on loan* 91/2 (1, 0);
Norwich City *on loan* (0, 0);
Brentford *on loan* 92/3 (14, 0); Brentford 92/3- (5, 0).

DIMITRI KHARIN 1992/93-

Goalkeeper. BORN: Moscow, Russia, 16.8.68.
HONOURS: Soviet Union/CIS/Russia caps.
GAMES: 5. GOALS: 0.
OTHER CLUBS: Moscow Torpedo, Dynamo Moscow,
CSKA Moscow.

DAVID HOPKIN 1992/93-

Right-winger. BORN: Greenock, 21.8.70.
GAMES: 2 (2). GOALS: 0.
OTHER CLUBS: Morton.

NEIL SHIPPERLEY 1992/93-

Forward. BORN: Chatham, 30.10.74.
GAMES: 2 (1). GOALS: 1.

STEVE LIVINGSTONE 1992/93-

Forward. BORN: Middlesbrough, 8.9.69.
GAMES: 0 (1). GOALS: 0.
OTHER CLUBS: Coventry City 86/7-90/1 (31, 5);
Blackburn Rovers 90/1-92/3 (30, 10).

GERRY PEYTON

DAVID HOPKIN

STEVE LIVINGSTONE

TED DRAKE MANAGER: MAY 1952-SEPTEMBER 1961

No Chelsea manager has refashioned the club more dramatically than Ted Drake. A fearless, rampaging centre-forward with Arsenal and England before the war, he succeeded Billy Birrell at Stamford Bridge in the summer of 1952 after serving a five-year apprenticeship at Reading. Determined that the Blues should at last fulfil their obvious potential and cease to be a team of big-name stars whose whole was invariably less than the sum of its parts, he abolished the club's old-established emblem, the Pensioner – putting an end to

one of music hall's more enduring jokes – and called on the supporters to be more partisan. Aiming to build a side with the courage and spirit that had characterised his own playing career, Drake signed a number of players from the Third Division and recruited others from amateur football, and their success in the top flight was to be a remarkable vindication of his judgement. In Ted's first season in charge, the Blues finished 19th, as they had 12 months earlier, but the changes he had made gradually took effect and in 1954/55 Chelsea won the League Championship.

The following campaign proved to be a sorry anti-climax and, with a number of players apparently past their best, Drake started to dismantle his title-winning team – prematurely, in the view of some observers. A genial Hampshireman with a sunny, idealistic view of the game, Ted now placed his faith in a youth policy and filled the side with the gifted youngsters emerging from the club's Juniors. There were days when Drake's Ducklings showed enormous promise, but too many fresh-faced teenagers had been thrown in at the deep end together and heartbreaking inconsistency was the predictable consequence. The seasoned players he signed to hasten his young charges' progress failed to make the expected contribution and there were suggestions that discipline at Stamford Bridge had become lax. The incomparable genius of Jimmy Greaves ensured that enough goals were scored to counter-balance the torrent conceded by a leaky defence, but when the little maestro moved to Italy in the summer of 1961 disaster was inevitable. After a discouraging start to the new season, the Chelsea directors decided that change was essential and after nine years Drake was relieved of his position.

TOMMY DOCHERTY MANAGER: JANUARY 1962-OCTOBER 1967

Tommy Docherty's passion and steely determination brought Chelsea agonisingly close to sustained success, but his turbulent reign was attended by unceasing conflict. He came to Stamford Bridge as a coach in February 1961 after a distinguished playing career with Preston, Arsenal and Scotland, but made a handful of first-team appearances the following season as the Blues slipped perilously down the table. When the decision was taken to replace Ted Drake, Docherty was put in charge of team affairs with the title of chief coach, and his self-confident, aggressive manner impressed the directors sufficiently for him to be appointed manager in January.

Nothing could be done to prevent relegation but Docherty lost no time in reshaping the playing staff, dispensing with the services of a number of stalwarts who had served the club well for many years. His remodelled team, built around the latest crop of youngsters to emerge from the Chelsea youth scheme, swept to promotion at the first attempt, eventually scraping into the First Division on goal average after the Big Freeze had interrupted their imperious progress. The Doc's fire and drive were superbly complemented by the tactical astuteness of his coach, Dave Sexton, and the exciting young team they had created became famed for fast, exciting football, based on non-stop running with the full-backs overlapping at every opportunity.

However, Docherty's Diamonds never quite fulfilled their potential. In 1964/65 they chased an unprecedented treble but only the League Cup was won, and an incident at Blackpool when eight players were sent home in disgrace after breaking a curfew seemed to poison the atmosphere in the dressing room. The following season the Blues reached the semi-finals of the FA Cup for the second season in succession and the semi-final of the Fairs Cup, but controversy was never far away and four leading players departed in quick succession. Doc's tough stance seemed to have been vindicated when the Blues led the First Division the following autumn, but then Peter Osgood broke his leg, and although Chelsea finally reached the FA Cup final, the old sparkle had gone. A disastrous start to the new campaign suggested that morale was at a low ebb, and when Docherty was suspended by the FA as a result of a dispute with a referee during a summer tour to Bermuda his departure from Stamford Bridge became inevitable.

DAVE SEXTON MANAGER: OCTOBER 1967-OCTOBER 1974

It now appears a little ironic that Dave Sexton should have been the players' choice to succeed Tommy Docherty. He had given up his position as Chelsea coach in January 1965 to manage Leyton Orient, and subsequently worked as a coach at Fulham and Arsenal before returning to Stamford Bridge. He would become the most successful manager in Chelsea's chequered history, but his relationship with his star players was never comfortable, and it seems clear that he would have been more effective had he been relieved of responsibility for matters such as contracts and discipline, and left to concentrate on the coaching at which he excelled.

The Blues advanced up the table in purposeful fashion following Sexton's appointment, finishing in sixth place, and the players he signed fitted in well. The frantic intensity of the Docherty days had gone for ever but the team played with style and spirit, and in 1969/70 they looked a match for any side in the country, winning the FA Cup and taking third place in the League. The following season brought the European Cup-Winners' Cup to Stamford Bridge and in 1971/72 the Blues reached their third Cup final in successive seasons, but Sexton's previously sure touch in the transfer market appeared to have deserted him. He signed a number of players without seeming to have a clear idea of the role he wanted them to fill and endless team changes gave the impression of a loss of direction.

A quiet, scholarly man who thought deeply about the game and rarely betrayed any emotion, Sexton appeared to have lost the respect of some of his players and the Blues' increasing inconsistency pointed to problems behind the scenes. There were persistent reports that he was engaged in a battle of wills with Alan Hudson and Peter Osgood and matters came to a head when the two stars were dropped in January 1974. Hudson was soon on his way but the board's reluctance to part with the popular stiker apparently prompted Dave to offer his resignation before the directors reluctantly gave him their backing. Osgood was sold, but Chelsea slipped to 17th place in the final table and, with the financial burden imposed by the building of a new stand making success on the field imperative, a disappointing start to the following season resulted in Sexton's dismissal.

RON SUART MANAGER: OCTOBER 1974-APRIL 1975

The task that faced Ron Suart when he replaced Dave Sexton could scarcely have been more daunting. Chelsea were haunted by the prospect of relegation, star players had left, morale was low and there was no money available for replacements. Suart was liked and respected, having been the club's assistant manager for seven years, and had the experience gained during nine seasons in charge at Blackpool to fall back on, but it was a situation where a fire-breathing evangelist was needed rather than a competent administrator.

An improvement in the atmosphere at the club was immediately apparent and Suart introduced a few of the talented youngsters who represented the Blues' hope for the future, but despite one or two encouraging performances, it was quickly apparent that he was no miracle-worker. The threat of relegation grew ever more real and in desperation the directors turned to Eddie McCreadie, with Suart moving 'upstairs'. He remained with the club until 1983, subsequently joining Wimbledon as chief scout.

EDDIE McCREADIE MANAGER: APRIL 1975-JULY 1977

Eddie McCreadie appeared to regard the task of managing Chelsea as a personal crusade to save the club from oblivion. He had just three games in which to stave off the threat of relegation when he was put in charge of team affairs and he responded to the challenge with the courage and defiance that had characterised his long and distinguished career as the Blues' left-back, dropping a number of his former team-mates and making 18-year-old Ray Wilkins captain.

Despite the new manager's bold gamble, the Blues went down and a massive financial crisis threatened to overwhelm the club. No money was available for transfers but Chelsea had to start winning if they were to survive. A fiery, passionate character who seemed to have based his management style on that of his old sparring partner, Tommy Docherty, McCreadie suffered agonies of frustration as his young team failed to perform. He built them up with extravagant praise and knocked them down with savage criticism until at last he found the winning blend. The following season they raced to promotion playing exciting, flowing football that brought the crowds flocking back to Stamford Bridge. McCreadie had achieved mission impossible. There seemed to be every reason to take him seriously when he declared that his exuberant young team was going to take the First Division by storm, but in July, outraged at the board's lack of appreciation for his efforts, he walked out and embarked on a new life in America.

KEN SHELLITO MANAGER: JULY 1977-DECEMBER 1978

As the manager of Chelsea's youth team, Ken Shellito had been responsible for the development of many of the young players who had regained the Blues' place in the First Division in such stirring fashion in 1977, and when Eddie McCreadie walked out he must have seemed the obvious candidate to take over. Philosophical and unfailingly cheerful, Ken was a very different personality from his old full-back partner and favoured a more measured, controlled style of football, but too many of the players at his disposal proved unequal to the challenge.

Ken strove mightily to keep the ship afloat and 16th place in the final table represented a creditable achievement. The introduction of Clive Walker prompted a flurry of goals, and a rousing Cup win against Liverpool pointed to a brighter future, but the following season Chelsea looked certain to go down almost from the first day of the campaign and after a humiliating farce when the directors flirted with Miljan Miljanic, the celebrated Yugoslav coach, Ken resigned. It was a sorry end to Shellito's long association with the club he had served with such distinction, but at least he had the satisfaction of knowing that no one could have tried harder.

DANNY BLANCHFLOWER MANAGER: DECEMBER 1978-SEPTEMBER 1979

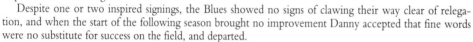

Danny Blanchflower was an idealist who longed to restore beauty and style to a game that had been defaced by cynicism and the win at all costs mentality. Since the end of his outstanding playing career with Tottenham his only involvement with professional football (apart from some journalism) had been as the part-time manager of the Northern Ireland team, so his appointment represented a brave gamble, to say the least. He encouraged the Chelsea players to enjoy themselves and attempted to liberate them from the shackles imposed by traditional coaching methods, but they seemed to lack the technique and imagination to put their new manager's ideas into effect.

Despite one or two inspired signings, the Blues showed no signs of clawing their way clear of relegation, and when the start of the following season brought no improvement Danny accepted that fine words were no substitute for success on the field, and departed.

GEOFF HURST MANAGER: OCTOBER 1979-APRIL 1981

Geoff Hurst was very nearly an extremely successful Chelsea manager. The former West Ham star and hero of England's 1966 World Cup victory came to Stamford Bridge in the summer of 1979 to act as Danny Blanchflower's first-team coach, and when the amiable Ulsterman departed he took over, initially as a caretaker. With Bobby Gould acting as his assistant, Hurst succeeded in getting the best out of the players he had inherited, but the experienced men he signed failed to make the expected impact and defensive shortcomings ultimately caused the Blues to miss out on promotion on goal difference.

The following autumn saw another stirring drive towards the top of the table. Often playing with two out-and-out wingers, Hurst's side produced some thrilling football but they were then afflicted by a mysterious inability to put the ball in the net, failing to score in all but three of their League matches from the start of December. Brimming self-belief quickly gave way to abject despair, and before the season was out Chelsea were once again looking for a new manager. However, most fans felt that a little more patience might well have seen the Hurst/Gould partnership put the club back on the right path.

JOHN NEAL MANAGER: MAY 1981-JUNE 1985

John Neal was the first manager with previous experience at another League club to be given the job at Stamford Bridge since Ron Suart, and his record at Wrexham and Middlesbrough suggested that he was likely to enjoy rather more success than the hopefuls who had tried their hand before him. His first season in charge brought little satisfaction apart from an exciting run to the FA Cup quarter-finals but, with the support of the club's ambitious new chairman, Ken Bates, Neal then set about restoring the Blues' fortunes. Determined to add resilience and drive to a side that had seemingly lost much of its heart, he recruited a number of seasoned professionals and the example they offered would prove invaluable.

Chelsea narrowly escaped relegation to Division Three in 1982/83, but that summer Neal signed seven new players and his rebuilt team stormed to the Second Division Championship, playing the most attractive football seen at Stamford Bridge for a decade, combining flair with energy and a steely determination to succeed. The club had seemingly been reborn and amid great optimism the Blues went on to finish sixth in the First Division the following season, but it was then decided that Neal, who had undergone heart surgery the previous summer, should make way for John Hollins. Neal was given a place on the board but that arrangement was not destined to last and his association with the club he had done so much to revive was soon severed altogether.

JOHN HOLLINS MANAGER: JUNE 1985-MARCH 1988

When John Hollins moved into the manager's office in the summer of 1985, success seemed guaranteed. As a coach, he had made an influential contribution to Chelsea's recent resurrection, and the young team John Neal had brought together had shown enormous potential.

Hollins lost no time in imposing his own ideas on the successful set-up he had inherited, tightening discipline and replacing the Blues' high-octane style with a more measured approach. Chelsea remained in touch with the leading bunch until Easter but injuries to Kerry Dixon and Eddie Niedzwiecki seemed to tear the heart out of the side and at Christmas Chelsea were firmly rooted at the bottom of the table. The tabloid press mounted a campaign of unprecedented viciousness in an effort to force the personable young manager out of his job and there were unending stories of dressing-room unrest, but John showed commendable courage and, with the steadfast support of the chairman, guided the team back to a respectable position.

Substantial changes to the playing staff during the summer appeared to put the club back on course, but then Niedzwiecki was injured again and the Blues' season collapsed. The press set to work once more and after four months without a League win a change became inevitable. Once again a lack of previous experience in the hot seat had seen a Chelsea manager ill-equipped for his task.

BOBBY CAMPBELL MANAGER: MAY 1988-MAY 1991

Bobby Campbell put Chelsea back on an even keel after three seasons of turmoil, but he never really seemed likely to lead them to a secure place among football's elite. He was brought to Stamford Bridge by Ken Bates to act as John Hollins's first-team coach and when Hollins departed he took over as manager. He could not prevent the Blues from going down but the improvement in team spirit after his appointment was obvious.

The cheerful Liverpudlian adopted a pragmatic approach to the task in hand and his judgement was vindicated when Graham Roberts and Peter Nicholas, the two battle-scarred veterans he had signed during the summer, led the Blues to a crushing Second Division Championship triumph. Campbell had not enjoyed too much success during his previous spells as a manager at Fulham and Portsmouth but when Chelsea briefly topped the First Division table the following autumn playing cultured, flowing football it seemed that the decision to appoint him had been inspired.

The Blues finished the season in fifth place and the arrival of Andy Townsend and Dennis Wise in the summer suggested that they could expect to challenge for honours in 1990/91, but the team failed to fulfil their obvious potential and after a bitterly disappointing defeat at the hands of Sheffield Wednesday in the Rumbelows Cup semi-final it became clear that Chelsea would look elsewhere.

IAN PORTERFIELD MANAGER: JUNE 1991-FEBRUARY 1993

Despite frantic transfer activity, Ian Porterfield never seemed to have the squad he wanted during his brief spell as Chelsea manager and it was hardly surprising therefore that success remained elusive. A thoughtful Scot who had proved his worth at Sheffield United and Aberdeen, he was not top of the club's short-list when the decision was taken to appoint a new manager, but he had made a favourable impression when he spent 16 months at Stamford Bridge as Bobby Campbell's assistant and seemed to have a real feeling for the club.

The Blues reached the FA Cup quarter-finals during his first season at the helm but 14th place in the final League table was a disappointment. Porterfield proved to be an astute bargain-hunter but Tony Dorigo and Gordon Durie were never adequately replaced and the loss of Paul Elliott through injury the following autumn was a serious setback. Ian encouraged his young side to play attractive, constructive football and by Christmas they were in a position to challenge for the title, but defeats in the Coca-Cola Cup quarter-final and FA Cup third round within a week left their season in tatters. Confidence evaporated with alarming speed and after two months without a win Porterfield was shown the door.

DAVID WEBB MANAGER: FEBRUARY 1993-MAY 1993

Like some jobbing plumber called out to plug a leak, David Webb was summoned back to Stamford Bridge to halt the Blues' ignominious slide towards the relegation zone. He had achieved creditable results with meagre resources at Bournemouth, Torquay and Southend and received a warm welcome from the Stamford Bridge crowd, who remembered him as the swashbuckling defender whose goal had won the Cup in 1970.

With his engaging mixture of breezy amiability and steely determination, Webb succeeded in restoring the spirit and pride that had seemingly been lacking, but insisted on a dour, utilitarian style of football that did not please the purists. He succeeded in hauling the club to mid-table respectability but – somewhat surprisingly – at the end of the season it was announced that his three-month contract had not been extended.

PLAYERS' STATISTICS

Player	Season	LEAGUE			FA CUP			LEAGUE CUP			FULL MEMBERS' CUP			EUROPE			TOTAL		
		App	Sub	Gl	App	Sub	Gl	App	Sub	Gl	App	Sub	Gl	App	Sub	Gl	App	Sub	Gl
Allen C	1991	15	(1)	7	4	(1)	2	0		0	3		0	0		0	22	(2)	9
Allon J	91-92	3	(11)	2	0		0	0	(2)*	0	1	(1)	1	0		0	4	(14)	3
Anderton S	58-61	76		2	3		0	1		0	0		0	2		0	82		2
Aylott T	77-79	26	(3)	2	1		0	2		0	0		0	0		0	29	(3)	2
Baldwin T	66-74	182	(5)	74	21		5	14	(3)	6	0		0	11	(3)	7	228	(11)	92
Bannon E	78-79	25		1	0		0	2		0	0		0	0		0	27		1
Barnard D	91-	9	(8)	1	0		0	0	(1)	0	0		0	0		0	9	(9)	1
Barness A	92-	2		0	0		0	0		0	0		0	0		0	2		0
Barron J	1965	1		0	0		0	0		0	0		0	0		0	1		0
Bason B	72-76	18	(1)	1	0		0	2	(1)	0	0		0	0		0	20	(2)	1
Beasant D	88-	133		0	5		0	11		0	8		0	0		0	157		0
Birchenall A	67-69	74	(1)	20	10		3	7		3	0		0	4		2	95	(1)	28
Block M	57-61	37		6	2		0	0		0	0		0	1		0	40		6
Blunstone F	52-63	317		47	24		4	3		2	0		0	2		0	346		53
Bodley M	1987	6		1	0		0	1		0	1		0	0		0	8		1
Bolland G	1961	2		0	0		0	0		0	0		0	0		0	2		0
Bonetti P	59-78	600		0	57		0	45		0	0		0	26		0	728		0
Borota P	78-81	107		0	2		0	5		0	0		0	0		0	114		0
Boyd T	1991	22	(1)	0	2		0	2		0	5		0	0		0	31	(1)	0
Boyle J	64-73	188	(10)	10	24	(1)	0	21		1	0		0	20	(2)	1	253	(13)	12
Brabrook P	54-61	251		47	12		4	4		4	0		0	3		2	270		57
Bradbury T	60-61	29		1	0		0	0		0	0		0	0		0	29		1
Bridges B	58-65	174	(2)	80	17		9	5		3	0		0	7		1	203	(2)	93
Britton I	72-81	253	(10)	33	15		0	11		1	0		0	0		0	279	(10)	34
Brolly M	72-73	7	(1)	1	1		0	0		0	0		0	0		0	8	(1)	1
Brooks J	59-60	46		6	2		0	4		1	0		0	0		0	52		7
Brown D	63-64	10		1	1		0	2		1	0		0	0		0	13		2
Bumstead J	78-90	318	(24)	38	20	(1)	3	29	(5)	1	12		2	0		0	379	(30)	44
Burley C	90-	7	(5)	0	0	(1)	0	0		0	2		0	0		0	9	(6)	0
Butler D	61-62	18		0	0		0	0		0	0		0	0		0	18		0
Butler G	1967	8	(1)	0	0		0	0		0	0		0	0		0	8	(1)	0
Canoville P	81-85	53	(26)	11	2	(3)	1	12	(6)	3	0	(1)	0	0		0	67	(36)	15
Cascarino T	91-	19	(1)	4	2		0	0		0	0		0	0		0	21	(1)	4
Chivers G	78-82	128	(5)	4	7		0	8		0	0		0	0		0	143	(5)	4
Clare J	1980	0	(1)	0	0		0	0		0	0		0	0		0	0	(1)	0
Clarke S	86-	183	(4)	6	9		1	11		1	12		1	0		0	215	(4)	9
Cliss D	57-61	24		1	0		0	0		0	0		0	0		0	24		1
Coady J	86-87	9	(7)	2	0		0	0	(1)	0	1	(1)	1	0		0	10	(9)	3
Cooke C	65-72	204	(8)	15	28	(1)	3	18	(1)	3	0		0	17		1	267	(10)	22
	& 73-77	85	(2)	7	4	(1)	0	4		1	0		0	0		0	93	(3)	8
Crowther S	58-60	51		0	4		0	1		0	0		0	2		0	58		0
Cundy J	90-91	40	(1)	2	6		0	6		0	4		0	0		0	56	(1)	2
Davies G	84-85	11	(2)	6	2		0	0		0	0		0	0		0	13	(2)	6
Dempsey J	68-75	161	(4)	4	15	(1)	2	15	(2)	0	0		0	9		1	200	(7)	7
Dickens A	89-91	39	(9)	1	0		0	3		0	4		3	0		0	46	(9)	4
Digweed P	1987	3		0	0		0	0		0	0		0	0		0	3		0
Dixon K	83-91	335	(4)	148	18	(2)	8	40	(1)	25	20		12	0		0	413	(7)	193
Docherty J	1978	2	(1)	0	0		0	0		0	0		0	0		0	2	(1)	0
Docherty T	1961	4		0	0		0	0		0	0		0	0		0	4		0
Dodds B	86-88	0	(3)	0	0		0	0		0	0	(2)	0	0		0	0	(5)	0
Donaghy M	92-	39	(1)	2	1		0	5		0	0		0	0		0	45	(1)	2
Dorigo T	87-90	149		11	4		0	14		0	13		1	0		0	180		12
Driver P	80-82	25	(19)	4	0	(1)	0	0	(1)	0	0		0	0		0	25	(21)	4
Droy M	70-84	263	(9)	13	21		4	17	(2)	2	0		0	1		0	302	(11)	19
Dublin K	83-86	50	(1)	0	5		0	6		0	5	(1)	0	0		0	66	(2)	0
Dunn J	62-65	13		0	3		0	0		0	0		0	0		0	16		0
Durie G	85-90	119	(8)	54	6		1	11		7	9		1	0		0	145	(8)	63
Elliott P	91-	42		3	5		0	2		0	5		0	0		0	54		3
Elmes T	1980	2	(2)	0	0		0	0		0	0		0	0		0	2	(2)	0
Evans B	1960	32		0	1		0	4		1	0		0	0		0	37		1
Falco M	1982	3		0	0		0	0		0	0		0	0		0	3		0
Fascione J	64-68	22	(7)	1	0		0	3		0	0		0	2		0	27	(7)	1
Feely P	70-72	4	(1)	2	0		0	0		0	0		0	0		0	4	(1)	2
Fillery M	78-82	156	(5)	32	11		3	9		6	0		0	0		0	176	(5)	41
Finnieston S	74-77	78	(1)	34	4	(2)	1	4		2	0		0	0		0	86	(4)	37
Fleck R	92-	28	(3)	2	1		0	6		1	0		0	0		0	35	(3)	3
Francis S	81-85	71		0	10		0	6		0	1		0	0		0	88		0
Freestone R	86-88	42		0	3		0	2		0	6		0	0		0	53		0
Fridge L	1985	1		0	0		0	0		0	0		0	0		0	1		0
Frost L	77-79	11	(3)	5	0		0	1		0	0		0	0		0	12	(3)	5
Garland C	71-74	89	(3)	22	7		1	15		8	0		0	0		0	111	(3)	31
Garner B	72-78	94	(11)	31	9	(1)	5	2	(2)	0	0		0	0		0	105	(14)	36
Gibbs D	56-60	23		5	2		1	0		0	0		0	0		0	25		6
Gilkes M	1991	0	(1)	0	0		0	0		0	0	(1)	0	0		0	0	(2)	0
Godden T	85-86	34		0	1		0	2		0	1		0	0		0	38		0